THE FILM USER'S HANDBOOK

Still of Captains Courageous—*a film popular with all audiences.*

THE FILM USER'S HANDBOOK

A Basic Manual for Managing Library Film Services

by

Dr. George Rehrauer

R. R. BOWKER COMPANY
A Xerox Education Company
New York & London, 1975

Published by R. R. Bowker Co. (A Xerox Education Company)
1180 Avenue of the Americas, New York, N.Y. 10036
Copyright © 1975 by Xerox Corporation
Printed and bound in the United States of America

Library of Congress Cataloging in Publication Data
Rehrauer, George.
The film user's handbook.

Includes index.
1. Libraries and moving-pictures. I. Title.
Z717.R4   025.17'73   75-15884
ISBN 0-8352-0659-9

to
ANNA, MARY, and LIL,
the 3 sisters
of my play

CONTENTS

ILLUSTRATIONS

FIGURES

TABLES

FORMS

EXAMPLES

PREFACE

What is new in film service and use? A provocative question. A reading of Orrin Cocks's article, written some 60 years ago and reprinted as the prologue to this book, will suggest the answer "not much," for indeed nearly all of the potentials and problems of using films in libraries and schools that he predicted in 1914 are still with us today.

It is the goal of *The Film User's Handbook: A Basic Manual for Managing Library Film Services* to give an overview of film services, provide information about and recommendations for film use, and suggest patterns and potentials for the future. *The Film User's Handbook* is intended for those persons, libraries, or institutions that are either considering, beginning, or enlarging film service or use. A basic approach that assumes little or no prior knowledge about the subject on the part of the reader is used. However, since it is a one-volume compendium of data relating to film as well as to film service and use, the book may also be used as a reference aid by the experienced professional.

Although my intent is to present a body of modern original material, the book's nature and purpose require the inclusion and discussion of certain topics that have been covered to some degree in earlier sources. However, it is the viewpoint and the demands of the seventies which must govern the use of film in libraries.

The sequence of presentation begins with some background and history of the development of film and motion pictures, as well as of the recognition and acceptance of the value of film service. Hence, Part I defines some terms, states the rationale for film service, and presents a selected chronology of some of the important dates and events in the evolution of film and film service. Film aesthetics are briefly reviewed in a discussion of the nature and influence of what most people now consider the art form of the twentieth century.

Part II discusses the factors that should be considered in preparing for film service; standards, finance, policies, and systems are described. How to build a film collection is explained by examining the reservoir of existing films and suggesting ways of locating or obtaining them. The essential processes of selection and evaluation are outlined and the role of other media in supporting a film collection is noted. Cataloging, circulation, and storage of films are also treated, as are some methods and practices for the care and maintenance of films. A section on the design and presentation of film programs follows; in it program notes, study guides, program evaluation, and local film audiences are defined by text and example. The selection, evaluation, and use of hardware are discussed, since these are important aspects of film service. The final chapter provides a summary of the problems and potentials of film service.

The first two appendixes contain examples of existing practices described by Helen Ransky and others and a fine essay by David Brown on materials for film study. Other appendixes provide a lengthy bibliography and lists of film periodicals, associations and organizations, distributors, and equipment manufacturers. Many of the names, titles, and sources referred to in the text are more fully documented in these lists. A glossary of terms and an index conclude the volume.

I express my appreciation to my friend, Enos Hernandez, who not only created the drawings but also assisted wholeheartedly in the myriad other tasks that a volume such as this demands; also to my editors, Deirdre Boyle, Madeline Miele, and Filomena Simora, all of whom offered so much valuable direction and advice, always with sensitivity and strength; to David Brown, Helen Ransky, and John Saylor for allowing me to reprint their work; and to Larry E. Beilin, Morey Berger, James F. Burns, Nadine Covert, Joseph Di Stefano, Kathryn Evans, John Gerardi, Theo Haynes, Ray Howe, Donald Krim, Elaine Mason, Lynn F. Miller, Eugene Mittelgluck, Ed Pason, Betty Braxton Preston, James E. Reedy, E. L. Richardson, Hal Sherman, Dr. Louis Snyder, Jack B. Spear, Betty Torricelli, and Helen K. Wright for their assistance and cooperation.

I am grateful to the following libraries and associations for allowing me to reproduce certain materials: the American Library Association, Camden Regional Film Library, Educational Film Library Association, Indiana University Audio Visual Center; Monmouth County Library, New Jersey State Museum, New Rochelle Public Library, the Public Library Association, Special Services Film Library of New York, the Westchester Library System, and the Woodbridge County Library. I also thank the following companies for furnishing material for this book: Eastman Kodak Company, Educational Products Information Exchange, Fides Press, Films, Incorporated, Learning Corporation of America, Research Technology Incorporated, and United Artists Corporation.

Finally, my gratitude is expressed to those students who have explored film form and use with me in both formal and informal settings. From them I have gained much.

GEORGE REHRAUER

Graduate School of Library Service
Rutgers, The State University
New Jersey

PROLOGUE

LIBRARIES AND MOTION PICTURES—AN IGNORED EDUCATIONAL AGENCY

By Orrin G. Cocks, Advisory Secretary, National Board of Censorship

[*This article appeared originally in* Library Journal *September 1914.*]

The libraries of the United States have failed to see the educational value of motion pictures during their period of growth in the last 15 years. These have now become overwhelmingly commercial and are supplied daily to over 17,000 motion picture houses. The libraries propose entering the field by exhibiting films which are peculiarly suitable for instruction and enlightenment. They must pay the price for their earlier indifference!

For years, the National Board of Censorship has been urging the development of the use of educational films. It has found many difficulties in the way, including an inertia on the part of schools, colleges, libraries, and churches. It is necessary to state these facts if librarians throughout the country are to realize the obstacles in the way of securing satisfactory programs.

There is no question but that splendid films are in existence. The manufacturers abroad and in the United States have scoured the world for scientific, literary, historical, artistic, scenic, and nature films. These manufacturers hold the sample copies of possibly 15,000 subjects, a part of which can be bought outright if desired. The trouble is not with the film supply, but with the ability of occasional renters to obtain from exchanges what they want, when they want it and at a satisfactory price.

In order to explain this technical situation, some facts should be given. There are a number of elements entering into the production, distribution, and exhibition of motion pictures. The raw stock of celluloid from which films are made has a certain life. The film base is usually inflammable. Before pictures are manufactured or exhibited it is necessary to obtain splendid cameras, studios, staging, and highly paid actors and actresses, or to search diligently for proper out-door settings for subjects. The proper use of the camera is an art in itself. The skillful direction of people and scenes to obtain illusions is also a highly technical business; even the production of travel, scenic, and scientific pictures with a minimum waste of film requires a high grade of artistic ability. When once the picture has been constructed, prepared with subjects and sub-titles, and has been submitted to the National Board of Censorship, it must be advertised, circulated among exchanges throughout the states of the Union, and await its demand by the exhibitors. In most cases, the man directing an exchange orders only a partial list of the films manufactured by the group of producers with whom he has affiliation. He rents the films to the exhibitors in circuits immediately around his city. The price for a day's use varies with the number of times it has run, the demand for the picture, its original cost, and the number of reels or parts.

All this process has been built up because of the regular daily demand of the people for entertainment and enlightenment. Let me emphasize the fact that the demand is regular. The manufacturers also know the percentage of film subjects demanded, whether it be thrilling, tragic, humorous, artistic, or educational.

The libraries which desire motion picture films are scattered. They make demands upon the exchanges only occasionally. They insist that films having comparatively little popularity in the commerical houses shall be furnished them. It is only natural that these exchange men who obtain their living from the regular demand of the commercial exhibitor are little interested in meeting the occasional request of the libraries for service.

The manufacturers and exchange managers realize that the increasing use of motion pictures in libraries, colleges, schools, and churches will, necessarily, draw away somewhat from commercial houses. They have cast their interest in with the commercial exhibitor and are loyal to him.

Another fact which should be stated is that librarians sometimes demand a concession in price. This has been the case many times in and around New York. They also have not always been business-like in the return of films.

The following firms of manufacturers announce that they have libraries of educational films which can be obtained:

The General Film Company, 71 West 23d St., New York City;
The Pathé Frères, 1 Congress St., Jersey City, N.J.;
The Eclair Film Company, 126 West 46th St., New York City;
Thomas A. Edison Company, 239 Lakeside Ave., Orange, N.J.;
The Gaumont Company, 110 West 40th St., New York City;
The Hepworth American Film Corporation, 110 West 40th St., New York City;
George Kleine Company, 166 North State St., Chicago, Ill.

There may be others, but these are the larger manufacturers. It is possible to obtain their books of educational films upon request. It does not follow that the films noted in these books can be obtained upon demand. Correspondence with the companies will undoubtedly make clear the conditions. A further fact is also important. The manufacturers of films withdraw from circulation most of their film subjects after they have been in circulation from 3 to 6 months. This gives them the opportunity to construct new films and to increase the profit of a lucrative business. Unless films are purchased outright, as time goes on it becomes increasingly difficult to obtain some of those which have been most beautiful and inspiring.

I desire to speak of solutions for these difficulties later. In the meantime, let us consider motion picture projecting machines and booths. Since the celluloid films are inflammable—though many of them are slow burning—it is necessary to protect audiences. Hence the fire-proof booth. Since pictures tend to flicker as they pass by upon the screen, it is important that a good grade of projection machine be obtained for regular exhibition. This minimizes the eye strain. Since most films are of standard size with standard perforations for exhibition, it is economical to obtain machines which will permit the display of the regulation film. The ordinary machine costs about $225 and a fire-proof booth about $100. Many companies are experimenting to produce satisfactory small machines that cost in the region of $100. This has been accomplished for small rooms and limited uses. Advertisements can be found in the motion picture trade papers.

A word about the psychology of audiences. Exhibitors everywhere testify that their patrons cannot be held with programs which are exclusively educational or consciously inspiring. The so-called educational picture has been used in many theatres as, in the motion picture slang, "a chaser." When these appear, the crowd leaves, making way for a new audience. An increasing number of exhibitors, however, recognize the appeal of the rest of these technical pictures and hold their audiences with them. A warning should be given to librarians against an attempt to furnish instruction at the expense of entertainment. A well-balanced program will produce a far more satisfactory result than a program which excludes laughter and thrills.

It ought to be clear by this time that it is no easy work to provide a regular program of a high grade. It cannot be done by a librarian who looks over a stock booklet and quickly makes two or three selections from likely subjects. This business should be left to someone who makes it a large part of his or her duty. He can obtain the films if the library is within striking distance of an exchange centre for films, but time, ability, patience, and money must be expended.

A final statement should be made about obtaining films. From the standpoint of the library or the school, the present system is unsatisfactory. The commercial companies with large stocks of films are not particularly interested in the occasional trade of institutions for education and enlightenment. Several organizations are in a process of development which aims to cater to the forces of enlightenment in the community. It must be said that this demands large capital for the purchase of films and keen business ability to maintain a circulation which will be profitable. The organizations which have been launched are based largely upon the plan of circulating a set program in 52 circuits composed of 7 members each. This will enable such a company to furnish 360 institutions with a five-reel program once a week at the initial expense for 230 reels of film. It makes it difficult, however, to obtain a varied program or to have it more often than once a week. The weekly rental for such a service will probably range from $10 to $25.

Another solution which would be more satisfactory for schools and libraries is the annual appropriation by the state of a sufficient sum to allow the purchase of a number of the best films each year by the state libraries or the state department of education. This increasing library of films could be held for circulation throughout the state at a nominal rental for libraries and schools. A committee skilled in the demands of these institutions for certain classes of films could make the selection. Such a plan pre-supposes, however, a far more general demand than there is at present for such purposes. The only other solution which has occurred to thinkers on this subject is the purchase at a large initial cost of a supply of films for rental and exhibition by some philanthropists or philanthropic foundation. Even this plan would have the disadvantage of being located in one section of the country and unable quickly and economically to supply the demands in various parts of the country. It would appear that either these social service film exchanges must develop rapidly and satisfactorily or public demand must cause the creation of state film libraries. In the meantime, libraries must make the best use possible of the commercial film exchanges or co-operate far more than they are at present doing with the motion picture exhibitor who is in their vicinity. Both librarians and teachers will be surprised to find a willingness on the part of many such men to furnish entirely satisfactory programs if audiences of library patrons, school children and their parents will be guaranteed.

To supplement Mr. Cocks' article the *Journal* on its own responsibility prints below a selected and, it believes, an authoritative list of manufacturers of inexpensive machines and of companies which furnish educational motion pictures, in the hope that librarians who are interested in the use of motion pictures in the library may find the information of value.

Machines which can be furnished for a price around $100 are as follows:

Pathéscope, Pathé Frères, 115 East 23d St., New York City;
Kineclair, Eclair Film Co., 126 West 46th St., New York City;
Phantoscope Mfg. Co., Bond Bldg., Washington, D.C.;
The Animatograph, Victor Animatograph Co., Davenport, Iowa;
Edison Home Kinetoscope, Thos. A. Edison, Inc., Orange, N.J.;
Nicholas Power Co., 90 Gold St., New York City.

These machines operate under different mechanical devices, with various forms of lighting, projection, protection of film, etc. Some of them advertise that the fire hazard is reduced to a minimum, and we believe all but one use the standard size of film. Screens, tickets, equipment, etc., may be obtained from the American Theatre Supply Co., 218 West 42d St., New York City. Any one of the companies mentioned will be glad to send complete information concerning their machines in response to inquiries.

There are at least three bureaus which have declared themselves ready to furnish film service of the kind desired in libraries, though no guarantee can be made at present that service can be obtained except within, possibly, 200 miles of New York. There is little doubt about the satisfactory character of the films they furnish. These bureaus are:

The Community Service & Film Bureau, Rev. Charles Stelzle, managing director, 200 Fifth Ave., New York City;

The Church and School Social Service Bureau, Rev. Wm. Carter, president,
18 East 41st St., New York City;

The Motion Picture Bureau, Edward W. Robinson, Singer Bldg., New York
City.

Besides these, the following large companies have educational departments:

The General Film Co., Educational Dept., 71 West 23d St., New York City;

Gaumont Co., Congress St., Flushing, L.I.;

Pathé Frères, 1 Congress St., Jersey City, N.J.

Large commercial exchanges of the great film producing companies have
many educational subjects on their shelves, and libraries and schools in different
parts of the country desiring to obtain programs should make a more serious effort to discover what these subjects are. Any motion picture exhibitor will tell the
names of these exchanges, and an examination of their resources will show the
investigator the great possibilities already existing for arranging programs well
suited to production either in library or school.

PART ONE
Background
for Film Service

CHAPTER 1
Rationale
for Film Service
in Institutions

Although it was written 60 years ago, Orrin Cocks's article contains many statements that are pertinent today. He notes, for example, that many libraries have still to acknowledge the educational value of the excellent motion pictures that are available today. Also, the planning of quality programs continues to demand knowledge and dedication, and the challenge of financing such programs remains great. Clearly the search for and development of new technology in the area of film production continues.

Yet some of the difficulties mentioned by Cocks have diminished or vanished. Although it is not total, acceptance of film by both the professional librarian and the library patron is increasing. Selection and acquisition of films is more efficient today than in 1914. Threats and cries of outrage from commercial theater owners have all but vanished, and the quality of motion pictures has increased appreciably.

In the last quarter of the twentieth century we readily accept the idea that institutions such as libraries, schools, museums, churches, and colleges offer film service. We recognize that we can no longer rely exclusively on one communication medium but must deal with several. As evidence of this acceptance, current published standards and guidelines for these institutions now contain some statement about nonprint services. Although varying in length and detail, all these statements indicate the importance of nonprint materials as part of the experience institutions offer their students, teachers, patrons, or users. The question today is not *whether* to include nonprint materials, but how to select, use, and store them along with other materials.

The primary rationale for including films in collections is that they are the most powerful communication medium of our time, of use in offering ideas, information, values and advice; in persuading; in encouraging discussion; and in providing many other experiences.

Indeed, film has been likened to books in many ways—it has even been called "visual literature." In certain ways, however, print and nonprint materials are quite different. Films appeal to both eye and ear, and communicate with a unique efficiency. Moreover, their physical form requires not only a machine for decoding, but also appropriate storage, handling, distribution, and use. Film is the art form of the twentieth century and as such plays an important part in our lives. Because of television, people are becoming more oriented to visual images than to print. To disregard the most popular communication form of our century in favor of an older one would be the equivalent of teaching Latin in our schools instead of English. This point may be clarified by considering the communication changes that have occurred throughout history. As man progressed from spoken sounds to symbols and then to handwritten pages and finally to printing presses, each change supplanted in part the existing communication system. Thus today's individual finds communication via sight and sound the preferred and predominate form of communication in life. Institutions that ignore this fact about their audiences are consigning themselves to rapid obsolescence. People are not interested in a turn-of-the-century service.

Film audiences comprise not only readers but also that 75 to 80 percent of the American population that does not, and probably never will, care for books. Hence, institutions can use audiovisual materials (e.g., through "outreach" and "community information center" projects) to expand their services to include people who are neither students nor readers. Moreover libraries, schools, or churches have access to films that are more varied and of higher quality than those shown on television. The economic pressures indigenous to the television industry dictate programming that is aimed at a mass audience. A compromised product which pleases few people is often the result. By selecting entertaining, informative films, presenting them in pleasant surroundings, and providing appropriate supportive materials as well as facilities for group discussion, institutions can provide an extremely valuable social and educational experience.

As a form of communication, film approaches a universal language. As with any language, the grammar of film should be learned before one tries either to create or use film with maximum effectiveness or view it with a comprehensive understanding. The fear, reluctance, and refusal of personnel in institutions to learn this new language and its grammar has hindered the growth of film service. (Compare, for example, the number of professionals in any library who can give a book talk with those who can give a film talk.)

There are other reasons why film service has been slow in developing in certain institutions, and these reasons are humanistic rather than logistic. Misuse or misunderstanding of film by users is uppermost. It is the greatest disservice to any art form to use it to promote either another medium, a building, or a service. Film is unique unto itself and should not be relegated to a shill position. To show a film in order to get students to read is poor methodology. To link book, film, and other media together in order to provide a total experience is more desirable and honest. To use films to draw persons into a library so they can make use of the other services is once more to assign to film a burden that it should not have.

Film should be shown for its own sake and not as a come-on for some other service that needs patron support.

The major problem facing schools, libraries, and universities today is all too obvious: recognizing and meeting client needs. These institutions must decide whether they exist primarily for their own perpetuation and personal security or to provide needed service for their users. Unless they opt for the second, alternate institutions will inevitably become their replacement.

Evidence which supports this possibility can be seen in declining enrollments, the rise of the free university, open classrooms, Montessori schools, and other alternatives to traditional learning. The audiocassette and the forthcoming videodisc or cassette, like community media centers and local cable television systems, will have far-reaching significance for existing institutions.

The refusal of these institutions, through oversight or shortsightedness, to adapt to their users' needs and preferences would be both counterproductive and unrealistic. Conversely, the intelligent use of film by and within such institutions is one way in which they can participate effectively in the process of change.

CHAPTER 2
The Evolution
of Film Service

Events in three major interrelated areas have contributed to the present state of film service in libraries, museums, and schools: the emergence of motion pictures as a mode of communication and as an art form over the past 75 years; the use of these motion pictures in educational situations; and finally, the appearance of film service in libraries during the three decades that followed World War II.

Man's efforts to represent motion in a two-dimensional form go back to the prehistoric paintings found on the walls of caves. Although the motion picture is basically a twentieth-century phenomenon, film history per se began in the sixteenth century with the invention of a primitive camera, and it is with this event that the following chronology of selected historical highlights begins.

1519	First practical demonstration of a camera obscura by Leonardo Da Vinci.
1824	Presentation by Peter Mark Roget (of *Thesaurus* fame) of a theory on the persistence of vision.
1837	Louis Daguerre devises the first photographic process which reproduces an image on a silvered metal plate.
1870–1893	Eadweard Muybridge (in the United States) and E. J. Marey (in France) experiment with photographs and eventually make films of animal and human locomotion—crude cameras and projectors were employed.
1876	The American Library Association (ALA) is established. Members include libraries, librarians, library trustees, and others interested in the responsibilities of libraries in meeting the educational, social, and cultural needs of society.
1889	The Kinetoscope is invented by William Dickson, an associate of Edison. Using a filmstrip drawn through a camera by sprockets, it

offers the first known motion picture. A public showing follows in 1894.

1895   First public showing by the Lumière brothers of the cinématographe—a camera, developer, printer, and projector of motion pictures.

1896   The vitascope, developed by Thomas Armat, is introduced at Koster and Bial's Music Hall on New York's Herald Square. The motion picture as we now understand it has come into being.

The earliest motion pictures ran for only a minute or so—as a curiosity or a side show—but, as film technology developed and audience sophistication grew, the length of films increased.

The years 1896–1915 are characterized by most historians as the developmental period of the narrative film, which culminated in such feature films as D. W. Griffith's *The Birth of a Nation* and *Intolerance*. The documentary, the educational film, the commercial film, and the newsreel also appeared during this period.

1909   "Books will soon be obsolete in the schools. Scholars will soon be instructed through the eye." *Thomas A. Edison*

1910   The *Catalogue of Educational Motion Pictures* is published by George Kleine in New York City. The first instructional film catalog on record, it lists 1,065 titles among 30 major categories in its 336 pages, and asserts that films cover "the works of textbooks without their dryness . . . and [can] yet impart a knowledge which cannot be gained by mere reading."

1912   Film depository collections given to land-grant colleges by the Department of Agriculture result in the first educational film collections in this country.

1914   "The cinema tells its story to the illiterate as well as to the literate; and it keeps its victim (if you like to call him so) not only awake but fascinated as if by a serpent's eye. And that is why the cinema is going to produce effects that all the cheap books in the world could never produce." *George Bernard Shaw*

Orrin G. Cocks argues for the acquisition, circulation and presentation of motion pictures by libraries in his article, "Libraries and Motion Pictures—An Ignored Educational Agency."

1917–1922 School systems in Chicago, Newark, Detroit, Kansas City, Los Angeles, Buffalo, New York City, Atlanta, Pittsburgh, Berkeley, and Sacramento establish film collections.

1919   Film libraries are begun in extension divisions of colleges and universities, state departments of education, normal schools, and museums. A contribution by the U.S. Bureau of Educational Motion Pictures to several institutions of about 100 reels of war films, which are to be distributed free of charge to the areas served by these institutions, stimulates the movement. Later these collections are enlarged by contributions of commercially sponsored films.

1920-1921 Eastman Kodak, Bell and Howell, and Victor-Animatograph adopt 16mm as the standard gauge for nontheatrical film. Previously, 28mm, 22mm, 21mm, 17½mm, 15mm, 11mm, and 9½mm were used.

1922 The first practical color reproduction system is introduced to the public by Dr. Herbert Kalmus, who names it Technicolor.

1923 The National Education Association establishes a Department of Visual Instruction—a clearinghouse of information and activities for educators concerned with visual instruction.

Eastman Kodak develops a 16mm nonflammable cellulose acetate film base, along with a camera and a projector to be used with it.

Lee De Forest demonstrates the first sound-on-film talking pictures. The idea is abandoned for want of interest.

1924 The ALA appoints a Committee on the Relations between Libraries and Motion Pictures and establishes the Visual Methods Committee.

One of the chief factors limiting the use of films in schools and libraries during this early period was the possibility of fire. The 35mm flammable stock on which films were printed made a fireproof projection booth essential. Later, a portable 35mm projector that could be used to show nonflammable film was introduced, but its success was hampered by problems relating to its size, weight, and power source. It was not until 1923 that technicians produced a practical 16mm camera, projector, and compatible nonflammable film. Wide acceptance of these innovations occurred only during the thirties.

During the mid-twenties, the American Library Association indicated concern about the noncommercial showing of films by establishing a Visual Methods Committee in 1924. For the next 15 years arguments were proffered for the inclusion of film in libraries but inadequate film distribution, high costs, poor selection policies, and a general lack of experience restricted progress in this area.

1925 At the ALA conference in Seattle, the Committee on Relations between Libraries and Motion Pictures recommends that (1) urban libraries contain information on sources of film; (2) a selected group of libraries be encouraged to collect and distribute films in their areas; (3) the office of executive clerk be established at the ALA or at the offices of the Motion Picture Producers and Distributors of America. The major responsibility of the office would be to develop and implement a program of cooperation between public libraries and motion pictures.

1927 The first successful sound-on-film talking pictures are introduced by Theodore Case in the Fox Movietone News.

1928 Kodacolor for 16mm film, a complex three-color system using filters, multiple lenses, and special projectors, is introduced.

1929 The Cleveland Public Library cooperates with a local movie theater to publicize the film *Scaramouche* by furnishing a bibliography, books, etc., designed to supplement or enrich viewing.

1932   Sound on 16mm film is made practical by a continuous optical reduction printer designed by Alexander Victor. The projection speed for 16mm machines is increased from 16 to 24 frames per second.

1934   The U.S. Office of Education is asked for information about the film movement in this country by the Rome Congress on Educational Films. Projects, studies, and surveys on film use are initiated.

At the conference in Rome the 16mm format in film becomes the accepted standard for the educational film. Film use increases in the schools of Germany, Italy, England, France, and the United States.

1935   The Kodacolor system is replaced by Kodachrome film, which uses reversal methods and dyes. Kodacolor becomes available commercially in 1939.

The Museum of Modern Art Department of Film is established to preserve representative motion pictures and related material.

1936   "It will be to the advantage of libraries to supply borrowers with film rather than to have them handled by a separate agency." *H. W. Wilson*

1938   The American Film Center is established by a Rockefeller Foundation grant. Using the British Film Centre as its model, the American organization extends assistance to anyone involved with film, including, of course, film libraries. It provides a complete service—film selection, study guides, equipment, and an operator. Its purpose is to promote and develop the distribution and use of motion pictures for educational and cultural goals.

1939–1945 About a dozen large urban public libraries organize their holdings of film and begin film services.

1940   The ALA renames the Visual Methods Committee as the Audio-Visual Committee, which in 1948 becomes the Audio-Visual Board.

Interest in film service in public libraries began in the thirties. It was not until World War II, however, when the effectiveness of 16mm film in training became apparent, that film service in libraries really began to grow. The forties were characterized by the formation of film centers, film councils and committees, etc., and culminated in two experimental programs that used film circuits, or groups of institutions formed to select, buy, show, and distribute motion pictures. Larger urban libraries also began to build film collections during the forties. (There were exceptions, in the form of pilot projects and experiments, of course; but the approximate eras were as indicated. For the most part, film service in public libraries was relatively new.)

1942   The National 16mm Advisory Committee is begun as a cooperative group of film organizations formed to assist the national government in the use of film on the home front—for bond sales, civil defense, morale, etc.

The U.S. government becomes the largest producer, distributor, and user of films. During the war, the government made more than 4,000 films and bought more than 54,000 projectors.

Educational Motion Pictures and Libraries by Gerald Doan Mac-Donald is published by the ALA. A study sponsored by the Joint Committee on Educational Films (ALA, American Council on Education, American Film Center, and the Association of School Film Libraries), it concerns the use and circulation of educational films in all kinds of libraries.

1943   The Educational Film Library Association (EFLA) is founded. Originally housed in the American Film Center, it survives the dissolution of that organization because it depends on membership fees rather than grants. Currently, EFLA has 1,800 members and a house staff of seven.

1946   "The old library outlook is over and done with. . . . If libraries do not adopt these [new] methods, the essential job of popular education to which they once enthusiastically dedicated themselves will pass on to others." *Documentary filmmaker John Grierson to 1946 ALA Convention.*

The Film Council of America emerges out of the National 16mm Advisory Committee. Its attempt to initiate a film council movement throughout the country is successful at first but quickly fades. The Department of Visual Instruction of the NEA changes its name to the Department of Audio-Visual Instruction (DAVI).

About 35,000 16mm projectors are in use for educational film showings. Very few of the government projectors find their way into civilian life.

About 600 national, state, and local film libraries are operating; this includes city and county school systems, state departments of education, university extensions, commercial organizations, etc.

1946–1947   The Carnegie Corporation gives the ALA funds to encourage audiovisual services in libraries and to establish a film advisory service at ALA headquarters. Standards for public library film service are formulated.

1946–1949   Approximately 70 larger libraries establish collections and services, which also include rentals from university collections. Some experimentation with film circuits begins in northern California. Canadian libraries begin to form film cooperatives.

1947   The American Film Center is discontinued after a grant from the Rockefeller Foundation is withdrawn. Only the Educational Film Library Association survives. The rights to the AFC periodical *Film News* are purchased by Rohama Lee, who still publishes it.

Film advisory service begins at the ALA, underwritten by a grant from the Carnegie Corporation and supervised by Patricia Blair.

1948   Two demonstration projects are funded by the ALA and the Carnegie Corporation. Based primarily on models developed in Canada, the projects are set up in Ohio and Missouri.

1949   A report of the Public Library Inquiry is published as *The Information Film* by Gloria Waldron.

Approximately 84 public libraries are circulating films.

1949–1951   The Missouri Libraries Film Project, begun as an experimental project under an ALA–Carnegie grant, is continued after support is withdrawn. The ten cooperating libraries offer film service to 21 counties and one city.

The Northern Ohio Regional Film Circuit is set up in a high-population industrial area; consisting of ten public libraries, this successful venture continues after external support is withdrawn.

1950   The magnetic striping of 16mm film is introduced, enabling makers of noncommercial films to add a sound track to their films. Problems of noncompatibility limit acceptance.

1950–1953   Many states—Indiana, Washington, California, Texas, Rhode Island, Minnesota, Connecticut, South Dakota, Wisconsin, Tennessee, Massachusetts, New Jersey, etc.—begin film cooperatives.

During the fifties the increased use of films in educational institutions and training programs—supplemented by the visual experiences provided by television—constituted the final argument for placing films in libraries. Problems of finance, handling, and training, among others, still existed but standards published during the fifties and sixties indicated, by the space they devoted to film collections, that most professionals accepted film service. The multimedia concept adopted by the school libraries was accepted—if not implemented—by other libraries: public, academic, and special.

1951   About 100 larger public libraries in the country circulate more than 36,000 films.

1952   The Illinois Film Cooperative begins, using the collection of 9,000 films (3,000 titles) at Illinois University as a central pool. The state library and all public libraries in the state participate.

1953   The U.S. Office of Education reports that 2,660 institutions, companies, and organizations, including about 166 public libraries, rent or lend films.

1955   Grace Stevenson's survey of public library film catalogs is published.

The demand for films in the Illinois Film Cooperative is so great that limitations have to be imposed. Curtailment of service suggests the formation of several cooperatives or circuits within the state.

1956   *Cooperative Film Services in Public Libraries* by Patricia Blair Cory and Violet F. Myer is published by the ALA via a Carnegie grant.

Standards for Public Libraries takes note of film, stating that larger systems should have 250 films, with 25 titles added each year.

1959   The Film Council of America is discontinued after the withdrawal of support by the Ford Foundation.

The decline of commercial motion picture theaters was counterbalanced by a renewal of interest in good films. Film societies, colleges, libraries, and schools began to exhibit a wide variety of films with greater frequency.

During the fifties and sixties, foreign films and short films became important elements in the programs of many American institutions. In library, museum, and university film departments attention was directed to the need for sources of information about films, selection and acquisition aids, and bibliographic control of films.

1960   Missouri Libraries Film Cooperative includes 33 members with 40 packets in circulation (14 titles in each packet).

A revival of 8mm film begins; this gauge is the most advantageous one for the amateur filmmaker because of size, cost, and equipment factors.

1961   The National Directory Project begins under the sponsorship of the Educational Media Council, using government (NDEA) funds. The publication of a directory of nonprint materials is the first imperative task of this project.

1962   *Films for Public Libraries,* a selection tool, is published by the ALA.

1964   *The Educational Media Index* (14 volumes), the result of the work of the National Directory Project, is published by McGraw-Hill. Reaction is mixed and no subsequent editions appear.

Marshall McLuhan's *Understanding Media: The Extensions of Man* is published.

1965   EFLA's *Film Evaluation Guide* is published. Based on EFLA review services, data are given on some 4,500 short films produced from 1946 to 1965.

1966   Seven film cooperatives are operating in Illinois but the trend is for library systems to assume responsibility for film service.

1967   The Film Library Information Council (FLIC) is founded. Serving 412 members, FLIC gathers and disseminates information about films. It publishes a periodical, *Film Library Quarterly,* and a directory of film libraries in North America.

The American Film Institute is founded. With more than half of the American films made since 1896 either destroyed or lost, the Institute sets out to recover and restore much of the remainder. Among its other functions is the organization of data about the history of motion pictures—as both an industry and an art form.

1969   *The Index to 16mm Films* is published by the National Informa-
            tion Center for Educational Media and gives data for about 30,000
            short films.

1970   The Department of Audio-Visual Instruction of the NEA changes
            its name to the Association for Educational Communications and
            Technology (AECT).

            *Guidelines for Audiovisual Materials and Services for Public Li-
            braries* is published by the ALA.

1972   Tom Brandon, former president of Brandon Films, estimates there
            are more than 1,000 public library film collections in the United
            States.

1975–?   The number of institutions using film continues to increase. The so-
            phistication of the viewer has grown appreciably, making an in-
            telligent presentation and use of film essential. Certain events noted
            in the chronology will tend to repeat themselves with slight varia-
            tion—circuits will form and dissolve, bibliographic control of films
            and film-related material will receive greater attention, and the
            presence of films in libraries will be accepted as commonplace.

CHAPTER 3
Aesthetics:
The Nature of Film

For the past 70 years film has been a part of everyone's life—directly or indirectly. Yet, if asked to explain what film is or what makes it both a unique, popular art form and a potent educational medium, most people cannot respond. Perhaps it is a case of taking something for granted—it exists, it works, so why question it? In the sections that follow, a response to these questions is essayed, first by discussing the innate qualities that give film its identity, and then by exploring film's relation to and effect on its viewers.

WHAT IS FILM?

Film—A Language

Film has all the characteristics of language. Its symbols can be arranged in a specific order: it has a *grammar* of shots, scenes, sequences, and whole films. *Punctuation* is provided by cuts, wipes, fades, dissolves, superimpositions, and other devices. Its *style* is determined by positions of the camera, the use of various lenses, movement, acting, dialogue, sound, editing, music, lighting, design, and other factors.

If *communication* can be thought of in very general terms as the transmittal of information or emotion from one entity to another, then film is certainly a basic mode of communication. To effect this communication, the filmmaker uses symbols that the viewers know or recognize, arranging them in some more or less conventional order determined by style and creativity. If unfamiliar symbols or an obfuscating style are used, communication will not occur.

Film Aesthetics

Aesthetics is that branch of philosophy which deals with what is beautiful—chiefly with theories of beauty's essential character. Tests by which beauty may be judged, and its effect upon the human mind are also considered.

The term *film aesthetics* embraces three elements: characteristics, judgment, and effect. We deal with some characteristics, or qualities, that give the film its identity or uniqueness when we consider *image, movement* and *space, sound, time,* and *color*.

This section describes briefly, and in general terms, some of these qualities. For detailed, in-depth discussions of the aesthetics of film, the following books are recommended: *The Art of the Film*, by Ernest Lindgren; *The Cinema as Art*, by Ralph Stephenson and J. R. Debrix; *Elements of Film*, by Lee R. Bobker; *The Film Experience*, by Roy Huss and Norman Silverstein; *Film Form* and *The Film Sense*, by Sergei Eisenstein; *The Film Idea*, by Stanley J. Solomon; *Film Technique and Film Acting*, by V. I. Pudovkin; *Film World*, by Ivor Montagu; *Grierson on Documentary*, by John Grierson; *Theory of Film*, by Siegfried Kracauer.

The Visual Image

Since film is a series of still photographs, the elements of composition, lighting, and focus are of primary importance. *Composition* denotes the spatial relationships among objects in a frame. Different effects can be achieved, depending on the arrangement of lines in the frame, since straight lines and angles can be used to suggest rigidity or strength, while curved, sloping, or arched lines may suggest harmony or grace. Broken lines can be used to convey a sense of disorganization or unrest; spirituality can be expressed by vertical lines, while rest and ease are sometimes implied by horizontal lines.

Large masses connote power and strength, whereas small ones may be used to indicate weakness, loneliness, alienation. Geometrical shapes offer certain meaning—squares and circles relating to equality while triangles suggest conflict.

An *intimacy* is attainable by means of film that cannot be obtained with any other medium. For example, the close-up on a large screen may reveal every detail of a character's face, and of his or her emotions and reactions. At times we are brought to an intimate contact which may cause embarrassment, discomfort, or even pain.

Lighting in films is sometimes categorized as low key, normal, or high key. It is used to create moods, to give a feeling of depth, and to make the image aesthetically pleasing. For example, when a communication of depression, mystery, or tension is desired, low key lighting may be used. The resultant image is composed mostly of darker colors, greys and black predominating, with only a few highlights. Similarly, high key lighting can intensify desert scenes, musical numbers, or certain action sequences. The image here is composed of brighter colors and highlights. Names or labels in lighting are difficult to pin down since the filmmaker creates whatever type of lighting is appropriate to the image he desires.

Focus refers to the clarity of the image. For certain effects, it is not unusual for the image to be fuzzy—or intentionally out-of-focus; on the other hand, *deep focus* implies that the depth of field is large. Most objects within the image frame are in clear focus regardless of their distance from each other. This results in a perspective or depth effect.

Movement and Space

Another basic characteristic of film is movement. The names "motion pictures" and "moving pictures" given to this art form are quite correct—the pictures create an illusion of movement for the viewer. By using tracks, vehicles, booms, panning, helicopters, zoom lenses, and other devices, camera movement in films is accomplished. The use of space then becomes unlimited, since the filmmaker can travel from a long shot to a closeup or from a high angle to a normal angle view.

Space relationships may be changed quickly in films. Not only can locations be manipulated with ease, but comparative sizes of images and their apparent distance from each other can be easily changed by changing camera position, movement, or lens. In addition to the arrangement of lines and shapes and camera movement, the effectiveness of a frame depends upon the eye of the beholder. At what angle and from what distance is the frame being observed? A high angle suggests vulnerability, loneliness, isolation, whereas a low angle of view conveys power to the image.

Distance offers additional meaning to the image—a close-up indicating a detailed communication while a long shot generalizes.

Movement of the shapes within the image conveys meaning. A movement from left to right is regarded by most viewers as positive while a movement from right to left is negative. For example, an army "advances" toward the right but "retreats" to the left.

Sound

Sound in films comprises dialogue, narration, sound effects, and the music on the film's audio track. Although it is undeniably an important element in the contemporary film, most filmmakers consider sound subordinate to the visual image. However, its effect on the total film experience cannot be ignored and should not be underestimated.

Time

Another unique quality of film is its ability to compress, expand, or exaggerate time. This manipulation of time can be accomplished by a flashback or a flash forward, by parallel editing, split screen, stop-motion or single-frame shooting, and other techniques. While certain manipulation of time is possible on stage and in the novel, the wide freedom to use time is not found in those media. For example, with split screen techniques, several actions happening at the same time can be seen and heard simultaneously. Then, too, to exaggerate, or speed up time is most awkward to accomplish in the theater and in books, while it is relatively simple in film. Think of a comedy chase, the budding of a flower, or Dr. Jekyll's transformation to Mr. Hyde.

Color

The trend today is to use color film. This can be unfortunate, since the black and white format is far more suitable for certain subjects. Realism in film is tradition-ally considered more convincing in black and white than in color. The character-istics of color film may have a tendency to make the unattractive appear less so. In addition, certain uses of color are so eye-catching that they disrupt the com-munication flow by visual distraction. Nevertheless, there are instances, ranging from travel films through certain scientific applications, in which the use of color film is a decided advantage.

Summary

In this section we have seen how film aesthetics relate to image, movement and space, sound, time, and color. Obviously, other factors such as costumes, settings, acting, and special effects have to be considered, but a discussion of all such ele-ments of film aesthetics is beyond the scope of this volume. However, attention must be given to the most important creative element in filmmaking—that of as-sembling the finished product—a procedure called *editing*.

Film Editing

To understand the editing procedure, it is helpful to be acquainted with the com-ponents of film: a *shot*, the basic unit, consists of the footage exposed during any single operation of the camera. It may be a fraction of a second to ten minutes or longer in duration. The only limitation is the amount of film the camera can hold. A *scene* is made up of shots that are related by location or time. A *sequence* consists of several scenes that form a coherent whole. It can exist by itself with some meaning, since it has a beginning, middle, and end.

Editing is the process of selecting and arranging shots into scenes, scenes into sequences, and sequences into films. The number of sequences in a film varies, depending on the film's subject and treatment. A short film may have only one sequence, whereas feature films may have more than a dozen. A specific concept in editing developed by the Russians, particularly Sergei Eisenstein, is known as *montage*. In part, the montage theory suggests that each shot bears a relationship to the shot before it and the one following it, and the cumulative effect of all three is different than the sum of their contents. A different use of the word "montage" refers to a set of brief shots arranged to present a change—that is a passage of time, the deterioration of a relationship, etc.

Subjectivity

A characteristic of film is its *subjectivity*. Arguments occur frequently as to whether the camera can ever be objective. The camera, by selecting those images it wishes us to see and presenting them in detail with emphasis, and at times with intimacy, is hardly objective. Efforts are made at objectivity but they must be la-beled partial. Film cannot be purely objective.

In a different sense character subjectivity can be shown in film. The thoughts, reminiscences, and sights of a person may be shown on film with effectiveness. We are made privy to the physical, mental, and emotional visions of another person by the concrete images appearing on the screen.

The filmmaker selects images and in doing so may provide an *emphasis*—an underlining or a repetition for effect. Control of what is emphasized rests with the filmmaker, for he selects angles of view, focus, specific details for close-up, and ultimately how the attention of the viewer can be channeled in the direction he wishes.

Film—A Popular Art Form

Argument on the pros and cons of this statement is about exhausted by this time. Although Europe recognized film as an art form years before America did, acceptance is fairly widespread now. If a popular art may be characterized by its ability to give lasting pleasure to groups and by having aesthetic qualities of beauty and good taste, then film qualifies. The question whether the moral tone of the person experiencing film is improved can also be answered affirmatively.

As a collective form of communication, film borrows spatial art and composition from painting and photography. To those arts, it adds motion. Its resemblance to the novel in literature is easy to establish, as are influences from dance, drama, and music. Attempts have been made to show its derivation from architecture.

Film or Motion Pictures?

Common usage in recent years has made the word "film" synonymous with "motion picture," although film also denotes the raw stock used for taking photographs, the broad field of film art, and the act of making a motion picture. For the purposes of this discussion, a motion picture is a series of still pictures, reproduced by a chemical process on cellulose acetate strips that have been coated with light-sensitive emulsions, which when projected at the appropriate speed, convey the *illusion* of motion. In the context of this book, motion pictures are almost always called films.

WHAT CAN FILM ACCOMPLISH?

Film and the Audience

The viewing of a film by an audience of one or thousands has some of the characteristics of ritual, in that it usually takes place in a dark room with the viewer seated, his attention fixed on a rectangular screen at the front of the room. Distraction is minimal because in physical conditions such as these a person tends to focus on the brightest portion of his field of vision (in this case the lighted screen). The eye is attracted by the movement, color, and size of the images, as well as the sound. People are curious about and interested in what happens to others, and the viewing experience optimally satisfies that curiosity.

A person becomes part of a film audience for many reasons. If a previous filmgoing experience has been positive, each new viewing promises to be pleasurable.

In many circumstances filmgoing revitalizes the viewer by providing diversion or stimulation. The viewer is aesthetically pleased by the frame, the sense of order, the beginning, middle, and end, and by the ability of the film language to communicate some information or emotion clearly.

Viewing a film as part of an audience satisfies a gregarious need. The communal feeling can unite a group or at least facilitate a dialogue between non-communicating groups. The common background of the shared experience supplied by the film gives a minimum concrete base upon which to begin.

Viewers can also be expected to identify and empathize with characters portrayed on the screen. What the actor pretends to experience the viewer may imagine himself to feel. (A physical reaction to an incident depicted on the screen is not unusual for some people.) It is theorized that a viewer can let off steam by vicarious participation in aggression or violence. He can be moved by the sadness of death, the emotions of love or friendship, and the frustration of hopeless struggle, hunger, or alienation.

These feelings occur because film conveys the illusion of reality more forcefully than any other medium. This convincing illusion intensifies the viewer's feeling. A temporary suspension of disbelief takes place as the viewer watches the events on the screen; he subscribes temporarily to the fallacy that "seeing is believing" and "the camera does not lie." The camera's apparent objectivity creates an impression of authenticity; the unreal (illusion, dream worlds, fantasy) is made to seem real. Fortunately, viewers do not ordinarily react to filmed incidents by loud rejoinders, active body movement, or violence. Reaction is generally limited to the emotions and does not include an active body response.

Film's Power over Audiences

We are aware of many things that film can do, but there has been relatively little research on the effects of film on different audiences. Most existing research has been in the area of education. Not nearly as much has been done in such areas as society, recreation, or information.

Nevertheless, there is general agreement that films can:

convey ideas	impart information
explain	summarize
create/develop attitudes	comment/editorialize
entertain	offer catharsis
stimulate/deepen appreciation	solve problems
influence conduct	provide for wish fulfillment
encourage habit formation	persuade
motivate action	foster values
illustrate	change taste
demonstrate	provoke thought
delineate policy	present ideals
affect behavior	

For further information on the effects of film on audiences and individuals, the reader is directed to Payne Fund Studies, a summary of which appears in *Our*

Movie-Made Children, or to the research findings summarized in volumes such as *Instructional Film Research 1918–1950*.

Film and Education

Education and entertainment are usually thought of as the two main uses of film. They are not mutually exclusive. Films are an essential educational medium for many reasons. Foremost, they are not affected by the unpopularity of verbalism and can therefore reach audiences that are resistant to print and lecture. They can provide a convenient alternate to museums and travel, and they can teach certain kinds of skills and concepts, as well as provide motivation for learning others. This facility of film for broadening knowledge and fostering skill comes about in several ways.

Film provides visual experiences not otherwise easily secured. Viewing foreign lands, examining certain vocations, observing the people, customs, and rituals of remote places are all eminently possible via film.

Film provides each student a front-row seat at demonstrations, experiments, and exhibits. Certain activities may be too difficult, costly, or dangerous to perform repeatedly before "live audiences"; others may require more specialized talent or skills than the teacher possesses. By means of film, experiences involving items that are only infrequently available can be reproduced at will.

Films can clarify actions or processes which might be difficult or impossible to depict or describe in any other manner. Examples include animal locomotion, rocket launchings, x-ray cinematography, zoological studies and nuclear research. With auxiliary devices such as telescopes, microscopes, and polarizers, much that is unavailable to the naked eye can be made visible.

Films can recreate a historical incident, personage, or period with a fidelity to locale and detail not obtainable with other media. Films make it possible to revisit the past and to imagine more vividly the particular mood and tempo of an era.

Abstract and theoretical concepts can be concretized with film, usually via animation. Certain "laws" or concepts in the fields of mathematics, chemistry, physics, mechanics, and industry can be expressed and explained most clearly on film. Statistical data, for example, can be presented extremely vividly by film.

A record of history may be kept on film. Newsreels and documentaries enable us to "relive" history. A recording of civilization has always taken place, but film enables us to *see* history.

Films provide opportunities to develop critical thinking. The rich material present in certain films challenges the viewer and helps to sharpen this talent/skill. It should be noted that films do not develop critical thinking by themselves, but provide a wide range of material on which the critical faculty can be exercised.

The film image is usually concrete and highly specific. The impression it makes on the viewer is therefore a precise one. For example, two viewers can describe a character or a setting in retrospect with more concurrence than two readers can recall a verbal image.

Film encourages experimentation. Many underground or avant-garde films are instances of expèrimental filmmaking. Pure film, simultaneous images, multi-images, abstractions, superimpositions, distortions, and computer films are examples of film's potential for new and different uses.

Summary

In addition to being a popular art form, film fulfills the functions of a mass communication medium. It entertains, informs, teaches, and prescribes for its audience. At times film can appeal both intellectually and emotionally, providing the viewer with catharsis, wish-fulfillment, revelation, identification, or escape. Even personal problems that cannot be faced directly can be helped when viewed through a third person's story flashed on a screen. The anthology of experiences that film can treat is wide, and the styles used to present them are many—narrative, nonnarrative, fantasy, documentary, realistic, symbolist, avant-garde, abstract, etc.

Finally, film facilitates the global village concept of McLuhan. Before the television era of instant world communication, film exhibition was changing the geographical, cultural, and social isolation of various areas of the world. Today film provides much of the content of television and the combination of these media makes us all world citizens.

FILM'S PHYSICAL ATTRIBUTES

Raw Stock Manufacture

Film is a strip of flexible material (base) over which a coating (emulsion) of photosensitive chemicals has been applied. The manufacture of raw stock begins with the changing of short cotton fibers into esters of cellulose by a chemical reaction. Mixing these esters with solvents results in a thick viscous fluid which is force-filtered to remove impurities. When spread on a large rotating drum, this fluid quickly forms a thin sheet which is peeled off in one rotation. After drying and curing, the sheets are wound on spools and cured in storage vaults.

After a period of time, the spools are sent to a coating room where they are dipped into a silver nitrate solution, cured, and rewound on spools. After more curing, the wide film stock is split into 35mm, 16mm, and 8mm widths.

The description just presented has been simplified for conciseness. Since so many types of film are made from raw stock, numerous other steps must be taken in the manufacturing process. Color film may require three emulsion layers, since each layer is sensitive to only one of the three primary colors.

Gauges

Film stock can be cut into any width, or gauge; and throughout its 80 or so years of existence, film has appeared in many widths. Today the widths are standardized to some extent, with the four formats shown in Figure 1 prevailing. Tables 1, 2, and 3 list the differences in running times, film lengths, and frame separation between sound (magnetic track) and picture (optical track) for 8mm, Super-8mm, and 16mm film.

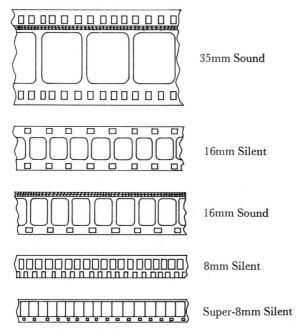

35mm Sound

16mm Silent

16mm Sound

8mm Silent

Super-8mm Silent

Figure 1. Film gauges.

35mm Film

The motion picture industry uses 35mm film. The area provided by this gauge is used differently in such processes as Cinemascope and VistaVision. Older films were shot and projected so that the film image was in a height-to-width ratio of 1 to 1.33. Wide screens offer the ratio of 1 to 2.35. Camera speed and projection speed is 24 frames per second, which allows 90 feet of film to pass the lens in one minute of running time. The 35mm film can be reduced to the 16mm or 8mm format by the film laboratory.

16mm Film

Both professionals and amateurs use 16mm film. Recent improvements in film technology have made it possible to enlarge 16mm to 35mm film for exhibition at movie theaters with little sacrifice of image quality and sharpness. Many smaller commercial institutions, including airlines, show first-run films in this format. Because of the portability of the film and its accompanying equipment, it is used by many schools and colleges in training young people. Editing is physically much easier with this format than with 8mm film, and the expense involved in filming with it is much less than with 35mm film. The projected image is large enough for most audiences today. Sound speed for this format is 24 frames per second, which allows 36 feet of film to pass the lens each minute. The 16mm format can be enlarged to 35mm film or reduced to 8mm film by the film laboratory. Nearly all the feature films available for rental or sale today were shot with 35mm film that was subsequently reduced to the 16mm gauge.

Table 1. Running Times and Film Lengths for Common Projection Speeds

	8mm (80 Frames per Foot)		Super-8 (72 Frames per Foot)		16mm (40 Frames per Foot)	
	Projection Speed in Frames per Second					
	18	24	18	24	18	24
	Running Time and Film Length					
Time	Ft.+Fr.	Ft.+Fr.	Ft.+Fr.	Ft.+Fr.	Ft.+Fr.	Ft.+Fr.
Sec.						
1	0 18	0 24	0 18	0 24	0 18	0 24
2	0 36	0 48	0 36	0 48	0 36	1 8
3	0 54	0 72	0 54	1 0	1 14	1 32
4	0 72	1 16	1 0	1 24	1 32	2 16
5	1 10	1 40	1 18	1 48	2 10	3 0
6	1 28	1 64	1 36	2 0	2 28	3 24
7	1 46	2 8	1 54	2 24	3 6	4 8
8	1 64	2 32	2 0	2 48	3 24	4 32
9	2 2	2 56	2 18	3 0	4 2	5 16
10	2 20	3 0	2 36	3 24	4 20	6 0
20	4 40	6 0	5 0	6 48	9 0	12 0
30	6 60	9 0	7 36	10 0	13 20	18 0
40	9 0	12 0	10 0	13 24	18 0	24 0
50	11 20	15 0	12 36	16 48	22 20	30 0
Min.						
1	13 40	18 0	15 0	20 0	27 0	36 0
2	27 0	36 0	30 0	40 0	54 0	72 0
3	40 40	54 0	45 0	60 0	81 0	108 0
4	54 0	72 0	60 0	80 0	108 0	144 0
5	67 40	90 0	75 0	100 0	135 0	180 0
6	81 0	108 0	90 0	120 0	162 0	216 0
7	94 40	126 0	105 0	140 0	189 0	252 0
8	108 0	144 0	120 0	160 0	216 0	288 0
9	121 40	162 0	135 0	180 0	243 0	324 0
10	135 0	180 0	150 0	200 0	270 0	360 0

Reprinted by Permission of Eastman Kodak Company

8mm and Super-8mm Film

Although this narrow gauge is associated largely with the beginning filmmaker, it is being put to other uses with growing frequency. For example, 8mm films are used for portions of news telecasts. Material produced originally in larger formats is being transferred to this gauge, and its potential in cassettes has yet to be decided. As original film, it is more fragile, hence more difficult to handle and edit, than the wider gauges. As the least expensive format, it is most suitable for the aspiring filmmaker's initial experiences in film creativity.

Projection and camera speeds with the 8mm gauge are 18 frames per second. Adaptation for sound or television requires a speed of 24 frames per second.

Table 2. Typical Running Times of Films

	Film Format					
Feet	8mm		Super-8		16mm	
	Projection Speed in Frames per Second					
	18	24	18	24	18	24
	Inches per Second					
	2.7	3.6	3.0	4.0	5.4	7.2
	Film Length and Screen Time					
	Min Sec	Min Sec	Min Sec	Min Sec	Min Sec	Min Sec
50	3 42	2 47	3 20	2 30	1 51	1 23
100	7 24	5 33	6 40	5 0	3 42	2 47
150	11 7	8 20	10 0	7 30	5 33	4 10
200	14 49	11 7	13 20	10 0	7 24	5 33
300	22 13	16 40	20 0	15 0	11 7	8 20
400	29 38	22 13	26 40	20 0	14 49	11 7
500	37 2	27 47	33 20	25 0	18 31	13 53
600	44 27	33 20	40 0	30 0	22 13	16 40
700	51 51	38 53	46 40	35 0	25 56	19 27
800	59 16	44 27	53 20	40 0	29 38	22 13
900	66 40	50 0	60 0	45 0	33 20	25 0
1000	74 4	55 33	66 40	50 0	37 2	27 47
1100	81 29	61 7	73 20	55 0	40 44	30 33
1200	88 53	66 40	80 0	60 0	44 27	33 20

Reprinted by Permission of Eastman Kodak Company

Table 3. Number of Frames Separation between Sound and Picture*

	8mm	Super-8	16mm
Magnetic Track	56	18	28
Optical Track	—	22	26

*Figures given are for reel-to-reel projection in which the sound precedes the picture. A proposed standard places the sound 28 frames behind the picture for cartridge-loaded films.

Reprinted by Permission of Eastman Kodak Company

Since the individual frame on 8mm film is smaller than on Super-8mm, there is a difference in comparative footage lengths. At the normal speed of 18 frames per second, 13 feet of 8mm film pass the lens in one minute. Because of the difference in sprocket arrangement and frame size, 15 feet of Super-8mm pass by in that same minute.

PART TWO
Developing Film Programs in Institutions

CHAPTER 4
Preparing for
Film Service and Use

STANDARDS

One of the most valuable functions that professional associations can engage in is the promulgation of standards for their member institutions. Usually association standards consider philosophies, personnel, materials, financing, and other pertinent topics. They are meant to be used as measures by existing institutions or as guidelines for establishing and building service organizations. Government agencies, professional associations, and producer groups often develop standards that are designed to provide manufacturers with information about minimum requirements for products. This type of standard is not considered in this discussion; only the organization or institution standard is pertinent.

The American Library Association (ALA) with its many member groups is most active in publishing standards for the use of professionals in the field. Since most library associations have accepted the concept of including both print and nonprint materials in collections, it is usual for some statement to that effect to appear as a philosophy. For example, in the ALA's 1968 *Guidelines for Audiovisual Services in Academic Libraries* we find: "Academic libraries have the responsibility of supplying students and faculty with resource materials regardless of format." The statement further emphasizes that the materials are not limited to the printed word.

The American Association of School Librarians (AASL) endorsed the concept of the media center more than a decade ago. Its commitment to the use of all types of learning materials is a well-known and accepted fact. In 1967, a Joint Committee of the American Association of School Librarians of the ALA cooperated with the Department of Audiovisual Instruction (DAVI) of the National Education Association (NEA) in developing certain standards for personnel,

35

equipment, and materials for junior and senior high schools. These were later published as *Standards for School Media Programs*, the materials (software) section of which gives no figure for the number of films to be owned by a school of 250 or more pupils. Instead it is recommended that such schools should have access to 3,000 titles. In the equipment (hardware) section the *Standards* suggest one 16mm sound projector for every four teaching stations, along with two more to be located permanently in the media center. For larger schools, five projectors are recommended for the media center and one for every two teaching stations. The recommendations for 8mm projectors are higher, with 15 for a media center and one for every three teaching stations. This would include, of course, the single-concept loop projectors which are quite effective for individual or small group use.

Guidelines for Audiovisual Materials and Services for Public Libraries

Perhaps the most detailed standards pertaining to films and film service are contained in the American Library Association's booklet, *Guidelines for Audiovisual Materials and Services for Public Libraries*, written by members of the Public Library Association (PLA) and published by the ALA in 1970. Permission has been granted by the ALA to reprint certain of these standards here. After an opening statement, which avers the equality of nonprint and print materials in public library collections, the following are among the standards suggested for 16mm film collections.

MATERIALS

For effective regional or community public service, a minimum of 300 16mm film titles is required.

It is understood that a regional or central library starting audiovisual services from scratch may not reach 16mm minimum standards in one year, but should do so over a period of three years.

Not less than 20 percent of the library's or system's materials budget is recommended for audiovisual materials.

Nonprint resources need repair and replacements at the rate of 10 percent to 15 percent per year of the AV materials budget. (For example, if 100 films are to be added to a collection in a given year, $22,000 will be required. $220–$330 should be added for repairs and replacement.)

Minimum additional 16mm titles, per year, after the base is achieved, is 30.

Where circulation demands for a title exceed 8 a month or 40 a year, it is recommended that a duplicate print be added.

COLLECTION SIZE

Minimum Standards for Size of Collection

Population	No. of 16mm prints	No. of 16mm prints added per year
150,000– 299,999	300	30
300,000– 499,999	400	40
500,000– 749,999	600	50
750,000– 999,999	1,000	100
1,000,000–2,499,999	2,000	150
2,500,000–4,999,999	2,500	200
5,000,000 and over	3,000	200

STAFF

Minimum Standards for Serving the Collection

Formula: Staff/No. of 16mm prints + Staff/Area in Sq. Mi.
+ Staff/Population = Total Staff Required.

No. of 16mm Prints	Staff Required
Under 400	1
400– 599	1½
600– 999	2
1,000–1,499	2½
1,500–1,999	3
2,000–2,499	3½

For each additional 500 prints add ½ staff.

Area in Sq. Mi.	Staff Required
Under 300	1
300– 999	1½
1,000–1,499	2
1,500–1,999	2½
2,000–2,499	3
2,500–2,999	3½

For each additional 500 sq. mi. served add ½ staff.*

Population Served	Staff Required
Under 150,000	1
150,000– 299,999	1
300,000– 499,999	1½
500,000– 749,999	2
750,000– 999,999	2½
1,000,000–2,499,999	3
2,500,000–4,999,999	3½
5,000,000 and over	4

For each additional 1 million population served add ½ staff.

Not applicable to an agency giving service on a statewide basis.

SPACE AND EQUIPMENT (16mm Film)

For a system or regional service center serving a population of 150,000 with a staff of three . . . a minimum space of 1,000 square feet is needed. This includes actual floor space for film storage, inspection equipment, trucks, standard library shelving for a reference collection, equipment storage cabinets, vertical files, two desks, booking files, public service area, small screening room, and movement space. It is strongly recommended that additional space be allocated or planned to accommodate the growth of collection and staff as indicated in the table cited above.

For the establishment of library or systems service, a minimum of $3,500 is required for equipment: two 16mm projectors, $1,100; one hot splicer, $250; one cold splicer, $50; one set hand rewinds, $50; one motor rewind, $450; two screens, $150; shelving or shelf racks, $300; five four-drawer files, $500; miscellaneous (cement, leader fibre cases, cans, gloves, labels, trucks, etc.), $650; total, $3,500.

Where library circulation exceeds 50 prints per day, it is recommended that automatic inspection equipment be considered.

Special venting or ventilation may be needed for use of film inspection or cleaning machines. The service area should be adequately wired, providing electrical outlets (with the required power supply) at counter top as well as baseboard levels. Screening rooms should have light controls convenient for use by projectionist. Ductwork, conduits, and other facilities should be planned as part of the building or renovation program. Shelving 48 inches wide, 18 inches deep, and 7 feet high is required for shelving 300 films.

Within the system area served there should be at least one public meeting room large enough to conduct all types of audiovisual programming for groups of 100 or more.

STATISTICS

AV statistics are important in planning budgets, in allocating staff, and in decision-making processes affecting future service. Standardization is imperative so that statistics may be used for such planning purposes and for comparison with systems and among public libraries nationwide.

Size of Collection—Counting

In order to achieve uniformity of data reported, the following definitions are to be used: *Title count:* For each type of audiovisual material the title count is the number of items which would be represented in the library catalog by main entry. (A film of four parts would be one. A series of four independent films would be four.) *Item count:* For each type of material, the total number of all titles (title count plus duplicates). *Physical package count:* This is the equivalent of a count of the number of volumes in a book collection. For each type of material, the count is by the number of individual slides, reels of tape, discs in albums, etc.

Annual additions and withdrawals of holdings for each type of material must be kept.

NOTE: Circulation figures for materials that are comparable to books in cost and use are reported on the same basis as books. Attendance figures which may be relevant for other materials have been indicated as "optional."

The showings and attendance records required are a measure of service a library or system provides through films, television, and similar materials. They indicate the per viewer cost of providing the material.

Examples: If eighty people use a $10 filmstrip per year, that is 12½ cents per person circulation.

If twenty-four people take out an $8 book in a year (i.e., twice a month), that is 33⅓ cents per circulation.

If 7,000 people see a $200 film in a year, that is less than 3 cents per person circulation.

Although the PLA describes 8mm film as valuable and useful, it does not set numerical minimums. Instead, large libraries or systems are advised to have a minimum collection of more than 100 in any format (loop, silent 8mm, Super-8mm, etc.) in order to provide effective service.

Space

Recognizing that providing space for film service may be difficult in many libraries, we gathered the following optimum-condition suggestions from reports by and discussions with experienced film librarians.

The film service area should be the location in which user and professional come together. Thus part of the area should be designed for patron use and the other for staff activities.

The patron area should contain all the informational material necessary for introduction to, and proper use of, the service. Books, periodicals, and catalogs about films should be located in this area. Carrels can be placed here if there is a need for them—for example, for a collection of 8mm single-concept loops. Sufficient furniture should be provided for patron comfort, and the area should be decorated as tastefully as possible. A desk with one or more telephone lines should be provided for the film staff.

The staff activities section should include space for storage, inspection, shipping, and previewing.

The storage area should maintain a temperature (70°F) and relative humidity (40%) conducive to film preservation. Shelving should be provided for the projected maximum size of the collection. It should be possible to reach films with ease and rapidity.

The inspection–shipping area should be large enough to accommodate incoming and outgoing films, whether they are new, returning from circulation, or being sent to patrons. This is the area where reels, cans, shipping cartons, and other supplies are kept, so storage space for these items must also be included. The movement of personnel or carts in this area must be unimpeded.

A preview room for films may be a part of this area, although the general meeting room or auditorium generally serves this purpose.

Administrative offices may be located in this area but usually only very large film libraries make this provision.

Personnel

The number of persons employed for film service will depend on such factors as level of service (state, regional, district, system, or local), population, area, size of film collection, and financial support.

On the local level the most frequent assignment of film personnel is on a part-time basis. A public or school librarian spends only a portion of her time on film service. As the other factors listed above grow larger, so does the professional time needed to offer adequate service.

Persons concerned with film service fall into three major performance categories—administrative, professional, and nonprofessional.

Administrative Level

In addition to general administrative knowledge and skills, personnel on this level should be familiar with:

1. Literature of films, including pertinent reference tools
2. Uses of films
3. Costs
4. Film programming
5. Problems of film service
6. Community served and its film needs
7. Film resources available

Among the many skills and duties required at this level are:

1. Analyzing film budgets
2. Providing staffing
3. Attending conferences, meetings, etc.
4. Interpreting film service
5. Justifying film service (accountability)
6. Interpreting film user statistics
7. Supervising film personnel

Professional Level

Most film personnel operate on this level, at times assuming some of the responsibilities of both the administrative level and the nonprofessional level.

The person at this level knows:

1. Resources of films, including pertinent reference works
2. Uses of films
3. Equipment operation
4. Librarianship
5. Community
6. Extent of nearby film collections
7. Film availability

Duties and skills include:

1. Arranging previews
2. Planning film programs
3. Creating and designing film catalogs
4. Selecting films for preview
5. Offering advice and suggestions on films
6. Organizing an information center on film—a film reference service
7. Attending conferences, meetings, institutes, film festivals, etc.

8. Keeping up-to-date with film literature
9. Collecting/interpreting statistics on film service (borrower comments, preview evaluations, etc.)
10. Using public relations vehicles to inform users of film service (newsletters, newspaper articles, etc.)
11. Supervising nonprofessionals

Nonprofessional Level

The person at this level has secretarial as well as audiovisual technical ability and knowledge. Duties and skills include:

1. Operating projectors
2. Inspecting film
3. Scheduling film
4. Repairing film
5. Gathering statistics from record cards, etc.
6. Ordering replacement footage
7. Keeping catalog files
8. Preparing notices of film showings—posters, signs, etc.
9. Making inventories
10. Packing, shipping and unpacking films
11. Evaluating film's physical condition
12. Delivering film to classroom, post office, etc.
13. Typing film requests, orders, etc.

Deployment of personnel engaged in film service varies widely. In many situations today, providing film service is a part-time responsibility of a single professional. This person usually has a bachelor's or master's degree in librarianship and is in complete charge of a media center, public library, or special library. Nonprofessional assistance may be available from students, volunteers, or aides.

In larger situations the opportunity for specializing in film service increases and it is not unusual to find more than one person assigned that responsibility. Academic libraries, college film libraries, county/district libraries, and state libraries usually require several people.

In all cases the person at the professional level, rather than the administrator or nonprofessional, is the essential element in the success of the service. The administrator must understand the service and its requirements, while the nonprofessional performs those tasks which deal with the maintenance and physical operation of the service. The heart of the service—selection, acquisition, advisement, and use—remains the domain of the professional.

FINANCING FILM SERVICE

To obtain software, hardware, supplies, and personnel for film service necessitates an appreciable expenditure. Before beginning film service, a survey should be made to ascertain need, the existing film services available nearby, and most important, whether there is an adequate commitment of funds for the purpose.

Budget figures may be determined in a variety of ways; for example, as a

per capita amount based on the population served
percentage of the total institutional budget
straight dollar amount based on predicted expenses
combination of one or more of the foregoing ways

Factors of collection size, type of film library, population served, area served, type of area, and so forth will affect budget amounts.

In any inflationary period it may be futile to quote dollar amounts, but the ranges shown in Table 4 represent typical costs in the early 1970s for initiating film service. Personnel costs are not included in these data which are middle or average figures suggested to help the librarian ascertain total budget figures. The cost of many items can be well above the figures indicated—for example, certain short films can cost well over $250.

Continuing to provide film service after certain capital expenditures have been made will necessitate provision for the budget allotments indicated in Table 5. Other items to be considered may include replacement footage, contingencies, telephone, cleaning, or rejuvenation.

Table 4. Average Costs for Initiating Film Service in 1970s

A. Average Film Budget for Public and School Libraries

Item	Public Libraries	Schools (in a county film service)
Total film budget	$3,000–10,000	$200–3,000
Per capita appropriations	$2.50–4.00	$0.50–2.00
Nonprint services, % of budget	5–20%	5–20%

B. Average Film Rental and Purchase Prices

Film (unit)	Rental	Purchase/Lease
Short	$2.50–15	$125–250
Feature	$25–50	$500–900

C. Average Purchase Prices for Short Films

Short Film	Est. Cost per min.	Min. Cost per title
b&w	$5–10	$40
color	$10–15	$60

D. Average Film Equipment Purchase Prices

Equipment	Price
Motion picture projectors	$400–700
Manual splicing equipment	$40–75
Open film racks (150–300 reel capacity)	$130–200
Closed film cabinets (150–225 reel capacity)	$200–300
Reels, cans (2,000 ft.)	$3.50–5.00
Shipping cases	$4.00–6.00
Projection carts	$40–70

Table 5. Budget Expenditures for a Film Library

Budget Items	Average %
New films	65–85
Supplies	3–5
Insurance	4–6
Printing	5–7
Postage	3–5
Miscellaneous	0–12

FILM POLICY

The question of a written policy for film services is usually illustrative of the gap between theory and practice. Theoretically, most professionals agree that a written film policy should exist, and the rationale for it is easy to establish. In practice, however, many of these same professionals prefer "No Policy" as policy. The need for freedom in the selection and circulation of films is the usual defense offered. Other factors, such as institution size, type of audience, or geographic location can determine how necessary a written film policy is. Moreover, a poorly written policy is worse than no policy at all. If a policy is desired, there are definite items that should be considered for inclusion.

General Policy Questions

1. What is the purpose of the institution?
2. What is the philosophy of the institution regarding nonprint materials?
3. What is the purpose of the film collection?
   Who makes up the institution's anticipated public?
   Where are they getting their films now?
   Are they satisfied? If not, why not?
   Are they entitled to free film service at general public expense?
   Who gets free service?
   Who has to pay (i.e., buy a card)?
   Is a local film collection better than rentals or membership in a circuit?
4. How good is the collection? Are the films:
   The best available?
   Of use to the community?
   Effective in their communication?
   Representative of authority in subject content?
   Authentic in their presentation?

Selection Policy

1. Content
   Should the collection contain:
   a. Holiday films?
   b. Ethnic films?
   c. Educational films?

      d.   Art films?

      e.   Discussion films?

      f.   Films that treat controversial topics?

      g.   Religious films?

      h.   Vocational training films?

      i.   Sponsored films?

Should the collection:

      a.   Fill in the gaps of the print collection?

      b.   Duplicate subject matter found in other media?

      c.   Support the total library program?

      d.   Promote an understanding of today's world?

      e.   Emphasize significant social problems?

2. Probable Audience

Will the viewers be:

      a.   Children?

      b.   Young adults?

      c.   Students: Elementary? Intermediate? Junior high? Senior high?

      d.   Adults?

      e.   Senior citizens?

3. Film Techniques

Should the collection contain examples of:

      a.   Animation films?

      b.   Documentary films?

      c.   Iconographic films?

      d.   Photostatis films?

      e.   Nonnarrative films?

      f.   Narrative films?

4. Length

Should the collection contain:

      a.   Short films?

      b.   Feature films?

      c.   How many of each?

5. Color

Should the collection contain:

      a.   Black and white films?

      b.   Color films?

      c.   How many of each?

6. Rationale

Should the purpose of the collection be:

      a.   Entertainment?

      b.   Education?

      c.   Survey?

      d.   Prescription?

7. Who Recommends
   Should additions to the collection be suggested by:
   a. Individuals?
   b. Committee?
   c. Library patrons?

8. Who Approves
   Should additions to the collection be chosen by:
   a. Individual responsibility?
   b. Committee responsibility?
   c. Individual with administration approval?
   d. Committee with administration approval?

9. Handling Films
   a. Who catalogs?
   b. Who processes and numbers, inspects, attaches leaders and trailers, packages film containers?

10. Hardware, Software
    Should the collection include:
    a. Gauge
       (1) 35 mm? (2) 16 mm? (3) 8 mm? (4) Super-8mm? (5) Other?
    b. Sound Systems
       (1) Optical? (2) Magnetic? (3) Optical–magnetic?

11. Rental Films
    Should the service provide for rentals?

12. Discarding Films
    a. What criteria are used?
    b. What procedure is used?

13. Intellectual Freedom
    Does the collection include films representing all views?

14. Selection Criteria
    Does the film meet minimum standards as regards:
    a. Picture composition?
    b. Movement?
    c. Color?
    d. Sound?
    e. Treatment?
    f. Authenticity?
    g. Suitability?

15. Loan or Gift Films
    a. Are loan or gift films accepted?
    b. If so, on what conditions?

Circulation Policy

1. Circulation
   Does the collection serve:
   a. Individuals?
   b. Schools?
   c. Recognized groups only?
   d. Other libraries via interlibrary loan?
   e. Home use?

2. Length of Circulation Period
   Do the films circulate for:
   a. 24 hours?
   b. 2 days?
   c. Other time periods?

3. Fees/Fines
   Are there fees/fines for:
   a. Film use?
   b. Film damage?
   c. Late return of films?

4. Storage/Housing
   a. Where?
   b. How?

5. Catalogs
   If a catalog is planned:
   a. What format will be used?
   b. To whom will it be circulated?
   c. With what frequency will it be circulated?
   d. Will it be sold or given away?
   e. Who is responsible for its preparation?

6. Film Care
   What provisions are made for:
   a. Inspection?
   b. Repair?
   c. Replacement?
   d. Preservation/conditioning/rejuvenation?

7. Hardware
   What provisions are made for:
   a. Storage?
   b. Maintenance?
   c. Circulation?

8. Reserving Films
   a. By whom may films be reserved?
   b. How long ahead may they be reserved?

9. Limitation of Use
   Are the films to be used in free showings only?

Examples of Film Policies

A sampling of different film policies follows in Examples 1–7. Because it is not possible to include every type of institutional policy, representative specimens are presented as models for those who are formulating their own statements. The arrangement of the examples proceeds from the smaller institution and collection to the larger. Example 1, the Westchester (New York) Library System, is typical of an early general film policy designed to promote film service among several small member libraries. The role of the New Rochelle Public Library reflected in Example 2 is one of paternal leadership; a letter from the director of that library notes some recent changes. The selection policy of the Monmouth County (New Jersey) Library is reprinted in Example 3. A general policy for the Camden (New Jersey) Regional Film Library appears in Example 4; the regional library usually serves several counties. The film selection policy of the Special Service Film Library of New York State appears in Example 5, and the circulation, acquisition, and service policies of a large eastern university appear in Example 6. How motion pictures satisfy the purposes of a library is taken from the Indiana University Audio Visual Center and reprinted as Example 7.

Example 1. Westchester Library System Film Service and Selection Policy

FILM SERVICE

Film service is professionally recognized as an integral part of public library service, along with various other nonbook media.

Recent studies tend to show that the ultimate cost of circulating films compares favorably with the cost of book circulation. The high initial cost of films, however, and the special techniques required for their maintenance make for difficulty in including films in budgets of most medium and small libraries. Cooperation throughout the Westchester Library System makes it possible for every library in the System to offer film service to its community.

Film Service Staff

By means of a contract with the Westchester Library System, the New Rochelle Public Library provides audiovisual services for the System. The Film Service has a staff consisting of a specialist who coordinates film service throughout the System, assisted by a full-time senior clerk and a half-time page. Staff salaries are provided by the System, and the staff members are part of the New Rochelle Public Library staff.

The Film Collection

The film collection is an aspect of the Library's educational rather than of its recreational program. Most of the films are short, nonfiction titles that have been produced for audiences of adults. A few discussion films on topics of particular importance to young adults, especially teen-agers, are included for extracurricular programs. Films for children are chiefly stories suitable for out-of-school programs.

The holdings are mainly 16mm sound films, although a few filmstrips of children's picture books are acquired. Films have been obtained either by gift or long-term loan, or by purchase. The largest number of films have been purchased. Funds for this purpose have been appropriated cooperatively by the New Rochelle Public Library and the Westchester Library System. These two funds vary according to the proportion of use in New Rochelle as compared with the use in the remainder of the System.

Films on deposit for long-term loan are sponsored films of general interest, including those deposited by local offices of Civil Defense and Social Security.

The New York State Library, Division of Library Extension, lends to the Westchester Library System small groups of about 15 films for periods of several months. Other films from the N.Y.S.L. may be ordered for special programs at any time, upon request by the WLS Film Service.

Several films in the collection have been donated by organizations and interested individuals.

Film Distribution

Films are available free of charge to adult members of WLS libraries for nonprofit, nonclassroom use. Films borrowed from the New York State Library cannot, for legal reasons, be used by schools in any way.

Films from the collection at the New Rochelle Public Library are, upon request of the borrower, sent by the regular WLS Motor Delivery Service to libraries outside the immediate vicinity of New Rochelle.

The New Rochelle Public Library publishes annually in the early fall a Film Catalog that describes the films available for the coming year with procedures for their circulation.

Film Information Service

All WLS libraries are provided with copies of the Film Catalog for use by their patrons. Limited information and advice about films is available at many libraries, particularly at the central libraries of the System. The New Rochelle Public Library maintains a reference and advisory service on all aspects of films for use by patrons of WLS libraries.

Source of films not listed in the Film Catalog can be suggested, and help is available in locating suitable films on many subjects for special purposes. Film information resources available at the New Rochelle Public Library are the following:

1. A file of descriptions and objective evaluations of many thousands of films, arranged by title
2. A file of information about films arranged by subject, including slides and filmstrips on various subjects
3. Film catalogs of major film distributors, public libraries, universities, and government film libraries
4. Catalogs of 8mm films, feature films in 16mm, silent films, tapes, and filmstrips, as well as 16mm sound films
5. Film discussion guides
6. Audiovisual equipment manuals
7. The major audiovisual periodicals
8. A list of local projectionists and rental equipment
9. Indexes and guides to films

Films for use in adult programs may be previewed by appointment at the New Rochelle Public Library.

Film Equipment

The New Rochelle Public Library owns two 16mm sound projectors, including one with screen donated by the Soroptimist Club of New Rochelle for use within the Library or for use with shut-ins outside the Library. A projectionist trained by the Film Service staff is required when the Library's projector is used. The Library also owns an opaque projector, a gift of the New Rochelle Art Association, that is available for use by any WLS library.

The Westchester Library System owns two 16mm sound projectors and a three-inch projection lens, two sizes of screens, an overhead projector, a slide and film-strip projector, and a record player, for use by any member library. Training in 16mm projection by the Film Service staff is a prerequisite for using the motion picture projectors.

FILM SELECTION*

Film selection is consistent with the selection of other materials for the public library. Films are chosen primarily for their educational, informational, and cultural values for all ages, keeping in mind the unique position of the library as an agency for adult education.

Criteria for Film Selection

The same general principles used in the selection of books and other materials are used in evaluating films. Content, authenticity, suitability for the intended audience, and similar qualities are subject to the same scrutiny.

Because of the powerful impact of visual and audio presentation and because the motion picture is essentially a medium for group viewing, the selector must employ special criteria. Among them are:

1. The film content must be valid, true to fact, true to life, true to text (if based on writing). It should contain no half truths nor generalizations.
2. Subject matter should be either timely or timeless.
3. It should be presented in a manner suited to its content, with no condescension, no loaded words, avoiding cheapness, preachiness, and coy humor.
4. The film is an art form and should be judged for its style, imagination, originality, and other aesthetic qualities in much the same manner as books are judged.
5. A film should have the following technical qualities:
   a. Imaginative photography, sense of movement and change
   b. Good, clear, understandable sound
   c. Imaginative narration or dialogue
   d. Good color quality. If color is used, it should definitely add to the film. Some films are best in black and white. Is the black and white clear?
6. Does the film have unity? Is it a cohesive whole?

Factors Affecting Film Selection

1. *Probability of Use.* The usefulness of the film in the region served is a prime factor. A film that would be used by a small number of viewers is avoided, unless it is of exceptional importance.

---

*This section is based in part on film selection statements of *The Booklist and Subscription Books Bulletin* of the American Library Association, the Enoch Pratt Free Library of Baltimore, and the Seattle (Wash.) Public Library.

2. *Unavailable Films*. Many films are not available for purchase or lease by libraries which do not charge a fee. This excludes from selection almost all theatrical feature films, most religious, and many business films.

3. *Educational Values*. In most cases films are used by groups and families for specific and serious purposes—to raise questions for discussion, to change attitudes, to improve skills, to impart information, to give cultural background. This means that films are selected that will be useful in the educational program of the borrower, whether it is a club or church program, a training course in a business situation, or a learning experience in the family. Because of this factor, social, psychological, ethical, and safety aspects are considered in relation to the film's usefulness.

4. *Films for Adults*. Topics selected cover a wide range of general adult interest, with only occasional consideration of films of an instructional nature that are sufficiently important to be widely used, such as those in the field of safety. Although entertainment feature films are generally considered to be outside the scope of the public library's film collection, such films may be acquired occasionally because of their cultural or social values, or because they present examples of motion picture history.

5. *Films for Young Adults*. Since young adults (teen-agers) are interested in many of the same topics that interest adults, few films are selected particularly for young adults. Films for use outside school that deal especially with the problems of teen-agers and are suitable for discussion may be selected for purchase.

6. *Films for Children*. Stories on film suitable for use in out-of-school programs for children are selected with particular care to assess their qualities of storytelling and characterization. Certain films in the general collection will also be enjoyed by children—films about animals and nature study, for example.

Films are not selected for use in the curricula of private, parochial, religious, or public schools.

7. *Loans and Gifts*. A film that is accepted for loan or as a gift should have the same content value as one that is selected for purchase. Standards, however, are somewhat less exacting in relation to technical quality and timeliness.

8. *Curriculum Films*. Films produced primarily for classroom use are not included, since like other teaching materials, they are the responsibility of the schools.

9. *Holiday Films*. Holiday films are acquired only if they have potential use throughout the year.

10. *Restricted Films*. Films for professional audiences only or films which are thought to be unsuitable for showing without a trained discussion leader are not added, but inquiries are referred to other sources.

11. *Controversial Topics*. In film selection as in book selection, the library has the right to offer materials on all sides of an issue. This is more difficult to do with films than with books because the cost of films makes a balanced collection impossible and makes usefulness to borrowers the paramount consideration in purchase. A film is not excluded from selection because it may be objected to by some individuals or groups. The principle of intellectual freedom applies to the selection and retention of all types of library materials.

12. *Religious Films*. An attempt is made to acquire films of good quality, acceptable to many denominations, and explanatory rather than persuasive in nature.

13. *Special Interest Films*. Many films are made by or for organizations which support causes or charities. If such films are acceptable under the criteria for film selection, they are accepted as gifts or deposits only.

Discard Policy

Prints of films which receive a normal amount of use are discarded after seven to ten years. Discarded films are often replaced by newer titles rather than by new prints of the same film.

Responsibility for Selection

All films are previewed before purchase. In evaluating for possible purchase, the film specialist, Westchester Library System service consultants, librarians of member libraries, and whenever appropriate, community specialists take part in previewing. The decision to purchase or not to purchase is made by the audiovisual consultant, whose decisions are subject to the approval of the head of the Fine Arts Department, and ultimately by the director of the New Rochelle Public Library.

Approved November 20, 1963 by the New Rochelle Public Library

Example 2. Follow-up Letter from the Director of the Westchester Library System

Dear Dr. Rehrauer:

I would like to call your attention to a number of changes which have taken place since our film selection policy was originally approved in 1963.

As our collection grew we found it was not necessary to have a supplementary collection of films from the New York State Library. At the present time we receive copies of that library's catalog which are distributed to all of our member libraries. We do serve to transmit requests for films in the State Library collection for our member libraries.

The Westchester Library System now has two separate delivery routes and as a result it is possible to make deliveries of films to all libraries in the county, not just those outside of a certain service area.

The increase in the size of the collection, and of production costs, have made it virtually impossible to publish a new catalog every year. Instead, accumulated supplements are issued at semi-annual or shorter intervals.

While the New Rochelle Library still does circulate some equipment to other libraries, many more of the member libraries have purchased their own 16mm film equipment.

As a matter of practical fact, the discard problem seems to be relatively unimportant. The popular films are generally worn out within a relatively short period of time, and we have instituted a policy of replacing films still considered to be desirable. Many films now are purchased on a lease arrangement and as a result at the end of their normal life span are returned to the distributor.

In the intervening years since this policy was written, there have been a number of major administrative changes, particularly the fact that there is no longer a Westchester Library System audiovisual consultant. In her place there is now a film librarian on the staff of the New Rochelle Public Library who is responsible for the administration of film service. The previewing has become much more of a group process involving librarians from the various member libraries who make their recommendations to New Rochelle.

One final comment which is not necessarily covered by the scope of the policy, and that reflects the fact that there has been an evolving interest in specialized media other than 16mm film, such as videotape recording and mixed media presentations. At present the Westchester Library System is contemplating hiring a specialist, not necessarily a librarian, for the purpose of advising member libraries on this subject and development of programming in this area.

I trust this information will be helpful to you.

Very truly yours,
Eugene L. Mittelgluck
Director

Example 3. Monmouth County Film Selection Policy

OBJECTIVES

Films in the joint Monmouth–Woodbridge film library as well as those acquired independently by the Monmouth County Library are intended for entertainment and learning of patrons of the Monmouth County Library.

Films will be selected for use by libraries, home users, nurseries, clubs, religious groups, government agencies, service and educational organizations, and schools. Since children 14 and under represent over 30% of Monmouth County's population, a particular effort will be made to provide a representative number of suitable feature length and short films for them.

CRITERIA

The library will always try to choose films offering the greatest possible accuracy, pertinency, filmmaking quality and good taste. While the library seeks as early as possible available films on topics of current interest, a popular subject title will not be acquired without meeting other criteria. Classics of screen history and other useful and quality retrospective films will be acquired to meet demand and utility.

PROCEDURE

In selecting films the Film Librarian will be actively assisted by at least two other county librarians; the children's coordinator (or representative) and a Branch Librarian or other designated person. These three will represent Monmouth County in the joint Monmouth–Woodbridge Film Selection Committee. Other Monmouth librarians are welcome to attend film preview sessions but will not vote on selections. All Monmouth members of the Selection Committee will try to view all films added to the collection. When necessary they will review films being considered for withdrawal or replacement. They will always review a film on which a patron request for reconsideration of a film has been made and will refer such requests to the full committee for decision, which will be relayed to the complaining patron. Film user's reports will be routinely inspected for feedback of value of films being circulated to audiences.

Monmouth members of the Film Selection Committee will routinely initiate requests for previews of new films. Film review media, professional literature, and suggestions from patrons and other librarians will be used as aids in selecting new films for the collection.

Example 4. Camden Regional Film Library Policies and Procedures

GENERAL POLICIES

Who May Borrow Films

Individuals and nonprofit organizations may borrow 16mm films, without charge, for use within the state of New Jersey. Films may not be shown where an admission fee is charged, a donation requested, for fund-raising ventures, or for any course for credit or certificate in any teaching or training institute, primary through college. Visual materials produced primarily for the classroom are not included in the film collection. Teaching materials are the responsibility of the schools.

Hours of Operation

The film center is open Monday to Friday, 9:00 A.M. through 5:30 P.M.

Registration

Participating libraries should require borrowers to complete a registration form identifying the borrower's name, residence, phone number, and organization for which he is borrowing. Borrowers should also be required to sign a statement assuming responsibility for the return of films on time and in good condition.

Scheduling

General Rules

1. No borrower will be loaned more than six films or more than a total of 90 minutes of total running time per show date.

2. Due to the large number of requests and the possibility of late returns and damaged films, no film request can be guaranteed.

3. Confirmations cannot always be provided immediately upon request.

4. Requests must arrive at least one week in advance of the show date (pickup date).

Individuals

Individuals may call the film center directly to schedule films if they are picking up in either a participating library or the film center. The film center will register borrowers who pick up at the film center. If a borrower is picking up at a participating library he need only give his name and the name of his participating library along with his requests. The film center will confirm the request with both the individual and the participating library; the participating library is responsible for registering the individual before loaning the films.

Participating Libraries

Only participating libraries may use the WATS line for calling in requests. When taking requests, indicate the borrower's alternate choices; ask borrowers if they will accept film center substitutes when first and second choices are not available. For additional information, see "Scheduling Procedures" below.

Period of Loan

Films must be picked up the day they are scheduled and returned the following day at hours convenient to the participating library.

Overdue Fines

Overdue film programs should be charged a late fee of $2.00 per day.

Reports

Participating libraries are responsible for insuring that borrowers complete the "Report of Use" card found in every film case. This report is of great value to the film center and to other borrowers.

Damage

The film center will notify participating libraries of damage to films. It is the responsibility of the participating library to collect for damage costs or to discontinue service to a delinquent patron. Fines will be assessed at 35¢ per damaged foot of film to a maximum of $35.00. A lost film must be replaced at the original cost less depreciation.

Reference Service

Film indices, magazines, catalogs, film evaluations, and reviews are available for use in the film center. Qualified personnel will assist in program planning if given enough notice in advance.

SCHEDULING PROCEDURES

Before scheduling films from the film center, the following information should be obtained from the patron:

1. *Name, address, and phone number;* request patron to complete an application or registration form for your permanent file.
2. *Pickup date;* this is the date patron will come into the library to receive his films. If you are going to provide the delivery of films to local libraries in your service area, then the "pickup date" is the date patron will receive his films in his local library. In this case, you must determine *delivery date;* this is the date the participating library will deliver films to the local library in time for a patron's pickup date.
3. *Return date;* this is the date patron will drop off the films he has borrowed. Normally, the return date is 24 hours after pickup. If you have delivered films to a local library, and the patron returns them there, then you must determine *return from delivery date*; this is the date you have brought back a film you have delivered to a local library.
4. *List of films requested;* take requests according to the scheduling procedure outlined in "General Policies."

After obtaining the above information from a patron, you are ready to pass the following information along to the film center:

1. *Show date;* for all practical purposes, this is the same as the "pickup date" above. It is the date a film must be in your library to meet the show date of a patron. If you provide delivery to local libraries, then the "show date" is the date it must be in the participating library in time for delivery to the local library.

2. *Return date;* this is the same as "return date" above. If you deliver to a local library, then the "return date" is the "return from delivery date" above. In all cases it is the date the film is back in the participating library and available for pickup by the film center.
3. *List of films requested;* this is the list of film selections and alternate selections made by patron.

Example 5. Special Services Film Library Selection Policy

Films, along with various other nonbook media, are an integral and unquestioned part of a public library's service to its community today. Even though the cost of circulating films can be equated favorably with the cost of circulating books, the rather high initial cost of a film quite often prohibits small and medium-sized libraries from acquiring films of their own. Even if their budgets could include a few titles, there would be very little choice of subject matter in any one community. With these factors in mind the New York State Library, through the Library Extension Division, Special Services Section, embarked in 1958 on the task of building a film collection. It would serve as a statewide resource for people in small and medium-sized communities, and in larger communities and library systems with active film collections, as an in-depth resource supplementing their film collections, thereby spreading the high unit cost of films over the State through broad usage. The funds for this program were received initially from the Federal Library Services Act and continued under the Library Services and Construction Act.

By terms of the Federal legislation, materials purchased with these funds were for nonclassroom use. In addition to this basic mandate, film collections in several other State agencies needed to be considered. It was decided that wherever possible, the State Library collection would not duplicate their specific fields of interest or holdings. Close liaison is maintained with the New York State Departments of Commerce, Health, Conservation, Motor Vehicles, Mental Hygiene, and the Division of Youth to carry out this coordination and nonduplication of film purchases at the State level. Where duplication may occur, it must be justified by a broader public interest or answer needs in other areas of interest different from or beyond those of the specific State department's field.

PURPOSE

The purpose of the State Library film collection is to supply library systems and their members with films they do not have, might not expect to purchase, or cannot readily obtain. The present film collection covers a wide range of subjects for all age groups. As system film collections develop, the policy and subject emphasis of the State Library collection will be more highly selective to support the more general collections in the systems.

CRITERIA FOR FILM SELECTION

All films are 16mm sound, and wherever appropriate to the subject, are purchased in color. Visual materials produced primarily for classroom use are excluded. Films are selected for all age groups, with emphasis on subjects of educational, social, and artistic value. As the film collection increases, it is important to compare films in one subject area with others and in relation to the State Library's existing coverage.

The same general principles used in the selection of books are used in evaluating the content of films. Because of the powerful impact of audiovisual presentation and because the motion picture is essentially a medium for group viewing, the selector must use, within his ability to judge, the following special criteria.

For Adult Films

1. The content should be valid, true to fact, or true to text (if based on writing).
2. Subject matter should be timely—pertinent to community needs or problems; or should be of such cultural and social value as to be timeless.
3. The manner of presentation should be suited to theme and content, avoiding cheapness, condescension, preachiness, and coy humor.
4. As an art form the film should be judged for its style, imagination, originality, and other aesthetic qualities in much the same manner as books are judged.
5. The film should have unity, and be a cohesive whole.
6. If color is used, it should definitely add to the film.
7. All films should have the following technical qualities:
   a. Creative photography, sense of movement and change.
   b. Clear understandable sound.
   c. Imaginative narration or dialogue.
   d. Good print quality.

For Children's Films

The criteria for judging children's films are similar. In addition, however, several points must be emphasized:

1. A film based on a juvenile book is judged by its success in achieving a fresh interpretation consistent with the medium. A good book does not always translate successfully to film. Occasionally a poor book can be the basis for a fine film. Care should be given to the assessment of the film for the qualities of storytelling and characterization.
2. For nonfiction materials, in addition to authenticity, emphasis should be placed on films which offer a creative experience for children.
3. There are some films which may not meet all of the foregoing criteria, but should be considered for purchase because of their motivational impetus. That is, the children, after seeing a particular film, often ask for further library materials on the subject.

For Young Adult Films

Because the main characteristic of the young adult is "in-betweenness," many adult films and some children's films are equally suitable for this group. While, again, material should be selected that is supplementary to classroom demands, special emphasis is needed in two areas:

1. Films that deal especially with teenage problems, social, physical, psychological, and economic.
2. Films that could motivate or strengthen the disadvantaged, the potential dropout, or the nonlibrary user to further concern for self-education and social development.

FACTORS AFFECTING FILM SELECTION

The film is a language and medium in itself. But a film collection can and should integrate with and augment total library service, whether at the State, regional, or local level.

As system and intersystem audiovisual centers develop or expand, the quality and content of the Special Services collection will profoundly affect selection policy at the local level. While duplication is inevitable and expected at the system level, the State Library selection policy should begin to be more highly selective and specialized, and will:

1. Collect the classical, the outstanding milestones in the motion pictures. This would include the works of pioneer and creative film makers, as well as the classic comedies and comedians. Some of this material will be very expensive and difficult to locate. This should not be an archival collection. Some titles have both classical and archival value. Films should not be acquired because they are rare but because they have intrinsic reference value and add to the depth and utility of the collection.

2. Acquire some films because of their historical importance or their innate relation to the State's development. New York State history or American history pertinent to New York's history should be emphasized.

3. Purchase in subject fields in enough depth to assist the library systems in special program needs. To do this most effectively it would seem appropriate to purchase several films in the areas of: automation, astrophysics and relativity, alcoholism, juvenile delinquency, unemployment, industrial management, investment problems, urban development, population control, labor relations, international trade, retirement and the aged, business and management, water and air pollution, and other problems leading themselves to group discussion.

4. Acquire a selected group of films dealing with art, drama, music, dance, and related cultural subjects.

5. Procure a selected group of films dealing with librarianship, literature, publishing, information storage and retrieval, and related library and research areas.

6. Purchase representative titles of cinematographic art showing experimental camera work, direction, film editing, creative animation, sound effects and dimensions, creative color control.

In summation, the film selection policy of the State Library should ultimately parallel the policy of its book collection—the classical, the historically valuable, the expensive, the difficult to obtain, plus special subject areas covered in some depth that could support local library services to the community.

Example 6. Circulation of Audiovisual Materials—Eastern University Libraries

A. GENERAL POLICIES

Users

Anyone who may use Eastern University Libraries book collections in the library may use the nonbook collections in the library.

Borrowers

Anyone with a valid borrower's card may check out any AV software, excluding motion pictures (see special policy for motion pictures below).

Loan Period

AV materials, excluding motion pictures, will circulate for one week, with renewals possible.

Equipment

Equipment will not be loaned by the Dumas Library for outside use, although the library staff will keep a folder of suggested sources of equipment for loan, rent, or sale in the area. Equipment will be made available for in-library use of all materials, including motion pictures. If library equipment is not used, be sure the software is compatible with available equipment. Please ask for instructions in the use of any library equipment.

Motion Pictures

Borrowers: Eastern University faculty with valid borrower's cards may borrow films. Their representatives may pick up motion pictures if arrangements have been made by the faculty member.

Loan Periods: A period of 24 hours from the time of pickup from the Dumas Library or any Eastern University Library branch is customary. Requests for motion pictures should be made at the branch from which the motion picture is to be picked up.

Borrower assumes all responsibility for damage or replacement of motion picture while checked out to him, and is responsible for supplying a qualified projectionist.

Borrower must not attempt to repair damaged motion picture with Scotch tape, staples, etc., but should return damaged motion picture as is.

Due to conditions of purchase, fees may not be charged for any showings.

Maximum advance notice will assure availability of the film on dates needed.

B. AV MATERIALS AS A UNIVERSITY-WIDE RESOURCE: ACQUISITIONS GUIDELINES

Basic Objectives

The intent of this document is to describe the scope of the materials which the Dumas Library will acquire to serve as a University-wide resource. These guidelines are not intended to inhibit branch and campus libraries from selecting and acquiring materials to be maintained in their respective collections which will support local needs.

Procedures

1. Branch and campus librarians will act upon suggestions for materials. If they conclude that needs justify acquisitions, they may process orders from their available funds.

2. Requests not acted upon may be referred to the branch coordinator. He will present the input to a selection committee.

3. The members of this committee will include faculty members with particular interest and expertise in the media, the Associate Librarian for Public Services, and the University Bibliographer.

They will review the requests in the light of University needs and funds available; priorities will be assigned and purchases will be made accordingly.

Basic Guidelines

1. Instructional films produced exclusively for use in the classroom are not to be included.

2. Material will be added in support of specific programs and not as a purely entertainment resource.

3. Keep in mind that the materials are those for which campus and branch libraries may not be able to devote funds.

4. Materials will be considered for purchase as a university resource where use is too limited to warrant purchase by a branch or campus library.

5. Due to conditions placed on them at the time of purchase, materials selected are not to be used for programs charging admission.

C. FILMS: ACQUISITION AND SERVICE

Policy

As part of the library's resources the Eastern University Libraries are prepared to acquire a limited number of full-length films when the films are to be used to meet educational needs and when the extent of use is likely to be such that hiring will be uneconomic in the long run. For the present the film collection will be located in the Central Library and administered by Circulation Department through the Reserve Room.

It is not intended that funds will be used (1) to relieve departments from providing material usually required for teaching use in the classroom, or (2) to provide entertainment material for use by student organizations, but rather (3) to provide material for study and reference outside a classroom situation.

Procedures for Handling

Films will be bought as "University-wide services" and the concurrence of the University Bibliographer obtained (as with any other large expenditure) to recommendations made by branch librarians or faculty departments before purchase.

Films will be cataloged and processed (including an IBM book card) by Technical Services. The Processing Department will send new films to the Circulation Department where the films will be handled as Reserve material, i.e., charged to Reserve and held in closed reserve. A periodic printout will be used as a "book catalog" of holdings.

Films may be borrowed for a three-day period by a faculty member or his appropriately identified agent by a manual charge (hand-signed).

D. FILM CIRCULATION: PROCEDURES AND POLICIES

Borrowers

Films may be borrowed by an Eastern University faculty or staff member, with a valid borrower's card, for university use. Their representatives may pick up motion pictures if arrangements have been made by the faculty member.

Borrowing Procedures

1. For each date requested, fill out one Request Form with title(s), date requested and time, alternate date and time, borrower's name, department, phone extension, and home phone number. Borrower's name should be that of individual to be re-

sponsible for motion picture during showing. The same person should also sign that portion of the request form labeled Responsibility Clause.

2. Request forms should be sent to the branch from which the motion picture is to be picked up, at least two weeks prior to preferred pickup date. Pickup is possible from the Dumas Library or any of the Eastern University branch libraries. Branches are responsible for notifying patrons of final details. If you are dealing directly with the Dumas Library, send forms to Grace Rogers, Circulation Department. Confirmation details will be returned via campus mail. Films may be picked up for the confirmed date at the Circulation Department, Dumas Library.

3. The *loan period* for motion pictures is 24 hours from borrower's pickup at the library, unless special arrangements have been made.

4. Dumas Library will review and repair film upon return. Borrower will be billed directly for any major damage.

Additional Policies

1. Due to conditions of purchase, fees may not be charged for any showings.

2. Borrower assumes all responsibility for damage or loss of motion picture while checked out to him, and is responsible for supplying a qualified projectionist.

3. Borrower should not attempt to repair damaged motion picture with Scotch tape, staples, etc., but should return damaged motion picture as is.

4. Films may be requested up to a semester in advance.

Equipment

Film projectors are not loaned by Dumas Library for outside use. Faculty members are responsible for making their own arrangements for a projector and projectionist with the appropriate party. Please contact us if you need information regarding equipment source(s) on your campus.

To Avoid Film Damage in Projection

1. Know how to operate your projector and be certain it is in good working condition.

2. Be sure take-up reel is large enough and is not bent.

3. Before each showing, be sure to clean with the enclosed tissue the path on the projector along which the film runs. *Be especially certain to clean the film gate* where the film passes behind the lens.

4. Stop projector *immediately* if there are indications that the film is not running properly.

5. Never leave the projector while it is in operation.

Example 7. Purposes of Library—Indiana University Audiovisual Center

The motion pictures in the library have been selected on the basis of their contributing to the major purposes of the film library, which are (1) to provide a library of materials for university instructional and research purposes, (2) to provide schools with educational audiovisual materials for classroom and extra-classroom purposes, (3) to meet the needs of adult groups in the state for informational materials.

TYPES OF USERS

All materials are selected on the basis of their probable potential contributions to the information, enlightenment, and thinking of interested persons, educational agencies, and adult groups in Indiana.

Comprehensiveness is recognized as a valuable criterion in measuring the adequacy of a library. An attempt is made to include materials in as wide a range as possible of content areas, grade levels, treatments, approaches, and types.

GOOD FILM USAGE

All films are selected on the basis that the film will not be used as an end in itself or as the inviolable authority. Films are placed in the library on the basic assumption that they will be used as means to ends and as such will be preceded and followed by group discussion or other analytical follow-up interpretation and criticism.

In an effort to evaluate for the purpose of improving its services, the Center will welcome users' reactions and suggestions concerning the materials listed in the catalog and the manner in which they are presented.

Films on a particular subject considered satisfactory by one group will not necessarily be equally satisfactory to other groups. Discussion leaders, program chairmen, and teachers should, therefore, determine their appropriateness for use with particular groups.

SPECIALIZED FILMS

More and more the library hopes to make available highly scientific and professional films, as well as those that appeal to other specialized interests. As the more basic curriculum films and general interest films become available from other film libraries in the state, the University will be able to realize this objective.

UP-TO-DATE LIBRARY

The motion pictures in the library are constantly being evaluated in terms of their continuing usefulness. It is the intent of the library to circulate on an active basis only those films which are accurate in terms of man's present knowledge and are consistent with and contribute to currently accepted goals. Users' reactions to films provide a valuable criterion and are sincerely invited. Those films which, on the basis of evidence gained from users and evaluators, do not seem to meet these standards are withdrawn from circulation. Since the publication of the 1965 *Catalog of Educational Motion Pictures,* more than 700 titles have been withdrawn in an effort to maintain an up-to-date film library.

REFERENCE FILMS

Many films for which there is little demand are retired to the reference library. The reference library of films now has over 2,000 titles. Users interested in using an older film not listed in this catalog are asked to request the film by title. The library will be pleased to book any of these films.

COOPERATIVES, CIRCUITS, POOLS —
SOME ALTERNATIVES

The Film Cooperative

The film cooperative made its first appearance in this country in the late forties. Cooperation between libraries was not a new concept; interlibrary loans, book purchasing, and cooperative cataloging were common and accepted practices. It was the high cost of film service to the smaller library that brought the film cooperative into being.

With the acceptance of the idea of film service in libraries and the obvious demand for films by patrons and groups, it was inevitable that libraries should attempt to meet this need. The larger urban libraries serving a denser population and having larger budgets were able to establish their own collections. It was the smaller library that needed an alternative method. The cooperative film circuit proved to be a satisfactory solution. In this arrangement, several libraries join by contract in selecting a number of films, wide in variety, and of interest to the communities served by the libraries. The films are divided into packets which are put together with attention to subject, audience level, length, etc. There is one packet at each member library at all times; after a specific period the current packet is sent on to the next library in the circuit and is replaced by a different packet from another library.

Based upon a few early experimental programs begun in the late forties (see Chapter 2), a general pattern for film cooperatives appeared. The structure of such a cooperative can be shown by a theoretical model. It should be understood that many variations of the following schema appear in almost all existing film circuits. Some definitions may prove helpful:

A *cooperative* consists of several libraries joined together to provide film service; methods include acquisition, rental, circuit, or central pool.

A *circuit* is a group of libraries that routes packets of films on a scheduled basis. A member library has custody of each packet for a specific, uniform period of time and then arranges delivery of it to the next member.

The *packet* usually includes six or more films placed together as a unit package that is circulated in round-robin fashion among member libraries of a circuit.

The *central pool* is a film collection retained in one location which serves as the administrative center. Films from the collection are booked for specific periods by member libraries. After use the films are returned directly to the center.

The Structure of a Cooperative Circuit

Cooperatives may be formed by contracts, incorporations, or informal agreement. The last method is not often used for obvious reasons.

Membership is unlimited but most existing cooperatives seem to prefer 12 or fewer members. A larger membership will result in a proportionately reduced share of each circuit film for each member and in a proportionately increased cost of film handling.

Libraries entering an established circuit are usually required to pay an initial fee in addition to the yearly assessment. The fee is determined primarily on the value of the existing collection at the time of entrance. Any member library wishing to withdraw from a circuit relinquishes all ownership rights to the collection. Usually no compensation is granted to the retiring member.

When dissolution of a circuit occurs, the film collection is either (1) divided among the members; or (2) sold, with the cash receipts divided equally among the members.

With regard to voting, each member library has one vote. A quorum may transact business by majority vote. A two-thirds vote is necessary for the acceptance of a new member. A majority vote may terminate the circuit.

Budgets are used to maintain and improve service, and to determine member dues. They are based upon film purchases, replacement footage, insurance, contingency, stationery, telephone, postage, catalog publication, cleaning, processing, leader, mailing cases, reels, etc. Cost of personnel is usually not considered except in the instance when the circuit hires an administrator to oversee its entire operation.

Dues or fees must be stated explicitly in the yearly contract.

Elections are held once each year, when the officers are chosen and the various committees are organized. Officers include the chairman, who provides overall administration, represents the circuit to the public, calls general meetings, and presides at meetings; the vice-chairman, who screens and reviews new films, contacts producers, distributors, etc., and arranges preview meetings; the secretary, who takes minutes at meetings, handles general correspondence, prepares reports, and facilitates communication between members; and the treasurer, who collects dues, purchases films, supplies, etc., prepares the budget, and does any bookkeeping for the circuit. There are five types of committees.

The Preview–Selection Committee consists of small groups that perform the initial screenings, eliminating any films that are not suitable. This unit operates in accordance with a film selection policy and meets frequently to select those films to be shown to the total group.

The Allocation Committee divides the film collection into packets; balances each packet for subject matter, variety, audience level, color versus black and white, etc.; arranges routing of films so that second- or third-year films do not appear at the same library during the same month; creates the film catalog; and reviews all films in the collection each year for popularity, pertinence, physical condition, etc.

The Maintenance Committee makes decisions on major repairs to be made to films; repairs small damage; evaluates the physical condition of the films (sometimes based upon the number of splices: if there are more than 15, the film is considered in poor physical condition); arranges training sessions for projector operations, film repair, etc.

The Budget Committee prepares the yearly budget with the treasurer.

The Appointment Committee suggests new officers and distributes the work load (most members will work on several committees).

Meetings include general meetings, held bimonthly, and the location for meetings is rotated among the member libraries. Preview–Selection Committee meetings are held as needed—sometimes as often as several each month. Films recommended by the committee are shown at the general meetings.

Insurance coverage is usually an all-risk floater policy which covers all films in all locations. With regard to maintenance, the following requirements must be met: (1) Each member shall own rewinding and splicing equipment. (2) Member libraries shall check each film carefully after each showing and before it is sent on to the next library. (3) One staff member shall be qualified by training to perform the maintenance necessary. With regard to film circulation, each library is responsible for its own circulation policy: Do films circulate to schools? To individuals? No fee can be charged for the loan of films but fines may be charged if films are returned late. Records of audience size and reaction must be kept for each film circulation.

Those films no longer suitable for circulation or those appealing to a small specialized audience may be placed in a central collection. Member libraries may request films from this collection at any time.

Advantages of a Circuit

1. Films are available to all at a small or minimal cost to the library.
2. A professional film librarian may be hired by the circuit. The contributions this person can make to the circuit include selection, maintenance, and processing of films; preparation of catalogs, guides, and lists; etc.
3. A larger number and greater variety of films than a single library could otherwise afford are attainable.
4. The continual evaluation, enlarging, and rearranging of the packets prevents stagnation of the collection.
5. The system is more efficient in time and cost per unit showing than the central pool arrangement.
6. Supplementary materials such as catalogs, guides, and interim lists can be prepared more efficiently.
7. The contract, if properly drawn, can be a source of great strength for the circuit, since it provides an irrevocable commitment of funds, effort, and participation.
8. The quantity and quality of service can exceed that possible by a single unit.
9. A circuit is a good way to begin a film service that will eventually become either individual or system.
10. Film service may introduce borrowers to other library services.

Disadvantages of a Circuit

1. Each film is available for a limited period.
2. Programming within each library is more difficult.
3. Collections may be too general and too broad, thus failing to satisfy the specific needs of one community.
4. Films get much harder use in a circuit than in one library. We can estimate that a film deteriorates three times as fast because of more use by different persons.

5. There is a lack of professional staff trained in film librarianship in most libraries.
6. Emergency programs or immediate special needs are difficult to satisfy.
7. Selection may involve conflicting personalities who must agree in making numerous decisions.
8. Previewing procedures are difficult to structure and standardize.
9. Members vary in their expertise in maintenance (splicing, rewinding, packing, etc).
10. There is always difficulty in trying to get a group of libraries or librarians to agree. Competition, suspicion, and misunderstanding of the circuit's function are not uncommon factors in any circuit operation.
11. Film care may not always be adequate.

The Structure of a Central Pool

In the central pool plan films are housed by one central organization—usually a state university or a state department of education. The existing collection of these state institutions serves as the base upon which a larger collection is built. Member libraries may request sets of films for specific periods (e.g., four weeks). One week is set aside for delivery and return, thus allowing a three-week circulation period. A single title may be borrowed for a specific length of time also. The central organization usually is responsible for the repair and maintenance of the films.

Costs in this plan are predicated primarily on new films purchased, and the number of bookings supplied to the member libraries. Percentage of budget, type of library, and state subsidization are other factors considered here.

A variation of this plan is the establishment of several central pools within one state. With funding to come from federal/state sources, collections may be either initiated or enlarged, with all the films now serving a large fraction of the state rather than only a few communities, as in a circuit.

Each such center should have an advisory board representative of the communities being served. The board should formulate policy and assist in the selection of films. Formulation of the procedures for sharing the total resources of the centers is the responsibility of the center directors.

CHAPTER 5
Building the Film Collection

THE RESERVOIR OF FILMS

What exists as a reservoir of both short and feature films is hard to delineate exactly but some evidence as to its size and nature can be noted. For clarity, a distinction between a short film and a feature film may be helpful. A short film is arbitrarily defined as any film with a running time of less than 61 minutes; a feature film, one that runs 61 minutes or longer.

Films have been manufactured or created since shortly before the turn of the century. Although many of the silent films produced from 1896 to 1927 are available, their use by today's viewers is limited to film study and 8mm home projection for entertainment to satisfy curiosity or nostalgia.

The story values of the silent films are generally not appreciated today. Thousands of titles are available but the number of worthwhile, usable silent films—both short and feature length—is probably less than 500.

In the case of the sound feature film, a different circumstance exists. To the three uses cited above, story value, education, and discussion may be added. Many of the early talkies treat themes, personal dilemmas, and social problems that are still pertinent today. In 16mm distribution by either rental, lease, or purchase, more than 100,000 titles now exist. This is the film equivalent for books in print, although there is no single listing of the available titles. New films are being added to this group within a year or so after their commercial run—sometimes earlier than they are sold for television showings. The number of new feature films being made in the United States has declined since the demise of the major Hollywood studios, but world-wide production probably numbers several hundred new feature films each year.

Presently, then, we have the accumulation of Hollywood films, foreign films, and a relatively few silent films. Two other groups must be noted.

Short films have been with us as long as the features. Short theatrical silent comedies are still popular, since they define what James Agee called "The Golden Age of Screen Comedy." Nontheatrical short films of the silent era are not used to any extent today. Certain early sound documentaries are shown, but for the most part, short films are a post-World War II phenomenon. Tens of thousands of these films have been made since the end of the War. As indicated elsewhere in this book, the NICEM *Index to 16mm Educational Films* lists 70,000 titles and the EFLA *Film Evaluation Guide* considers 7,000—only a selected partial listing. The short films that the government makes are not fully accounted for and the short films produced elsewhere in the world are not represented to any extent in these two master indexes.

Finally, with the new technology embodied in the videocassette, videotape, or videodisc we may expect the production of audiovisual materials to approach and exceed the number of book or record titles currently being published each year.

The implications are obvious for the person who deals with this software. There is a great deal of it, much of it remains eminently usable, and it is essential that a total knowledge of all aspects of it be possessed by the responsible professional.

FILM CLASSIFICATION

The Feature Film

Feature films have always been made for entertainment, and as a product to be sold for profit. There are a few exceptions, of course. Some documentary films, propaganda films, and message films were made to inform or persuade with little attention to the entertainment/profit motive but they are comparatively few. Nearly all the feature films produced over the past 60 years are story narratives designed primarily for entertainment.

The feature film may be divided into subject categories which are called film genres. Among the most common genres are musicals, gangster films, westerns, mystery films, horror films, comedies, romances, dramas, adventures, biographies, social comment films, science fiction films, war films, and documentaries. Foreign films, compilation films, and animated films can be assigned to these various genres with ease. An experimental feature film such as Warhol's *Chelsea Girls* offers more of a challenge in classification, as do certain other avant-garde features. As yet, the number of such films is small.

The Short Film

Since the first film catalog of George Kleine in 1910, there have been attempts to classify short films. The obvious division was to establish two groups, "entertainment" and "educational," but early on many people realized that these categories were not mutually exclusive. Entertainment films could also educate, and later educational films did entertain. In 1922 W. M. Gregory divided short films into advertising, government, health, school, and reedited commercial films; a year later Frank N. Freeman suggested four categories: dramatic, anthropological/sociological, industrial/commercial, and scientific. During the forties Mark A. May suggested four other categories—demonstration, information, incentive, and provocative. A more detailed classification was proposed by F. Dean McClusky in 1948, when he suggested a dozen possible types of short films:

Narrative. A film with a complete story line enacted by actors, puppets, or animated figures.

Dramatic. A film used to complement the study of literature or drama—could be a speech, a scene, an act, etc.

Discursive. An orderly arrangement or presentation similar to a lecture, essay, or lesson.

Evidential. Film used for research or study, or even as evidence.

Factual Film. Newsreel, travelogue, etc., showing a single episode or a series of episodes that are not narrative or arranged in any structured way.

Emulative Film. Shows skills, behaviors, acts, etc., which the viewer is expected to imitate.

Problematic Film. An open-ended film with no answer: it supplies material for discussion, debate, thought.

Incentive Film. Propaganda, commercial, or message films; films designed for emotional persuasion.

Rhythmic Film. A film designed to create feeling and mood, such as an experimental, avant-garde, pure, or computer film.

Therapeutic Film. Film used for the rehabilitation of psychoneurotics (experimental).

Drill Film. A film that encourages viewer participation to facilitate learning.

Participative Film. A film in which the viewer participates for enjoyment or appreciation.

McClusky gives lengthy explanations of each film type; the broad general definitions above are offered for classification. Lewis Herman in his 1965 book, *Educational Films*, offers another grouping: skill, drill, loop, information, appreciation, documentary, science, attitude, provocative, orientation, and industry.

From the sampling of short film classifications just presented, it can be seen that there is no standard listing. Perhaps this is a good thing, since it allows for the individual, flexible approach. Certainly many of today's short films are more entertaining than films made for exhibition in movie theaters. Although some can be assigned easily to a specific category, others defy such ordering. Films today can reach over several categories and be justified for placement in each. With such limitations in mind, the following classifications of short films are suggested.

The entertainment film is a film made initially for theatrical showing with a subsequent transformation into film for TV, schools, or libraries. Feature films, cartoons, and two-reel comedies are examples. Its primary purposes are escapism, moralizing, uplift via identification. It is usually narrative, has a beginning, middle, and end, and uses characters.

The information film is intended to provide relatively objective information without editorial bias. It tries to present content without prescription.

The propaganda film exists to persuade, convince, cajole, etc. It is structured to present and extoll one viewpoint.

The documentary film presents information with bias and prescription limited to the selection and arrangement of the content or some suggestions for possible improvement of a problem or situation.

The experimental film lacks conventional structure/technique. It is more concerned with communicating a mood, feeling, or emotion than information or a story. It may or may not be a film about art.

Pure film does not undergo the chemical developing process; instead the visual is drawn directly on the film.

Alternate definitions for certain of these film classifications are offered in the glossary.

LOCATING FILMS

The first step in building a film collection is the designation of candidates for possible inclusion. By using the sources of film information and evaluation discussed below, along with personal methods for finding films, a group of possible nominees can be found. The titles of several publications are listed here, but for bibliographic and ordering data, see the appropriate appendixes at the back of this book.

Books, Indexes, Guides, Etc.

The person who wishes to evaluate, rent, purchase, or lease a film will find pertinent information in many books, sometimes in a convenient, usable form and at other times buried amidst much undesired content. The following books are efficiently organized aids that will assist anyone seeking such information about films.

Film Evaluation Guide (1946–1964)
   and Supplements I (1965–1967)
   and II (1967–1971)
Index to 16mm Educational Films
Library of Congress Catalog
8mm Film Directory

Feature Films on 8mm and 16 mm
*The Film Programmer's Guide to
   16mm Rentals*
Movies on TV
The Short Film
TV Movies

Periodicals

Any listing of periodicals must be selective and suspect. Announcements of new magazines arrive with as much frequency as sad notices of the demise of others. Changes take place in the frequency of publication and formats are constantly being redesigned. Requests for information about the following periodicals should be directed to them at the addresses listed in Appendix 4.

Films

Business Screen
Canyon Cinemanews
Cinéaste
Cinéfantastique
Cinema
Cinema Canada
Cinema Journal

Classic Film Collector
Continental Film Review
Count Dracula Society Quarterly
Critic
CTVD: Cinema-TV-Digest
The Exploiter
Film

Film Comment
Film Culture
Filmfacts
Film Fan Monthly
Film Heritage
Film Information
The Film Journal
Film Library Quarterly
Filmmakers' Newsletter
Film News
Filmograph
Film Quarterly
Films and Filming
Films in Review
Film Society Bulletin
Focus
Focus on Film
Inter/View
The Journal of the Popular Film
Journal of the University Film Association
Mise en Scène
Modern Screen

Monthly Film Bulletin
Motion Picture Magazine
Movie
Movie Life
Movieland and TV Times
Movie Mirror
Movies International
Movie Stars
Photon
Photoplay
Photo Screen
Screen
Screen Facts
See
Sight and Sound
Sightlines
SMPTE Journal
Soviet Film
Take One
Today's Filmmaker
TV and Movie Screen
Women and Film

Educational–Professional

Adult Jewish Education
Advertising and Sales Promotion
American Journal of Nursing
The American Biology Teacher
American School and University
Athletic Journal
Audio-visual Communications
Audiovisual Instruction
Booklist
Clearing House
Community Mental Health Journal
Cultural Information Service
Educational Screen and AV Guide
Encounter
Elementary English
English Journal
Grade Teacher
Illinois Education
Instructor
Journal of the American Medical Association
Journal of Geography

Journal of Reading
Junior Scholastic
K–Eight
Man, Society, Technology
Mass Media Ministries Newsletter
Media and Methods
Media Mix Newsletter
Medical and Biological Engineering
Mental Hygiene
Nursing Outlook
Preview
Previews
PTA Magazine
Scholastic Teacher
School Musician Director and Teacher
School Progress
Science and Children
Science Activities
Science News
The Science Teacher
Senior Scholastic

Social Education	Training in Business and Industry
Spectrum	Views and Reviews
The Speech Teacher	Vocational Guidance Quarterly
Today's Catholic Teacher	Your Church

Trade

Box Office	Independent Film Journal
Daily Variety	Motion Picture Daily
Film and Television Daily	Motion Picture Herald
Greater Amusements and International Projectionist	Screen Actor
	Show Business
Hollywood Reporter	Variety

General

After Dark	Ms.
Argosy	Nation
Christian Century	National Observer
Coast FM and Fine Arts	National Review
Commonweal	New Leader
Consumer Bulletin	New Republic
Consumer Reports	Newsweek
Cosmopolitan	New Times
Cue	New York
Ebony	New Yorker
Esquire	Oui
Evergreen Review	Parents' Magazine and Better Family Living
Family Circle	
Glamour	Penthouse
Good Housekeeping	Playboy
Harper's Bazaar	Playgirl
Harper's	Ramparts
Holiday	Rap
Humanist	Redbook
Ingenue	Rolling Stone
Ladies's Home Journal	Saturday Review
Liberty	Seventeen
Maclean's Magazine	Teen Magazine
Mademoiselle	Time

Producers' Catalogs

A rich source of information about films is the producer-distributor catalog. These usually free volumes give almost all the information found in the book sources with two exceptions—the number of films they treat is usually much smaller and there is no evaluation, only descriptive annotation. At times certain ones will give critical quotes taken from favorable reviews. The catalogs are available on request and it is possible to be placed on a mailing list to receive future editions.

Attendance at any national meeting of a profession that deals in part with media (education, librarianship, instructional technology, etc.) is an efficient way to build up a collection of film catalogs. Many companies have exhibits at these meetings and are eager to have you take a catalog or to place your name on the mailing list. You can be even more efficient if you bring along a supply of preprinted gummed address labels. The quality of the catalogs varies but the major distributors put out impressive volumes.

Macmillan Audio Brandon offers *16mm Collection of International Cinema—1974-1975*. Films Incorporated offers a number of fine catalogs, among them: *Films Incorporated—1972-1973; Rediscovering the American Cinema; A Half Century of American Film*; and *Dialogue with the World*. Another fine catalog is the *Catalog of Shorts, Selected Features and Serial Films for Film Study* prepared by Contemporary Films/McGraw-Hill.

These are representative of the several excellent catalogs available. No one need hesitate to place them on the shelves in a reference collection. In addition, many general readers along with film buffs will enjoy the literate text and many nicely reproduced visuals.

Government Catalogs

The Federal government publishes many film catalogs, most of them indirectly through the various government agencies that circulate film as a public relations gesture. The Department of Agriculture, the Navy, the Army, and NASA are some of the organizations that use films to inform the public of their services and contributions to the country. These catalogs list films that are available on free loan. Since each agency deals with producers independently, not all of the films become the property of the government.

A selected list of films for loan, rental, or purchase can be found in *U.S. Government Films for Public Education Use: Circular Number 742* and in *U.S. Government Films*.

Most state governments publish catalogs not only of the films made about their states but also of the films that they circulate on a free loan or modest rental basis. Often the circulating collection is administered by the state library.

Free Films—Catalogs

The danger in using free films is the exposure of a captive audience to commercialism. Free films *must* be previewed to determine their suitability for showing. With that understanding, this concentrated guide, the most famous catalog in this area, is a most valuable resource: *Educator's Guide to Free Films*, edited by John W. Diffor and Mary F. Horkheimer.

Evaluation Sources

Most of the periodicals listed earlier in this chapter not only describe but also evaluate films. The depth or degree of the evaluation varies from a summary letter—E (excellent), VG (very good), G (good), A (average), F (fair), P (poor)—to the extended essays found in certain better film periodicals. There are a few guides and sources that will aid the user by locating evaluations or by giving collections of film evaluations:

Film Evaluation Guide (1946–1964)   *Film Sneaks Annual*
  and Supplements I (1965–1967)   *Audio-Visual Resource Guide*
  and II (1967–1971)   *Media for Christian Formation*
Film Review Index   *Media Two for Christian Formation*
Multi-Media Reviews Index   *The Short Film*

Evaluation Services

Certain organizations sell a film evaluation service whose general plan is to send a certain number of reviews each month to subscribers. At the end of one year, the subscribers will have received several hundred reviews of short films printed on either file-sized cards, loose-leaf sheets, letter-size sheets enclosed in a folder, or some other easily filed format.

Three services of this type are EFLA Film Evaluations, Landers Film Reviews, and Training Film Profiles.

EFLA FILM EVALUATIONS (Educational Film Library Association, 17 W. 60 St., New York, N.Y. 10023). This service offers a collection of 36 film evaluations printed on individual 3-by-5-inch cards each month except July and August. Each card has the title, running time, color or black and white, cost, date of release, producer, subject area, evaluator, synopsis, uses, audience, technical evaluations, comments, ratings. Cumulations of the cards are published at intervals; at present three volumes are available: First volume (1946–1964), Supplement I (1965–1967), and Supplement II (1967–1971).

LANDERS FILM REVIEWS (Landers Associates Publications, Box 69760, Los Angeles, Calif. 90069). This service publishes a collection of 70–80 short film evaluations each month except June, July, and August. Reviews are sent on punched 8½-by-11-inch sheets which fit into a loose-leaf binder. Binder and approximately 700 reviews cost $35 in 1972. Back volumes and a cumulated title index are available.

TRAINING FILM PROFILES (Olympic Media Information, 161 W. 22 St., New York, N.Y. 10011). The emphasis in this service is on the training film, although other media are reviewed. Issued on 8½-by-11-inch sheets, each page resembles a study guide, with audience, category, content, synopsis, questions, related materials, evaluation, and distributor given. A yearly subscription costs $125 and a cumulation of the years 1968–1974 is available for $350.

Film Organizations and Associations

There are hundreds of national organizations that are concerned either totally or in part with film. They range from professional societies to information-rating services. Some are directly concerned with filmmaking, others with film use, and still others with film evaluation. Below is a selected listing of some organizations whose rationale for being depends to a large extent on films. Groups such as the Association for Educational Communications and Technology (AECT) are not named, since film represents only one facet of their numerous interests. Annotations and addresses for these associations appear in Appendix 5.

Academy of Motion Picture Arts and   American Federation of Film
  Sciences   Societies

American Film Institute
American Science Film Association
American Society of
Cinematographers
British Film Institute
British Universities Film Council
Canadian Science Film Association
Center for Understanding Media
Center for Visual Literacy
Conference on Visual Literacy
Consortium of University Film
Centers
Council on International
Nontheatrical Events
Dance Films Association
Educational Film Library
Association
Encyclopedia Cinematographica
Farm Film Foundation
Film Library Information Council
International Federation of Film
Archives

Mass Media Ministries
Motion Picture Association of
America
Museum of Modern Art Film
Library
National Audiovisual Center
National Board of Review of Motion
Pictures
National Catholic Office for Motion
Pictures
National Center for Film Study
National Council of Churches
National Film Board of Canada
The New York State Council of the
Arts
Psychological Cinema Register
St. Clement's Film Association
Scottish Film Council
Society for Cinema Studies
Society of Motion Picture and
Television Engineers
Teaching Film Custodians
University Film Association

For further information on organizations dealing with film it is suggested that the reader consult *Encyclopedia of Associations,* edited by Margaret Fisk, or *Audiovisual Market Place* (R. R. Bowker).

OBTAINING FILMS

Perhaps the largest restraint to the full utilization of films is the difficulty of obtaining them. Recent trends seem to indicate a lessening of tight control on film distribution with a long overdue effort by companies to make their product easily available.

During the thirties and forties when commercial motion picture exhibition was at its economic zenith, feature films were zealously guarded from private or institutional use. A few titles were available for rental but these were of inferior quality and offered no competition to the theater owner. Since the mid-fifties, however, renting films to schools, libraries, hospitals, and individuals has become an important element in the business of film distribution, and in the seventies outright sale or long-term lease of feature films to institutions began. The video-cassette-disc will eventually make films as accessible as books and recordings are now.

Film Purchases

The primary and most expensive method for acquiring films is outright purchase. It has always been possible to purchase most short films, the exceptions being films that had theatrical reissue value. With the shrinking of the number of commercial movie houses, producers looking for additional revenues placed certain of their films in the outright sale market. It is now possible to purchase feature films from a variety of sources. The available titles include many of the classic films—a decided improvement over the low budget Republic-Monogram-type features that constituted the feature sale market for many years.

Price structure changes because of the many factors which influence the film industry—demand, supply, competition, company ownership and policy, etc. In the early seventies a very general rule for estimating short film purchase cost was as follows: for black and white films, $5–$10 per minute of running time with a minimum of $40 per title; for color films, $10–$15 per minute of running time with a minimum of $60 per title.

Features could be purchased in a range of prices from $100 to $2,500. Prospective purchasers of features are advised to shop around among several distributors, since wide price variation exists. When several short films are purchased, it is sometimes possible to secure discounts or installment payments.

Any film that is purchased should be guaranteed. An inspection screening should take place soon after receipt, and if there is any technical flaw (a light print, poor color contrast, splicing, etc.), the film should be replaced by the distributor with an acceptable print. In line with this suggestion, it must be noted that there is some appreciable traffic in bootleg-illegal-pirate prints, and the purchase of these prints is a most questionable procedure. No guarantee is given when the seller is a mysterious company or individual with only a post office box number for identification. The owner of the copyright for the film can confiscate the pirated copy and seek damages.

One last generalization about film purchase is that any film which receives ten or more showings per year should be considered for outright purchase rather than rental. Multiplying a unit rental by a factor of ten usually approximates the purchase price.

Film Lease

The leasing of films usually extends over a period of time such as five years. In the contract signed in this arrangement the lessee agrees to return the print after the specified period of use. Sometimes the phrase "or the life of the print" is included. Thus if a film is not usable because of wear after three years, another five-year contract would have to be negotiated for a new print. Using this system, the leasing company can keep much tighter control on its product and it can be seen that the arrangement favors the company rather than the customer. With proper care, one print can be used for a longer period than five years.

Rental

Films used infrequently or for special instances should be rented rather than purchased. Again the customer is advised to consult several rental agencies, since a wide variation of rates exists for the same film. Tables 6 and 7 indicate such variations in rental costs. Rental terms and conditions vary: some companies demand a written contract or agreement, whereas others operate via the request letter. Most agreements note a limitation of one showing or a day's use. Extensions of the number of showings or days of usage are possible at increased rental fees. The user pays the return postage and any insurance required.

Table 6. Rental Cost Comparison—Short Films

Film Title	Indiana Univ.	Univ. of Michigan	Univ. of California	Mass Media Ministries Maryland	Contemporary Films, New York	Syracuse Univ.
A Chairy Tale		$2.75	$8.00	$10.00	$10.00	$3.50
An Occurrence at Owl Creek Bridge		$6.25	$14.00	$17.50	$20.00	$14.00
Adventures of*	$4.75	$4.50	$11.00	$10.00	$12.50	$6.00
American Time Capsule		$2.65	$10.00			$4.00
Fiddle Dee Dee	$3.20	$2.65	$7.00		$12.50	$3.50
Night and Fog	$3.15	$13.00	$19.00	$30.00	$30.00	$20.00

Table 7. Rental Cost Comparison—Feature Films

Film Title	Films Inc., New York, Chicago, Los Angeles	Twyman Films, Ohio	Janus Films, New York	Macmillan Audio Brandon, New York	Swank, New York	Wholesome Film Center, Boston	Clem Williams, Pittsburgh	Universal 16, Los Angeles
Citizen Kane	$50 – $180		$75 – $120	$45.00				
The Bank Dick		$75.00			$65.00	$75.00		$65.00
Golden Age of Comedy				$30.00	$37.50	$25.00	$27.50	
Duck Soup		$37.50			$85.00	$52.50		$85.00
The Chase		$47.50		$50.00	$52.50	$50.00	$67.50	$50.00
To Kill a Mockingbird	$125.00	$125.00			$125.00	$75.00	$100.00	$125.00

A sample rental contract is shown in Example 8. Anyone renting films under such an arrangement should be aware of the terms of the agreement.

Example 8. Terms of Film Rental Agreement

1. License: This film order is an application for a license to exhibit, under copyright only at the place and time designated herein, each of the motion pictures listed. Showings must be limited to the students enrolled in your school or members of your organization.

2. Payment: Licensee agrees to pay all amounts due including the minimum guarantee seven (7) days in advance of shipping dates. If an admission price or subscription fee is charged a correct written report (on forms furnished by United Artists Corporation) must be submitted to United Artists Corporation immediately upon the conclusion of the showdate indicating the number in attendance and the total amount paid for admission to each performance, together with a check for the balance due.

3. Advertising: The motion picture may not be advertised in newspapers, or on television, radio, or in any other public media. Campus showings may be exploited within the school itself for its own College or organization members.

4. Return of Prints: Immediately after completion of exhibition on the specified showdate, but no later than the following day, the print shall be deposited by licensee with a U. S. Post Office, postage and full insurance prepaid, for Special Delivery to United Artists Corporation. For each day's delay in depositing the print with the Post Office, as provided herein, licensee shall pay an additional charge equal to one day's rental. All prints and material furnished the customer shall always remain the property of United Artists Corporation subject only to the right of the customer to make use of such material in accordance with the terms under which the picture is licensed. Violation of any of the restrictions of use noted above are subject to penalties set forth in Section 101 of the United States Copyright Law carrying a liability of up to five thousand dollars ($5,000.00) for each violation.

5. Cutting or Alteration of Prints: The licensee shall exhibit each picture in its entirety and shall not copy, duplicate, subrent or part with possession of any print thereof, nor shall the licensee cut or alter same, and the licensee shall return each print in the same condition as received, reasonable wear only excepted.

6. Damage to Prints: Licensee shall pay cost of replacement of each linear foot of any print, lost, stolen, destroyed or damaged in the interval between delivery to and return thereof by licensee except while in transit as directed by United Artists Corporation.

7. Assignment: This licensee is not assignable by licensee without the prior written consent of United Artists Corporation.

8. Prevention of Performance: If licensee shall be prevented from exhibiting any picture (provided notice thereof be received by United Artists Corporation before its delivery of the print to the shipper) or United Artists Corporation from delivering any picture by any causes beyond their direct control, then this license in respect of each such picture affected shall terminate and revert to United Artists Corporation without liability of either party.

9. Changes in Writing: This license agreement is complete and shall not be changed except in writing signed by a duly authorized representative of United Artists Corporation.

The Agreement is reprinted here by permission of United Artists Corporation.

The quality of the films in rental collections varies with the number of titles, number of copies of each title, condition of prints, etc. Anyone renting films should insist on quality and service. If a print is multispliced and in poor showing condition, the user should not hesitate to ask for a replacement, a substitute film, or a dollar credit. However, refunds are hard to obtain.

Most of the large university film libraries have extensive collections and offer adequate rental service at a reasonable cost. Their collections contain titles from many distributors, while some individual companies specialize in the rental of their own films. For example, the film library at Syracuse University, in its thirty-sixth year in 1973, added nearly 3,000 titles since 1970. It is the third largest university film library in the United States with more than 10,000 titles in its collection.

The renter of a film is sometimes at the mercy of the previous user who is late in sending a title back, or the distributor who is lax about dates, or last but not least, the U.S. mail service. It is not too unusual to have a film arrive days after its scheduled showing. In other instances it may not arrive at all because of a lost, damaged, withdrawn, or stolen print. The booking person may neglect to inform the user even though a confirmation was made. If a rental film is vital to a program, it is wise to check with the distributor a week or so before the showing date.

Film Pools

Another method of obtaining films is through a pool. Institutions participate in an arrangement where yearly fees are collected for the purchase or lease of films, which are placed in a common pool. For example, the schools in one county may join together with the county superintendent's office to form a pool. The fee in this instance is usually determined by the number of students in each school; it is usually a figure that sounds small, such as 50¢ per student, but that totals large when all the schools in a county participate. For example, a population of 30,000 generates an annual budget of $15,000. The difficulty in such a school arrangement is the demand for the same films at the same time of the year. Unfortunately, schools are for the most part locked into fixed chronological presentations of their subject matter by similar curricula, textbooks, and methods.

For further discussion of this topic see Chapter 4.

Free Loan

Many sponsored films can be obtained on a loan basis with the only financial obligation being return postage and insurance. State libraries, government agencies, commercial companies, and other organizations offer these free loan films. Two difficulties arise with this source of films: the quality is inconsistent—films included are frequently lengthy hard-sell commercials, often offensive in their brashness; second, any good free film becomes popular rapidly, and the demand for it can cause booking waits of a year or more.

Evaluations of commercial free films are quite difficult to find and the user must be familiar with the film before using it because of its uncertain content and the commercial sponsorship. It is mandatory to preview any sponsored film before showing it to an audience.

SELECTING AND EVALUATING FILMS

In general, the evaluation and selection of films for inclusion in collections depends on two factors, procedures and criteria.

Procedures for Evaluation

It is impossible to preview all the potentially useful films and so discrimination in choosing which should be previewed must be practiced. Under the leadership of an individual (such as the librarian, the media center head, the audiovisual specialist, or the curriculum director) or of a committee, the selection of films to be previewed is made. Recommendations from teachers, patrons, students, and any other audiences served should be solicited by those responsible for making preview arrangements.

All requests for previews should be channeled through one person, who may represent a committee or an institution. This individual should not only request all preview films but should also be the person to whom purchased films are sent. Such a designation will minimize errors and losses and promote a fuller cooperation with the film companies. The demand for preview prints is almost always greater than companies can satisfy and these prints must be handled efficiently.

A screening or preview of a film is the second essential in the selection process. It involves a willingness on the part of the institution(s) involved to make a commitment of money, personnel, and materials. The large blocks of time needed for professionals to view and evaluate films, in addition to the forms, letters, catalogs, etc. that must be maintained, all contribute to the cost of previewing.

Previewing know-how or ability seems to be an acquired skill which is directly proportional to the amount performed. Experience seems to bring forth a more valid critical judgment.

The actual preview should be held so that a maximum number of evaluators may attend. Numerous screenings for fragments of the reviewing group should be avoided since they add directly to both the institutional and the distributor's costs.

Participants in the previewing process need not be limited to committee members. Parents, students, citizens, and teachers should be invited to screenings and their evaluation should be sought. Previews may also be held with full audiences or classes.

If possible, previews should be scheduled in the actual locations where the films eventually will be used. The effectiveness of a film may not be the same in both an auditorium and a classroom. *King Kong* simply does not play as well on a small screen as on a large one.

Previewing films should be a year-round activity. One of the most disheartening procedures is the rush to expend all remaining funds before the fiscal year is finished. Rather than lose the monies, the harried purchaser may use less effective methods and the quality of the final collection may suffer.

Final decisions are made by individuals, committees, or administrators. Since more films are usually recommended than there are funds available to purchase them, the judgment of the professional is called upon in these final decisions.

There are several possible preview arrangements with companies.

Loan: The company will allow you use of the film for a specified length of time.

Purchase–Preview: The film is purchased and then previewed. If it is not acceptable, it may be returned and a credit memo is issued for future purchases. This process is not recommended for obvious reasons. Tying up film funds with one particular company, returning software for credit, and dealing with individuals who have your money in their possession is not a desirable condition.

Preview–Purchase: If institutions agree to keep the preview copy, a discount of 10–20% may be offered. This procedure may be acceptable if the preview print is in good condition, for what you are buying here may be a used film.

At times film previewing plans are subject to some misuse. Previews are requested when there is absolutely no intention of purchase—in other words, a free loan film. The time agreement is often violated. Films are retained for a longer period and the number of possible previews is ultimately reduced. Finally, preview films are not handled with care and are returned to the producer with torn sprocket holes, burns, etc.

These abuses tend to discourage or even eliminate preview privileges. Since the preview is a beneficial arrangement made possible by the distributor, its value should be acknowledged by the user via greater sensitivity and effort in handling the films.

Post-Preview Activities

After the screening, a small but informed group may meet to discuss and evaluate the films. They may have at their disposal the reaction-evaluation of a class, an audience, lay persons, visitors, etc. But it is their professional expertise that is essential at this point. Using the accepted criteria for their institution, they discuss the film with respect to those criteria, and with respect to the other candidates for selection. Final approval of the films may rest with the administration or directors of the institution.

Summary

The process of selection of films involves three major steps: (1) *the Search*—Candidates for selection are found by searching the literature; examining producer catalogs; viewing films at conventions, professional meetings, festivals, or on TV; or talking with concerned individuals, such as other professionals, patrons, students, etc. (2) *the Preview*—Actual screenings of the candidates for selection are the heart of the process. (3) *the Evaluation*—Those best qualified to evaluate a film in terms of the institution's goals and criteria make recommendations, and final decisions are made from these recommendations.

Criteria for Evaluation

There are several general considerations that appear consistently in published criteria for evaluation.

Purpose—How well does the film advance the stated purposes of the institution? Institutional goals vary from entertainment to civic awareness to vocational training. Each film must be measured against these aims, and its probable use must be approximated.

Audience—How well does the film serve the audiences of the institution? Fragmentation of the mass audience into specialized groups has made identification of the audiences essential.

Color or black and white—The one selected by the filmmaker should best suit the subject matter. Not all films should be in color. Whichever medium is chosen, it should be used with appropriate skill (i.e., suitable contrasts in black and white photography, or the employment of full color values in color film).

Sound—The sound is subordinate to the visual and should supplement it. Dialogue, narration, music, and sound effects should be clear, distinguishable but not distracting.

Treatment—How the subject matter is presented is an important consideration. A biased account, distorted information, selective editing, partial coverage, etc. are all possibilities. Today's films are created for both specialized and general audiences. One challenge of the selection-evaluation process is to correlate the right film with the appropriate audience. The ability to predict audience reaction is essential and can only be approached by a sound study and knowledge of the socioeconomic characteristics of the audience—background, education, profession, etc.

Film aesthetics—How well does the film fulfill the requisites of good filmmaking? Since there is no established or accepted standard for film criticism, criteria for evaluation of films vary greatly. Some professional critics stress directorial technique, whereas others look for a total effect. Still others look for social consciousness, important themes, or comment on the condition of man. Individual differences among professional critics make for interesting reading but they may cause confusion in film evaluation for institutions. There is agreement on some aesthetic factors which measure film quality, however.

Pictorial composition—The arrangement of images, figures, lines, etc., within the film frame should be emotionally and aesthetically pleasing.

Film movement—The name "motion picture" implies movement and the filmmaker should use this unique characteristic of the medium effectively.

Authenticity—Reality and truth as contrasted with contrived fiction may be factors to consider in evaluating films. The many biographies filmed in Hollywood's golden era are negative examples of this aesthetic.

Other factors may be considered but the major classifications listed above are the ones that appear on most evaluation forms and criteria statements. Forms 1 through 7 represent a sampling of evaluation forms popularly in use. Starting with a general listing of criteria and then some general media forms (Forms 2 and 3), the set concludes with specific evaluation forms geared to individualized purposes.

Form 1. Summary Checklist of Criteria for Media Evaluation

1. Authenticity, Treatment
   a. Is the information accurate?
   b. Is it up-to-date?
   c. What are the qualifications of the author or producer?
   d. Is the presentation an honest one?
   e. Is the content valid (true to life, true to fact, true to text)?

2. Appropriateness, Purpose
   a. Does it contribute to the goals of the institution?
   b. Is the vocabulary suitable for the intended level?
   c. Are the concepts presented appropriate for the intended audience?
   d. Does it add information or dimension to materials already owned?
   e. Is the material relevant?

3. Technical Qualities, Aesthetics
   a. Are the visuals clear and aesthetically pleasing?
   b. Are the accompanying printed items appropriate?
   c. Is the sound clear, supportive, and meaningful?
   d. Is the material an acceptable length?
   e. Is it the best medium for the presentation of its subject?

4. Cost Accountability
   a. What unique contribution is provided by this material?
   b. Does the packaging indicate physical durability?
   c. Does the content indicate longevity or will it be "out-of-date" soon?
      Is it "timely" or "timeless"?

5. Utilization, Audience
   a. Can it be used in several different situations?
   b. Can it be used with different audiences?
   c. Can it fit into a sequence of experiences?
   d. Can it lead to other activities?

Form 2. Evaluation of Audiovisual Materials

I. Descriptive information of media: (Check one)

16mm film ____	record ____	map ____	slides ____
film loop ____	audiotape ____	model ____	combo or kit ____
S-8mm film ____	videotape ____	flat pictures ____	other _____
filmstrip ____	chart ____	transparency ____	(specify types)

Title _____

Producer_____ Subject _____

Vendor_____ Copyright Date_____ Price _____

Set_____ B&W_____ Color_____ Time_____ Speed ____

II. Audience Level: (Circle as many as applicable.)

| P | I | J | S | C | A |
| (K–3) | (4–6) | (7–9) | (10–12) | College | Adult |

III. Evaluation of material in terms of quality and application:

	Excellent	Good	Poor
1. Potential for stimulating inquiry	____	____	____
2. Potential for stimulating creativity	____	____	____
3. Clarity of message	____	____	____
4. Validity of content	____	____	____
5. Technical quality	____	____	____
6. Aesthetic quality	____	____	____

7. Note any other values important to you   _____

_____

_____

8. Toward the attainment of what objectives might this material be a contribution? _____

_____

_____

_____

9. Can it be used for individualized study? (Check as many as applicable.)

Small group work?   _____

Whole class?   _____

Other?   _____

IV. Do you recommend this material?   Yes ____   No ____

Name of Evaluator _____ Date _____

Has this material been tried with an audience? Please comment. (Use other side.)

Form 3. Media Evaluation Sheet

Medium _____Copyright Date _____

Title _____

Producer _____ Price (Sale or Rent) _____

Vendor _____ B&W or Color _____

Subject Matter Field _____ Speed _____

Audience Level_____ Running Time _____

Description of Content_____

_____

_____

Comments (Note authenticity, creativity, technical qualities, overall value.)

_____

_____

What objectives are served by this medium?

Narrative Film _____Film as an Art Form _____

Factual Information _____Procedures_____

Visual Identification _____Motor Acts_____

Concepts _____Attitudes _____

Has the material been tested with an audience? _____ With what results? _____

_____

Compare with other media covering the same subject area: _____

_____

Recommended _____ Value rating: Low   High

                                   1   2   3   4   5

Not recommended _____

Name of Evaluator _____ Date _____

Form 4. Film Evaluation Sheet

Evaluator _____   Date _____

   I. Film Data
      Title_____Distributor_____
      Producer _____Price _____
      Color or Black & White _____Running time _____

  II. Quality: A—highest   B—good   C—fair   D—poor
      _____ sound track (audio)
      _____ visual (cinematography)
      _____ suitability of musical background to visual
      _____ suitability of narration to visual
      _____ acting
      _____ color
      _____ organization of content

  III. Does this film meet needs of (institution name)? In what areas?

  IV. Does this film maximize the assets unique to motion picture film as a me-
      dium of communication? Or would another medium do the job more effec-
      tively?

   V. What is the purpose of the film from the director's and producer's point of
      view? Is the purpose achieved?

  VI. *Who* is saying *what* to *whom* in this film?

  VII. What can audiences learn from this film?

  VIII. How would *you* use this film?

  IX. Additional comments:

Form 5. EFLA Evaluation

Film Title: Running Time _____

Subject Matter Field: Date Produced _____

Producer:

Purchase Sources:

So. _____ Si. _____ B&W _____ Color _____ Sale Price _____ Rental _____ Free _____

Evaluation Institution: Date of Evaluation _____

Names and Titles of Evaluators:

Synopsis: (About 75–100 words, as detailed as possible. Do not use producer's summary.)

I. List the possible audiences, and the purposes for which the film could be used. Rate probable value for each purpose.

		Value	
Audience	Purpose	Low	High
1.		1 2 3 4 5	
2.		1 2 3 4 5	

II. Recommended age level: primary _____, intermediate _____, jr. high _____, sr. high _____, college _____, adult _____.

III. Structure (organization, editing, continuity):   1 2 3 4 5
     Picture quality (clarity, framing, color, etc.):   1 2 3 4 5
     Sound quality (audibility, voice fidelity, music, effects): 1 2 3 4 5

IV. Comment and General Impression: (Note here any special points as to authenticity, creativity, or attitude; also a brief statement of how the film affects you. Use back of sheet if necessary.)

V. Your estimate of the value of the film: Poor _____ Fair _____ Average _____ Good _____ Very Good _____ Excellent _____.

Form 6. Feature Film Evaluation Sheet

Title _____ Running Time ___

Genre _____ Release Date   ___

Director   _____

Cast   _____

_____

Literary Source _____Distributor_____

Sound ___ Silent ___ B&W ___ Color _____ Rental Cost _____

Purchase Price _____5-Year Lease Cost   _____

Synopsis:

	Low				High
Picture Quality (clarity, framing, color, etc.)	1	2	3	4	5
Sound Quality (audibility, fidelity, voice, sound effects, music, etc.)	1	2	3	4	5
Structure (organization, editing, continuity, etc.)	1	2	3	4	5
Aesthetic Quality (use of space, time, motion, etc.)	1	2	3	4	5

Is this film factually or historically accurate?   _____

Does it hold your attention throughout?   _____

Are the actors' performances convincing?   _____

Is this film relevant to today? _____ How?   _____

Audience Level   Possible Use (i.e., information, discussion, training,

(Check as applicable.)   appreciation, etc.)

Primary   _____   _____

Intermediate_____   _____

Jr. High   _____   _____

Sr. High   _____   _____

College   _____   _____

Adult   _____   _____

Sr. Citizens _____   _____

Related topics for discussion_____

Other Comments:

Form 7. Evaluation—A Different Approach

A more personal humanistic approach to film evaluation can be formulated. For example, Cecile Starr in the *ALA Bulletin* of April 1956 suggested such criteria as:

Does the film stimulate the heart and mind?

Does it prompt the viewer to think for himself?

Does it make the viewer feel a part of humanity and the world of nature?

Does it spur the viewer toward actions which are desirable in a democracy?

Other criteria, such as originality, creativity, and imagination, are often mentioned. These are more subjective than certain other measures and should be considered in that light.

SUPPORT MATERIALS FOR THE COLLECTION

Any collection of films can be made more noticeable, attractive, and serviceable if it is reinforced by other forms of media—books, periodicals, slides, posters, filmstrips, recordings, etc. Ways of correlating the various types of media are unlimited. Exhibits, programming, bibliographies, contests, and bulletin boards are practical methods of using a multimedia approach to film use and circulation.

Local Production of Support Materials and Copyright

In several of the suggested local production activities that follow, questions of copyright may arise. Until clear answers are available from the Federal government, any position taken with respect to copyright materials will be the decision of the individual. Some guidelines used in the past include:

1. The duplication of any copyright material is to be limited to a single copy.
2. The copy is to be used only for educational purposes.
3. The material which is duplicated must not be available in a similar format via commercial purchase.

Whether the locally prepared slide, audiotape, or photograph falls into the category of fair educational use is an individual decision. New government rulings and definitions are still forthcoming.

Books and Periodicals

With the deluge of film books available today, the knowledgeable professional will have little difficulty gathering titles on any film subject. A suggested basic reference collection follows. (See Appendix 3 for further data on these titles.)

The American Movies Reference Book by Paul Michael

Cinema Booklist and *Supplement 1* by George Rehrauer

Classics of the Foreign Film by Parker Tyler

Classics of the Silent Screen by Joe Franklin

The College Film Library Collection by Emily Jones

Feature Films on 8mm and 16mm by James Limbacher

Film Evaluation Guide (1946–1964) and Supplements I (1965–1967) and II (1967–1971) by EFLA

The Filmgoer's Companion by Leslie Halliwell

Index to 16mm Educational Films by NICEM

International Encyclopedia of Film by Roger Manvell and Lewis Jacobs

International Index to Film Periodicals 1972 by Karen Jones

Motion Picture Directors: A Bibliography of Magazine and Periodical Articles, 1900–1972 by Mel Schuster

Motion Picture Performers: A Bibliography of Magazine and Periodical Articles, 1900–1969 by Mel Schuster

Movies on TV by Steven Scheuer

A New Pictorial History of the Talkies by Daniel Blum and John Kobal

The New York Times Directory of the Film by the New York Times

The New York Times Guide to Movies on TV by Howard Thompson

A Pictorial History of the Silent Screen by Daniel Blum

The Short Film: An Evaluative	*Themes: Short Films for Discussion*
Selection of 500 Films by	by William Kuhns
George Rehrauer	*World Encyclopedia of the Film* by
	Tim Cawkwell and John M. Smith

Similar collections or groupings may be assembled on topics such as film-making, history, biography, aesthetics, and criticism. The scope or size of any permanent collection will depend upon institution variables such as its budget, audience, or purpose.

Periodicals that contain film information are noted at length in Appendix 4. Although there are many good ones, most institutions are limited to a few subscriptions. A recommended basic list for libraries might include:

Film Comment	*Booklist*
Film Culture	*Film News*
Film Quarterly	*Film Library Quarterly*
Films in Review	*Sightlines*
Sight and Sound	*Previews*
Take One	

A survey taken by the author in 1972 indicated that the periodicals in the first column were those most recommended by eight writers of film books and by three library buying guides.

Nonprint Materials

At this time, location and acquisition of nonprint materials about films is a challenge. Rather than being able to purchase commercial nonprint materials designed specifically for a film collection, the professional will have to rely on adaptation, ingenuity, and intuitive intelligence in assembling multimedia that will support the collection. The following discussion offers some ideas about such media and is based largely upon personal experience. Individual creativity, local production, and acquaintance with nontypical sources can be most helpful.

Posters

Posters have become a big business in recent years. A collection called "Personality Posters" appeared some time ago and was displayed in many book stores. Selling for a dollar each, they measure about 30 inches by 40 inches and feature famous film faces of the past (Theda Bara, Mae West, Laurel and Hardy, etc.). Some recent actors (Peter Fonda, Sophia Loren, Steve McQueen, etc.) are also included. Many of the older subjects are pictured in famous roles and thus provide visuals that were formerly difficult or expensive to obtain. Twenty-five dollars invested in these posters can establish a rotating, lasting, and usable collection of film posters.

Attractive posters can be obtained in many other ways. Certain magazines include them as foldouts which can be pulled out for use. Media producers have offered posters as an advertisement or inducement. A fine poster of W. C. Fields was obtainable from a manufacturer of projection screens. Recently, announcements of film festivals and competitions have been arriving in poster form and many are attractive and worth saving.

Figure 2. Locally produced movie poster.

A more specific source but one that may be more difficult in certain cases is the local movie theater owner, who usually has a pile of the commercially produced billboard posters (one, two, or three sheets) lying around yellowing with age. Unless you are on friendly terms with the owner, you may receive a suspicious reaction, economically motivated at this point in film exhibitor history.

Recently specialty stores in larger cities have begun to collect and sell this same poster material but at very high prices. Mail-order houses operating out of smaller towns exist but care must be exercised in ordering from them since some of their product is the reduction of the original poster to a much smaller size, sometimes to 8½ by 11 inches.

Museums such as the Smithsonian, the Museum of Modern Art, and the Museum and Library of the Performing Arts at Lincoln Center publish or sell film posters from time to time.

Posters made locally within an institution can be strikingly effective. Students can sometimes visualize a film in a way that the commercial artist cannot approach. Figure 2 is an example of such an effort. Care should be taken about the poster material used if the poster is to be retained or stored in the collection. Paper that can be rolled is preferable to the stiffer cardboard material.

Filmstrips

The Europeans have been ahead of us in this area. In the late thirties, a series of 15 filmstrips devoted to the history of the film in America, Great Britain, France, Russia, and Germany was produced in England. For a brief period they were available from Stanley Bowmar Company in New York. As recently as 1965 two of the strips were still obtainable from a Canadian distributor. One contains material on prescreen history that would be hard to duplicate in other formats.

In the late fifties, Educational and Recreational Guides Inc. had 12 silent filmstrips available. They correlated with feature films that had English curriculum value: *Richard III, Romeo and Juliet, Ulysses, Adventures of Robinson Crusoe,* etc.

In England, Educational Productions Limited, East Ardsley, Wakefield, Yorkshire, lists in its catalog some silent filmstrips that are based on films such as *Mutiny on the Bounty, A Man for All Seasons, Doctor Zhivago, Camelot.*

Several companies have produced a few sound filmstrips recently which are most promising. Educational Dimensions Corporation (25-60 Francis Lewis Blvd., Flushing, N.Y. 11358) offers five sets:

Literature and the Film has four sound filmstrips which show how a major literary work is interpreted in visual terms by a film director. Included are the novel *Oliver Twist,* the play *The Importance of Being Earnest,* the legend *Black Orpheus,* and the folk tale *Beauty and the Beast.*

Two Films by Bergman includes two sound filmstrips which trace Bergman's themes of innocence, truth, and reality in his films *The Virgin Spring* and *The Magician.*

The Art of the Film is composed of two sound filmstrips discussing the main elements of film using *Citizen Kane, The 400 Blows,* and *The Seventh Seal* as examples.

Cinema and Art: Expressionism and The Cabinet of Dr. Caligari is a sound filmstrip in which the classic German film is treated as a superpersonal vision with elements of genius, horror, and madness.

Cinema and Art: Surrealism and Un Chien Andalou is a sound filmstrip about the Dali–Buñuel film which explores the human subconscious.

Visuals for Teaching (Box 8455, Universal City, Calif. 91608) has another promising set of three filmstrips available. These titles are *History of Motion Pictures, Planning the Motion Picture,* and *Shooting the Motion Picture*—the latter two photographed at the Twentieth-Century-Fox studio in Hollywood.

A set of four color filmstrips with two cassettes entitled *What to Look for in Film* has been released by Eye Gate House (146-01 Archer Ave., Jamaica, N.Y. 11435). The individual titles are *The Elements of Film, Meaning Through Light, Meaning Through Sound,* and *Meaning Through Image.*

Pflaum/Standard (38 W. Fifth St., Dayton, Ohio 45402) offers a set of three sound filmstrips called *Freeze Frame* which covers the history of the American film. The three parts are independent accounts of *The Silent Film, The Studio Era,* and *Hollywood Faces Life.* This impressive set will provide a historical context for many film showings.

Finally, Media, Inc. (Box 424, Culpeper, Va. 22701) has produced a set of two sound filmstrips entitled *The Whys and Hows of Student Film Making.* While not so impressive as the preceding sets, these strips are designed to help teachers understand the role of filmmaking in education.

Slides

Some years ago a project was announced in France which would provide a set of slides to accompany or illustrate texts on such filmmakers as Renoir, Eisenstein, Welles, Godard, Buñuel, and Fellini. Approximately 120 slides are offered for each director and they may now be purchased at a price of $35 from an American publisher, First Media Press (1121 Carney St., Cincinnati, Ohio 45202).

More expensive are the slide sets offered by the Cherokee Book Shop (6607 Hollywood Blvd., Hollywood, Calif. 90028). Fifty slides appear in each of some 20 sets at a cost of $40 per set. Most of the material is about silent films and previews are advised before purchase.

A recent set of slides entitled *Film: A Reflection of American Values* has been published by the Center for Humanities (2 Holland Ave., White Plains, N.Y. 10603). This two-part sound slide set consists of 160 slides in two Kodak Carousel trays, two tape cassettes, two LP records, and a teacher's guide. Initial reviews of and reaction to this set have been most favorable.

Because so little is available commercially, one can use the Kodak Ectographic visual-maker to make slides of pictorial material which will aid the presentation of most films. For example, slides of D. W. Griffith are useful since most viewers are unfamiliar with his appearance. *Birth of a Nation* on slides conveys much of the artistry and controversial material contained in this early film and can be used without offending any member of the audience. Preceding the viewing of a horror film, slides showing each of the horror characters (Count Dracula, Mr. Hyde, the Phantom of the Opera, etc.) can help to introduce this film genre.

Other slides are used to indicate set design, lighting, production scope, filmmaking equipment, etc. Perhaps in the videocassette age, film clips will be available to illustrate these ideas or concepts at a reasonable price. Even then, there will be a place for the use of slides or filmstrips, or both, in film presentations.

Stills, Photographs, Pictures

Visuals in these categories may be obtained from many sources. (Figure 3 and the frontispiece are good examples of stills.) Again the commercial film dealers or the "memory" shops have large collections of stills which they sell at prices ranging from 25¢ to $8 each. The Museum of Modern Art has a film stills archive which has as its base one million stills covering American films of the twenties. This group of stills, a gift from *Photoplay* magazine in 1948, has been augmented by two million stills from recent films and some pre-1920 films. The cost of each still is $2 if a negative has already been made. If a negative is necessary, the cost is $4. Less expensive are the small folios of stills that the Museum publishes. Each has approximately one dozen stills centering about a personality, or a director, or a film genre (the horror film, Katharine Hepburn, Josef von Sternberg, etc.). Other museums and libraries housing film collections offer similar services.

CFS Films (7237 Canby St., Reseda, Calif. 91335) makes 8-by-10 black and white stills available for $1.50 each. They also assemble packages ("Famous Di-

Figure 3. Still of A Tale of Two Cities.

rectors," "Scenes from Classic American Films," "Comedians," etc.) which lower the unit price to about $1.00 per still.

Business corporations occasionally make pleasant and laudable contributions to film education at all levels. A recent example was the offer by the Bowery Savings Bank of New York to make available 13 large pictures (not posters) illustrating the series of silent film classics that they sponsored on public television stations. The cost via mail was $1.00 and you could pick up free copies at any branch of the bank.

Older magazines and newspapers are another source of film pictures. Be advised, however, that the older movie magazines have become collector's items and are offered for as high as $25 each.

With visual material either scarce or costly, perhaps investing a few dollars in a second copy of a paperback picture book and then dismantling it for its visuals may be justified. A book such as Richard Griffith's *The Talkies* is made up of articles and illustrations from *Photoplay* magazine over the years 1928–1940 and would be ideal for this purpose. Certain photographs can be photocopied with some degree of success from other volumes that are not available for dismantling.

Study prints would seem to be an excellent medium for much of film study, but at this writing few are available.

Recordings, Tapes, Cassettes

The major portion of available recorded material pertinent to films consists primarily of recorded film scores, usually taken directly from the sound track. The Schwann catalog lists several hundred in-print titles of film music recordings. Since many of these titles are produced to publicize the film, they are usually deleted from the catalog after a brief period. Because these "cutouts" are remaindered, it is possible to acquire an interesting collection at a modest cost. A nearby outlet for the remaindered records is necessary, of course, but most large chain or department stores frequently remainder recordings. There is evidence that the same procedure will take place with cartridges and cassettes. (The prerecorded reel-to-reel tape seems to have disappeared from the retailer's inventory.)

Many original sound track recordings of film music include supplementary print material in the album. The illustrations and text provided are often impressive in quality and quantity. Most cassettes and cartridges lack this material.

An interesting use of recorded film music is to adapt it to accompany silent films. For example, it is possible to analyze *Intolerance* from a printed script and then select appropriate mood music for the various scenes. Even though the match may not be perfect, viewers enjoy silent film much more with music added, and experience a more authentic presentation, since silent films were never "silent" but were accompanied by anything from a piano to a full orchestra.

Less ambitious and time consuming is the use of recordings made specifically to accompany silent films. The Schwann catalog lists several titles, such as "Music for Silent Movies." Records from the general collection may also be helpful. For example, an album of electronic music can be used rather effectively with *The Cabinet of Dr. Caligari*, while a Knuckles O'Toole ragtime piano record usually works well with the silent film comedies.

The spoken word recording, usually taken from sound tracks, has started to appear but mostly with cult personalities. The Marx Brothers, Mae West, W. C. Fields, and Laurel and Hardy are represented on albums containing excerpts from their films. It is possible to record the dialogue from films shown on television on audiocassette for future study or analysis. Under present rental arrangements, previewing or multiple viewings of a film by students becomes a time-space–equipment–money problem. The audiocassette used together with a printed script (and there are hundreds available) may help to prepare for the viewing of the actual film.

An interesting attempt to create new film materials is the publication of two audiocassettes by Thomas More Mediatapes (180 N. Wabash Ave., Chicago, Ill.). The titles are "Sex and Violence in the Film" by Roger Ebert, and "Movies and Morals," interviews of Andrew Sarris, Roger Greenspun, John E. Fitzgerald, and Gene Phillips, with Todd Brennan asking the questions. The first tape runs about a half hour and costs $6 while the second is about one hour and sells for $9.

Erwin Frankel Productions (153 W. 82 St., New York, N.Y. 10024) produces recordings of interviews with film directors. Designed for broadcasting over college radio stations, they are most suitable for school and library collections.

Pacifica Program Service (5316 Venice Blvd., Los Angeles, Calif. 10019) publishes a series of eight audiotapes entitled "Before You Trust in Critics." Liz Smith, Roger Greenspun, Richard Schickel, Joseph Morgenstern, Stephen Kanfer, Judith Crist, Vincent Canby, and Andrew Sarris are interviewed about their approaches to film criticism.

Films

The single-reel compilation film in this format is often useful in supplementing a 16mm feature. For example, in a consideration of acting in films, let us use a Bette Davis feature film (16mm) from the thirties. An 8mm compilation film called *The Unsinkable Bette Davis* offers a review of Miss Davis as a film actress during her golden years, 1932–1945. Short clips are shown from many of her films, and although the famous voice is missing, audiences are still fascinated. The cost for this excellent supportive material is about $6.

One other example is noteworthy. The "Odessa Steps" sequence from *Potemkin* is available on a single reel for $6. In the study of Eisenstein's montage principles, it can be used in two ways. The first time it is shown at regular speed and the second time at six frames per second. (Many 8mm projectors have several speeds.) Analysis is much easier with this technique.

Many other valuable films are available in the 8mm format, and the lack of sound is not always a critical factor.

Television

Material for film study is rather scarce on television and can be found usually in two rather separate areas—public television and the late night talk shows. The former has presented "The Silent Years," "Film Odyssey," and "Movies Great Movies." This kind of programming is one tiny indication of television's potential. The films are introduced, shown without interruption, and then discussed for a short period. Public television is treating its audience and the film medium with respect. Other showings of films on television have a very limited value because of the many insulting interruptions and the usual abridgment of the original film.

The second area is the talk show, where the viewer can see and hear directors and actors as they talk about their films. Quality here depends on so many variables that a satisfying program is a rarity.

Games

Only one game in the film area has appeared thus far. Called "Movie Moguls" it is not very informative, stimulating, or even interesting. The lack of creativity on the part of its authors is evidenced by the close resemblance to the structure of "Monopoly." What it does suggest is that much better games might be devised; certainly a simulation game on making a film from original idea to premiere showing is a possibility.

CHAPTER 6
Organizing Film Service

CATALOGING FILMS

Different methods of cataloging films are used. Manuals on cataloging nonprint materials have been issued by several state librarians' associations in recent years, and independent publications have also appeared. These how-to-do-it volumes prescribe differing approaches: some advocate color coding; others suggest placing the medium name above the call number; still others recommend using three letters beneath the call number; etc. Probably the best guide to cataloging nonprint materials, including film, can be found in *Non Book Materials—The Organization of Integrated Collections* by Jean Riddle Weihs, Shirley Lewis, and Janet MacDonald.

The procedure for cataloging films should be similar to that used for books, whether it be the Dewey, the Library of Congress Classification, or simple accession classification. In addition to the title card, there should be several subject head cards, since most films can be classified several ways.

Information on each card should include the words "motion picture" and whichever of the following apply: "16mm," "8mm," "Super-8mm" or "loop film in cartridge." Colored cards are sometimes used to denote films. Other information should include:

Title or subject heading	Sound or silent
Release date	Color or black and white
Director	Annotation
Producer/distributor	Audience level
Running time	Other subject headings

Examples 9–12 show selected catalog cards—two for short films, one for feature film, and one for single-concept loop. The feature film is given an accession number with each of the three reels numbered separately; other films are assigned Dewey numbers.

Example 9. Cataloging a Short Film

759.9492
INS   **In search of Rembrandt.** (Motion picture) National Educational Telvision. Released by Films Incorporated, 1971.

28 min. sd. color. 16 mm.

SUMMARY: Blends paintings and drawings with actual scenes to illustrate and document Rembrandt's mastery of technique, dramatic sense, and ability to humanize his subjects. Shows the reflective quality of his portraits and his skillful use of such items as helmets, swords, turbans, jewelry, and costumes.

1. Rembrandt Harmenszoon van Rijn. 1606-1669. 2. Art—Psychology.

REMBRANDT, HARMENSZOON VAN RIJN, 1606–1669
759.9492
INS   **In search of Rembrandt.** (Motion picture) National Educational Television. Released by Films Incorporated, 1971.

28 min. sd. color. 16 mm.

SUMMARY: Blends paintings and drawings with actual scenes to illustrate and document Rembrandt's mastery of technique, dramatic sense, and ability to humanize his subjects. Shows the reflective quality of his portraits and his skillful use of such items as helmets, swords, turbans, jewelry, and costumes.

1. Rembrandt Harmenszoon van Rijn. 1606-1669. 2. Art—Psychology.

ART—PSYCHOLOGY
759.9492
INS   **In search of Rembrandt.** (Motion picture) National Educational Television. Released by Films Incorporated, 1971.

28 min. sd. color. 16 mm.

SUMMARY: Blends paintings and drawings with actual scenes to illustrate and document Rembrandt's mastery of technique, dramatic sense, and ability to humanize his subjects. Shows the reflective quality of his portraits and his skillful use of such items as helmets, swords, turbans, jewelry, and costumes.

1. Rembrandt Harmenszoon van Rijn. 1606-1669. 2. Art—Psychology.

Example 10. Cataloging a Short Film

MAIN
ENTRY

155.5
IAM **I am.** (Motion picture) Wombat Productions, 1972.

  14 min. sd. color. 16 mm.

  With study guide.
  CREDITS: Producer, director, and writer, Gene Feldman; consultant, Lodema Burrows; photography, N. Kurita, Urs Furrer; editor, Michael Weiner.
  SUMMARY: Deals with the quest of a boy to discover who he is, what makes a person important, and how one gets to be somebody. Emphasizes the importance of introspection, fantasy, and attempts at forming meaningful relationships in the development of individual identity.

  1. Identity (Psychology) 2. Child study.

SUBJECT
ENTRY

155.5 IDENTITY (PSYCHOLOGY)
IAM **I am.** (Motion picture) Wombat Productions, 1972.

  14 min. sd. color. 16 mm.

  With study guide.
  CREDITS: Producer, director, and writer, Gene Feldman; consultant, Lodema Burrows; photography, N. Kurita, Urs Furrer; editor, Michael Weiner.
  SUMMARY: Deals with the quest of a boy to discover who he is, what makes a person important, and how one gets to be somebody. Emphasizes the importance of introspection, fantasy, and attempts at forming meaningful relationships in the development of individual identity.

  1. Identity (Psychology) 2. Child study.

SUBJECT
ENTRY

155.5 CHILD STUDY
IAM **I am.** (Motion picture) Wombat Productions, 1972.

  14 min. sd. color. 16 mm.

  With study guide.
  CREDITS: Producer, director, and writer, Gene Feldman; consultant, Lodema Burrows; photography, N. Kurita, Urs Furrer; editor, Michael Weiner.
  SUMMARY: Deals with the quest of a boy to discover who he is, what makes a person important, and how one gets to be somebody. Emphasizes the importance of introspection, fantasy, and attempts at forming meaningful relationships in the development of individual identity.

  1. Identity (Psychology) 2. Child study.

Example 11. Cataloging a Feature Film

MAIN
ENTRY

No. 6-122 **Foreign correspondent** (Motion picture) Walter Wanger
 6-123 Productions, 1940. Released by Films Incorporated.
 6-124   95 min. b&w sd. 16 mm.

    CREDITS: Director, Alfred Hitchcock; Scenario, Charles
Pennett, Joan Harrison. Cast: Joel McCrea, Laraine Day, Herbert Marshall, George Sanders.
    SUMMARY: A melodrama about a young reporter sent to
Europe to cover pre-World War II events. He becomes involved
in the kidnapping of an important diplomat.

    I. Hitchcock, Alfred, 1899– , Director.

AUTHOR
ENTRY

HITCHCOCK, ALFRED, 1899– , DIRECTOR

No. 6-122 **Foreign correspondent** (Motion picture) Walter Wanger
 6-123 Productions, 1940. Released by Films Incorporated.
 6-124   95 min. b&w sd. 16 mm.

    CREDITS: Director, Alfred Hitchcock; Scenario, Charles
Pennett, Joan Harrison. Cast: Joel McCrea, Laraine Day, Herbert Marshall, George Sanders.
    SUMMARY: A melodrama about a young reporter sent to
Europe to cover pre-World War II events. He becomes involved
in the kidnapping of an important diplomat.

    I. Hitchcock, Alfred, 1899– , Director.

Example 12. Cataloging a Film Loop

612.
REA   **Reabsorption.** (Motion picture) Hubbard Scientific Co. and Films Inc., 1972.

    4 min. si. color super 8 mm. (Kidneys)

    Loop film in cartridge.
    With study guide.
    SUMMARY: Animated sequences show how useful materials are reabsorbed into the blood stream and the kidney tubules while metabolic wastes are sent to the bladder for elimination.

    1. Kidneys. 2. Urine—Secretion.

KIDNEYS

612
REA   **Reabsorption.** (Motion picture) Hubbard Scientific Co. and Films Inc., 1972.

    4 min. si. color. super 8 mm. (Kidneys)

    Loop film in cartridge.
    With study guide.
    SUMMARY: Animated sequences show how useful materials are reabsorbed into the blood stream and the kidney tubules while metabolic wastes are sent to the bladder for elimination.

    1. Kidneys. 2. Urine—Secretion.

URINE—SECRETION

612
REA   **Reabsorption.** (Motion picture) Hubbard Scientific Co. and Films Inc., 1972.

    4 min. si. color. super 8 mm. (Kidneys)

    Loop film in cartridge.
    With study guide.
    SUMMARY: Animated sequences show how useful materials are reabsorbed into the blood stream and the kidney tubules while metabolic wastes are sent to the bladder for elimination.

    1. Kidneys. 2. Urine—Secretion.

CIRCULATING FILMS

Silent 8mm Films

In many libraries silent 8mm films are handled in ways that are more similar to the book collection than to the 16mm film collection. The service is to the individual rather than to the group.

Most of the principles that govern selection, previews, circulation, and storage of 16mm films are not applied to 8mm. Since the demand comes largely from those patrons who have home projectors—usually either 8mm and/or Super-8mm silent film projectors which use a reel-to-reel system—the procedures for handling 8mm films are dictated by this audience.

When a program of films can be obtained with ease and without cost from the library, the patron is usually interested. Since the available material on 8mm reels is entertainment—feature film excerpts, silent films, comedies, travel, cartoons, sports—setting up a collection is relatively simple. Many libraries shelve the 8mm films in their original cardboard boxes so that the titles show and allow the patron to browse and select. Special reservation bookings, constant inspections, and other procedures associated with 16mm films are not used here. Films can be listed in the card catalog or in a book catalog. The borrower follows the same procedure as in checking out a book. The time period is usually for one or two weeks.

Advantages of 8mm Film

The hardware exists in large quantity. Each year more than 700,000 8mm film projectors are sold and more than eight million are now in American homes. Experience indicates that most of these owners operate their machines carefully, and as a result there is minimal damage to the prints. It is not unusual to have as many as 75 circulations before signs of wear or damage appear.

Storage and shelf space required is small. Since most collections number only a few hundred titles, the problem of space is minimized. One standard three-foot bin fixture will be more than adequate. Then, too, most of the films will be in constant circulation. A survey reported in the *Library Journal* in August 1969 indicated that 26 out of 28 libraries offering 8mm film service had 56 percent of the titles in circulation, while 14 had over 74 percent on loan.

Specialized personnel are not required. Since the films are reshelved directly upon return and are not inspected, trained film personnel are not needed.

8mm films are inexpensive. The price of the 8mm single reel, which runs for a maximum of 10 minutes, usually ranges from $6 to $15. Color, Super-8mm gauge, and certain specialized subjects will increase the cost. Thus a collection of 50 or 100 titles can be obtained for a modest sum. A California librarian reported that every dollar spent on 8mm films was used by 225 people. Certain companies will allow a trade-in of used films for as much as 40 percent of their original value. This practice is not standard, however.

8mm film is an attraction. Libraries having 8mm circulating collections report that other services were made more familiar to the borrowers of these films, many of whom are not regular patrons.

Disadvantages of 8mm Film

Noncompatibility of 8mm. Since not all films will fit all machines, is it wise for libraries to spend funds for a format that is constantly changing? Since most of the home projectors are either 8mm, Super-8mm, or duals, the film format should be limited to these sizes. Super-8mm will become more popular as the use of regular 8mm film declines.

If the expenditure of funds for the circulation of 8mm films can be justified in a five-year period, the selection of a collection in a single or double format might be considered.

Diminishment of patron interest. Two claims are voiced with sufficient frequency to warrant listing here. The first is that the film borrower does not want to see the films more than once and, second, his initial enthusiasm for the collection diminishes in direct proportion with his length of ownership of the projector. Both these factors are cited as the major causes for a rapid loss of patron interest in 8mm collections.

Content of 8mm films is limited. Since the films made in the 8mm format are designed for home use, the emphasis has been on entertainment. Some professionals decry the lack of anything "substantial" on 8mm film. Comparison is probably being made with 16mm films and the prospective user will have to decide the validity of this argument.

Sound 8mm Films

Since there has been no standardization in this medium, most film libraries have avoided any large investment of funds in sound 8mm formats. Not only is the hardware noncompatible, but up to now there has been little interest on the part of film producers in converting their films into 8mm sound formats.

The 8mm Film Loop

The silent 8mm loop projector is a noncompatible system that is usually identified by a projector made by the Technicolor Company and a plastic cartridge which houses the film in a continuous loop. Sometimes called "single concept," the film program lasts from a minimum of 30 seconds to a maximum of 8 minutes and then repeats itself until the machine is stopped or the cartridge is withdrawn. Often that running time will allow for more than one concept to be developed; it depends upon the material presented more than upon the time available.

Thousands of titles are available in continuous loop cartridge format. Almost all are educational and designed to support instruction. Certainly some are entertainment—for example, portions of the Walt Disney Nature Series have been used to make loops, and there are stories, cartoons, and travel films available.

The cost of the cartridges depends upon length, color, and topic, with the price range currently from $15 to $25. The potential of this format for use in schools and special libraries is not yet realized.

As indicated elsewhere, the costs of sound 8mm film loop hardware and the software begin to approach that of 16mm sound systems. Film libraries have not become involved with the 8mm sound format to any extent.

16mm Films

The loan and circulation of 16mm films by public libraries is usually a group service rather than an individual one. Thus, some film libraries will only lend their films to groups or to individuals representing groups. No provision is made for one-person viewing.

Circulation rules vary widely, but some requirements are common enough to be called operating policy. They include the following:

1. Films may be borrowed on the presentation of a library card. In certain situations, further information may be requested.
2. Films are available to adults who represent groups—civic, political, etc.
3. Films are loaned free of charge. A small fee is sometimes requested for insurance against loss or damage.
4. All showings of the films must be free of charge; there can be no admission, no requested donation, or no fund-raising activity associated with the showing. This restriction does not apply to films that are rented from commercial sources rather than owned by the library.
5. Sometimes film service is restricted to certain groups. For example, films are not loaned for school use by some public libraries, since the schools have (or should have) appropriations for securing their films from other sources. It is argued that the function of the public library is to serve its audiences in the areas that the school does not. The adult audience should be a major focus for this service.
6. Films are not to be duplicated or copied.
7. Films may not be shown over any form of television.
8. The period of the loan is generally 24 hours with an extension to 48 hours on a weekend.
9. A report must be filled out following each circulation. Data usually requested include: (a) audience type(s); (b) audience size; (c) audience reaction; and (d) number of showings.
10. Borrowers who are late in returning a film are subject to fines. These vary, and may be based on an hourly rate or a daily rate, and sometimes on whether another patron has been inconvenienced or a group has been deprived of a showing.
11. The borrower is completely responsible for the film while it is in his possession. Damage determination is established by the preloan and postloan inspections. Fines are often based upon damaged footage. It is possible for a library to refuse film loans to a patron who continually returns damaged films.
12. The number of films available to one group or individual may be limited by either number or total running time. Four titles is the limit used by many libraries.
13. Film showings are sometimes restricted to a specific geographic area.
14. If films are mailed, financial responsibility for postage, insurance, etc. should be established and understood by both the library and the borrower.

Certain supporting activities to 16mm film circulation in libraries appear to be standard and in common usage:

Catalogs

1. Catalogs are produced on a yearly basis—sometimes using a supplement rather than a complete revision.
2. The catalogs are either locally produced or commercially produced.
3. Costs for the catalog may be recovered by making it available outside the library for a fee.
4. Films are usually listed alphabetically by title. Data such as running time, color or black and white, silent or sound, and date of release are given. The most important part of the listing is the annotation. Unfortunately many libraries use a précis of the distributor's description of the film and avoid evaluation. Finally, the appropriate audience level may be indicated.
5. Preceding the film list in these catalogs, there should be a statement of policy, a notice of library hours, and some mention of the other library services that support or complement the film showings.
6. A subject index is usually included and some of the better catalogs offer directions, suggestions, and hints on handling films, projectors, and programs.

Loaning Hardware

Free loan of a 16mm projector is the exception rather than the rule in public library services. Arrangements which include financial remuneration for a trained projectionist are possible in some libraries. Others train some key organizational personnel in the community and will loan a projector if these persons run it.

Preview Center

Another valuable service that is rare in libraries is the preview room or center. A patron usually has no opportunity to see the films he has booked but must rely instead on the advice of the film librarian or the catalog annotation. Both of these have occasionally been found wanting by patrons. Space and financial considerations dictate the possibility of this service. Its importance, however, is obvious.

CIRCULATION FORMS FOR 16MM FILMS

Control of films is an essential element of film service and demands attention, vigilance, and even creativity. The investment in a film title is comparatively large and it should be protected with proportionate effort and time as a type of insurance. Well-designed circulation forms can contribute much to the efficient control of films. Although they are mostly the product of a film librarian's assessment of a specific situation, they are affected by the input of both the administrator and the technician.

The use, detail, and arrangement of film circulation forms varies considerably. The descriptions and illustrations presented here are general and are meant to suggest rather than direct.

The first requisite in control is a record of the history of a film (Form 8) in a particular collection. This card, which "legitimizes" the entrance of an accepted film into the collection, offers a record of the life of a film in a particular institution—a physical description of the film, the conditions under which it was selected, how it was used during its life, and the type of withdrawal/retirement it received. It includes other information on previews, costs, replacement footage,

Form 8. History Card

Side One

Title _____ Distributor _____
Cost _____ Address _____
Running time _____ Date of release _____
Color _____ B&W _____ Sound _____ Silent _____
Preview ordered_____ Remarks _____
Previewed _____
Accepted _____ Rejected _____
Purchase Order _____ Received _____
Inspected _____ Invoice to bookkeeper_____
Reviews _____

Side Two

	Date	Footage	Cost
Replacement Footage:	_____	_____	_____
	_____	_____	_____
Cleaning Rejuvenation:	_____	_____	_____

Summary of Showings: 1974_____   1977_____   1980_____
                        1975_____   1978_____   1981_____
                        1976_____   1979_____   1982_____

Withdrawn _____ Trade-In _____ $ Credit _____
Other disposition _____

rejuvenation, yearly showings, etc. An alternate purpose is also served by the indication of those films which were considered, previewed, and rejected.

Once the film has been placed in a collection, a record of its circulation is essential. The master booking card (Form 9) is the form used to control individual circulations of a film. At the top of this form, the film title and the circulation year are indicated. In addition, the data that a patron is apt to ask about are noted: running time, color, number of reels, etc. Beneath this information the card is divided into a daily calendar with space provided to note pickup and return data. Holidays and weekends are marked off in advance to avoid error, delay, or confusion. A typical booking would be noted by marking off any two consecutive empty white spaces. Inspection of this card should indicate film availability at a glance.

Used simultaneously with the master booking card is the borrower's request form (Form 10). All of the necessary information about the borrower is found here. In addition to his name, address, and telephone number, it should show the

Form 9. Master Booking Card

Title _____ Producer/Distributor _____
Running Time _____ Color _____ B&W _____ Sound _____ Silent _____
Number of Reels _____ Year of Release _____ Print # _____

1974–75

	1	2	3	4	5	6	7	8	9	10	11	12	13	14	15	16	17	18	19	20	21	22	23	24	25	26	27	28	29	30	31
SEP	X	H				X	X	X						X	X		H			X	X	X				H		X	X	X	X
OCT			X		H	X				X		X		H		X			X	X	X					X	X	H		X	
NOV			X		H				H	X		X		H		X									H		X	H			X
DEC	X						X	X	H				X		X	X		X	X	X		X	X		H	X		H	X	X	
JAN	H			X	X					X	X		X								X			X		X					
FEB	X			X		X		X	X		H	H				X	H			X	X	X	X		X	X		X	X	X	X
MAR		X		X		X							X		X	X				X		X		X			X		X	X	X
APR	X		X			X					X		X					X	X	X	X	X	X		X		X		X		
MAY			X			X	X				X				X		X	X			X			X	X	H			X	X	X
JUN				X				X	X	X		X	X		X	X			X	X	X			X		X	X	X	X		
JUL				H	X																						H				X
AUG		X	X	X		X			X						X							X		X		X				X	X

| | 1 | 2 | 3 | 4 | 5 | 6 | 7 | 8 | 9 | 10 | 11 | 12 | 13 | 14 | 15 | 16 | 17 | 18 | 19 | 20 | 21 | 22 | 23 | 24 | 25 | 26 | 27 | 28 | 29 | 30 | 31 |

Comments _____

Form 10. Borrower's Request Form

ANDREWS UNIVERSITY
MOTION PICTURE REQUEST FORM

For Central Use Only
P-U _____
SND _____
DUE _____

MP Title(s):

1. _____
2. _____
3. _____
4. _____

Preferred Showing Date _____ Time _____
Alternate Showing Date _____ Time _____
Borrower _____ Library from which to be
Dept. & Campus _____ picked up _____
Ext. _____ Home Tel. _____

Responsibility Clause: I assume all responsibility for damage or replacement of the above motion pictures while in my possession.

Borrower's Signature _____ Date _____

Form 11. Computerized Request Form

CONFIRMATION COPY   WILSON LIBRARY – 314 MAIN STREET – WILMETTE, ILLINOIS

CUSTOMER NUMBER

```
0 0 0 0 0
1 1 1 1 1
2 2 2 2 2
3 3 3 3 3
4 4 4 4 5
5 5 5 5 5
```

FILM NO. _____
FILM TITLE _____
DATE REQUESTED _____
ALTERNATE DATE _____
SIGN _____

[ ] CONFIRMED AS REQUESTED
[ ] ALTERNATE DATE SEE CALENDAR (AT RIGHT)
[ ] NOT AVAILABLE

FILM NUMBER

```
0 0 0 0 0 0 0 0 0 0
1 1 1 1 1 1 1 1 1 1
2 2 2 2 2 2 2 2 2 2
3 3 3 3 3 3 3 3 3 3
4 4 4 4 4 4 4 4 4 4
5 5 5 5 5 5 5 5 5 5
6 6 6 6 6 6 6 6 6 6
7 7 7 7 7 7 7 7 7 7
8 8 8 8 8 8 8 8 8 8
9 9 9 9 9 9 9 9 9 9
```

No.	Calendar	Month
1	1 2 3 4 5 6 7 8 9 10 11 12 13 14 15 16 17 18 19 20 21 22 23 24 25 26 27 28 29 30 31	JAN
2	1 2 3 4 5 6 7 8 9 10 11 12 13 14 15 16 17 18 19 20 21 22 23 24 25 26 27 28 29	FEB
3	1 2 3 4 5 6 7 8 9 10 11 12 13 14 15 16 17 18 19 20 21 22 23 24 25 26 27 28 29 30 31	MAR
4	1 2 3 4 5 6 7 8 9 10 11 12 13 14 15 16 17 18 19 20 21 22 23 24 25 26 27 28 29 30	APR
5	1 2 3 4 5 6 7 8 9 10 11 12 13 14 15 16 17 18 19 20 21 22 23 24 25 26 27 28 29 30 31	MAY
6	1 2 3 4 5 6 7 8 9 10 11 12 13 14 15 16 17 18 19 20 21 22 23 24 25 26 27 28 29 30	JUN
7	1 2 3 4 5 6 7 8 9 10 11 12 13 14 15 16 17 18 19 20 21 22 23 24 25 26 27 28 29 30 31	JUL
8	1 2 3 4 5 6 7 8 9 10 11 12 13 14 15 16 17 18 19 20 21 22 23 24 25 26 27 28 29 30 31	AUG
9	1 2 3 4 5 6 7 8 9 10 11 12 13 14 15 16 17 18 19 20 21 22 23 24 25 26 27 28 29 30	SEP
10	1 2 3 4 5 6 7 8 9 10 11 12 13 14 15 16 17 18 19 20 21 22 23 24 25 26 27 28 29 30 31	OCT
11	1 2 3 4 5 6 7 8 9 10 11 12 13 14 15 16 17 18 19 20 21 22 23 24 25 26 27 28 29 30	NOV
12	1 2 3 4 5 6 7 8 9 10 11 12 13 14 15 16 17 18 19 20 21 22 23 24 25 26 27 28 29 30 31	DEC

Form 12. Film Showing Card

ATLAS PUBLIC LIBRARY
ATLAS, IDAHO

Please provide the following information and return this card with the film:

Film Title _____

Date Shown _____

Place _____

No. of Times Shown _____

Attendance _____

Audience Reaction _____

_____

Comments _____

Borrower _____

(Signature)

Form 13. Computerized Film Showing Card

MARK THE APPROPRIATE
BOX ON THE RIGHT HAND
SIDE WITH PENCIL.

YOUR FUTURE SHIPMENTS ARE
DETERMINED BY THE PROMPT-
NESS IN RETURN OF THIS FILM.

FILM DUE BACK
AT LIBRARY _____

NO. OF
SHOWINGS

1 2 3 4 5 6 7 8 9
□ □ □ □ □ □ □ □ □

MORE THAN 9 □

TOTAL ATTENDANCE

0 -   26   50   101   201   301
25   50   100   200   300   400
□   □   □   □   □   □

CONDITION OF
SHIPMENT

EXL GOOD POOR DIST
□   □   □   □

SUBJECT STATUS

OBSOLETE   NOT OBSOLETE
□   □

113

group he represents, the film title, date booked, and the hours of pickup and return. Request cards (Form 11) with space for this information can be distributed to frequent users for their convenience. Cards may also be filled out by the film librarian in taking telephone requests. The borrower's signature is added when the film is picked up.

In order to evaluate audience reaction and size, the film showing card (Forms 12 and 13) is used. Some of the basic information that appears on the borrower's request form reappears here, along with the number of times the film was shown, the size of its audiences, and their reaction. The card is usually placed within or on the film container. An attempt should be made to keep the information requested minimal, and the form should be designed so that it can be completed quickly and correctly.

The size of the library and/or its collection may necessitate the use of other forms, such as:

1. Confirmation cards (Form 14) which are sent to the borrower as both a record and a reminder.
2. Delivery receipts (Form 15), which are acknowledgment from the borrower that the films have been received. When films are delivered by messenger to the borrower, a delivery receipt is advisable.
3. Container notices (Form 16) or box notices (Form 17), which offer suggestions and advice on the proper handling of films and usually request cooperation in reporting any damage or deterioration.
4. Return labels (Form 18), which are enclosed in the film shipping box or container. Convenience to the borrower and clarity to the shipper are two strong arguments for their use.

Good practice demands that films be inspected and repaired—if necessary—after each circulation. The inspection record form (Form 19) provides a breakdown of the various operations and services given to a film before it is circulated again. Information on the inspection form will indicate troublesome projectors, careless users, deteriorating prints, and so forth. Information from these cards can be used in formulating policy, in preparing budgets, and in other operations of a film library.

Form 14. Confirmation Form

ANDREWS UNIVERSITY
CHICAGO, ILLINOIS

The film(s)

1._____

2._____

3._____

4._____

requested by_____is/are

_____ confirmed for pickup on:

_____ other:

Note: The loan period is 24 hours from the time of pickup at the Library unless special provision has been made.

Form 15. Delivery Receipt

Date _____

Films Delivered to _____

Titles:

(1) _____

(2) _____

(3) _____

(4) _____

(5) _____

Received by _____

Date _____

Form 16. Container Notice

Please rewind each reel onto its proper reel and retape end with masking or film tape.

Also, please indicate any of the following that you are aware of:

Leader Broken _____

Film Torn _____

Other Damage _____

_____

Poor Visual Condition _____

Poor Sound Condition _____

NEVER make any film repairs and never attach Scotch tape or other materials to the film. If film breaks, wind it overlapped on the reel and indicate place of break with an unattached slip of paper.

THANK YOU.

Form 17. Box Notice

1 MINUTE OF YOUR TIME CAN SAVE US
$20–$200:

Before each showing, please clean the path on the projector along which the film runs. Use the tissue provided, *especially on the film gate*—where the film passes behind the lens. *Any* dust here will scratch the entire length of film.

Please rewind each reel onto its proper reel and retape end with masking or film tape. Also, please indicate any of the following that you are aware of:

Leader Broken _____

Film Torn _____

Other Damage _____

Poor Visual Condition _____

Poor Sound Condition _____

Never make any film repairs and never attach Scotch tape or other materials to the film. If the film breaks, wind it overlapped on the reel and indicate place of break with an unattached slip of paper.

THANK YOU!

Form 18. Shipping Labels—Sending and Return

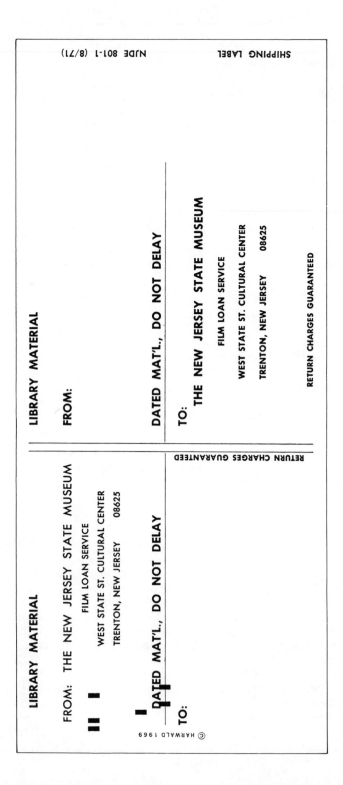

Form 19. Inspection Record

REEL NO.

TITLE:

PART ____ OF ____

Date	Insp's name	Borrower	Splices Made	Total	Sprocket repair	Cleaning	Footage	Comments

117

STORING FILMS

Storage conditions for films should be arranged to offer protection from dirt, dust, excess humidity or dryness, and extreme degrees of temperature. The possibility of damage from fire, water, physical surroundings, or chemicals should also be considered.

The most suitable location in a building is usually the average or middle one. Basements or top floors both evidence extremes of humidity which may be detrimental to film preservation. Within the room, the films may be placed in film cans and stored horizontally on shelves. These shelves should be located some distance from air conditioners, radiators, pipes, etc.

If steel cabinets are used, the films are stored on edge. The cabinets should be located so as to assure fresh air circulation and easy access.

In either case the room should be kept as free as possible from dirt and chemical fumes. Ideally, 16mm black-and-white films in active use should be stored at a relative humidity of 40 percent and a temperature of about 70 degrees Fahrenheit, but temperatures up to 75 degrees Fahrenheit or 80 degrees Fahrenheit and a relative humidity between 25 and 60 percent are acceptable. If other conditions of storage are necessary for an extended period of time, the film should be checked frequently for signs of trouble.

Since Kodak color films were first introduced, many improvements have been made in the stability of the dyes. However, all dyes are fugitive to some extent and they change in time. Heat, moisture, and light are the three factors that most affect the permanence of dyes. For maximum permanence, therefore, processed films should be stored where it is cool, dry, and dark.

A relative humidity of 40–50 percent and a temperature of 50 degrees Fahrenheit or lower are best for storage of processed color films. However, Kodak color films can be expected to have a useful life of many years if shown with care in good projection equipment and stored at ordinary room temperature (70 degrees Fahrenheit) and a relative humidity below 50 percent.

FILM CARE AND MAINTENANCE

Any film collection represents a considerable investment of time and money. Figured on an average of $200 per short film and with a depreciation factor of 15 percent per year, it is not unusual for a collection to be valued at $50,000 or more. The care of that collection becomes an item for serious consideration. Below are some suggestions and recommended procedures for maintaining the film collection. Films can have a long life if cared for properly. Two hundred showings are not unusual and some films are in good condition after six hundred or more showings.

Film Care

Before each showing, clean the film channel aperture and pressure plates with chamois or a soft cloth; use a solvent to remove wax or grease.

Film Threading

Always thread the film properly (see Figure 4):

Set the sprocket teeth directly in the film sprocket holes.

Lock the sprocket clamps.

Center the film in the channel so that the claws can engage the sprocket holes.

Allow adequate film loops when threading.

Test the threading by turning the manual control.

Stop the projector immediately at any indication of trouble. Recheck threading, restore lost loops, or correct any other apparent malfunction.

Do not overload the reel: the outside layer of film should be at least ½ inch in from the edge of the flanges.

Do not use bent reels; discard them.

Remain with projector and check its operation by observation, inspection, and manual examination of the sprockets on the film entering the take-up reel.

Films purchased by institutions should have leaders (green film) and trailers (red film) spliced to them as protection against end-of-reel damage. The name of the institution can be noted on the leader with Magic Marker pens. Several companies will preimprint leader film with the owner's name and other usual data.

Films should be inspected after each showing. Frequency of lubrication and cleaning varies with individual libraries. See the section on film repair treatment and rejuvenation.

Care should be exercised in rewinding films. The tension should be high enough to produce a tight roll, but not so high that it will cinch the film.

Common film defects are indicated in Figures 5 to 11 and suggested correctional procedures are noted. Other film defects are discussed in the following paragraphs.

Film Brittleness

Films that have been stored improperly, with poor conditions of heat and humidity, or films that receive very little use may dry out and become brittle. Threading a brittle film is difficult and it is much more likely to break during projection. A damp sponge or rag placed with the film in an air-tight container for a week or so will restore a brittle film. When using this technique, care must be exercised so that the sponge does not contact the film. Its only function is to supply moisture to the film.

Film Shrinkage

When film dries out because of nonuse, poor storage, or excessive heat and low humidity, shrinkage may occur. In such a case, the sprocket holes will no longer coincide or mesh with the sprocket gears, and a single showing can damage the film beyond repair.

Film Fungus

Mold or mildew can form on film surfaces if the conditions of cleanliness, heat, and humidity are suitable for growth. Usually a fungus condition can be corrected with film cleaner.

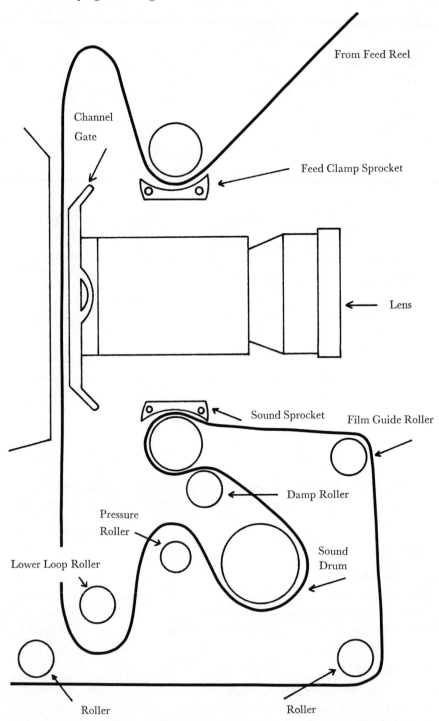

From Feed Reel

Channel
Gate

Feed Clamp Sprocket

Lens

Sound Sprocket   Film Guide Roller

Damp Roller

Pressure
Roller

Lower Loop Roller

Sound
Drum

Roller   Roller

Figure 4. Typical film threading diagram.

Film Maintenance

There are several possible methods of keeping a film collection in good showing condition, and with several basic and simple pieces of equipment, the smaller collection can be satisfactorily maintained. The following elements are needed: two manual rewinds, which should be secured or anchored to a wooden board or table; and a film splicer, which can be either a wet splicer (which uses film cement) or a dry unit (which employs clear sprocketed Mylar tape splices). To clean and lubricate the films, the appropriate fluids, some soft cotton cloths, and a pair of soft cotton gloves are needed.

This basic kit will allow for repair, lubrication, and cleaning of the films. Manual procedures are more tedious and time consuming than more sophisticated mechanical treatments but they are inexpensive and serviceable.

Cleaning and Lubricating Films

Film may be cleaned and lubricated by drawing it very slowly through a soft cotton cloth that has been moistened with a film-cleaning and -lubricating fluid. No other substance should ever be used; compounds such as water, oil, turpentine, soaps, detergents, and cleansers will destroy the film.

The cloth used should be lintless (cotton flannel), untreated with starch or softener, and white. From time to time it should be refolded so that the accumulated dirt does not scratch the film.

Splicing Films

For most film libraries primarily two methods of splicing films are used.

Dry splicing uses a pressure-sensitive gummed Mylar tape which is sprocketed so that it is a facsimile film. With a splicer, the Mylar tape is pressed onto the two adjoining ends of the film. The procedure is then repeated for the opposite side of the film. Care should be taken not to test the splice by pulling immediately after making the repair. Heat from the projector or aging will cure the splice.

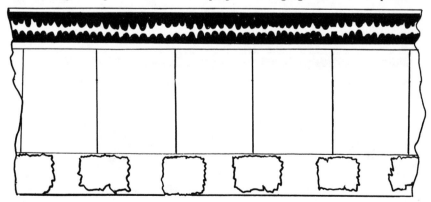

Figure 5. Film damaged by torn or enlarged sprockets. Prevention: *(1) Relieve tension on the gate or take-up reel. (2) Eliminate any jerking or erratic movement of the take-up reel. (3) Check to see if the shuttle is worn or needs adjustment. (4) Inspect film to see if it is worn out, too dry, or if the sprockets are enlarged. (5) Make sure there is no loss of loop either above or below the gate.*

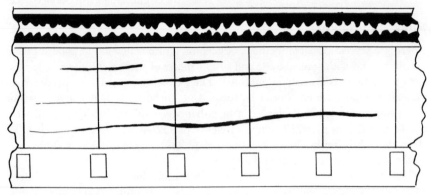

Figure 6. Film damaged by scratches. Prevention: *(1) Do not allow loose film to fall on floor, desk, etc. (2) Check to make sure rollers are not frozen. (3) Clean rollers, film channel, and gate regularly. (4) Do not tighten film after it is wound on reel (cinching).*

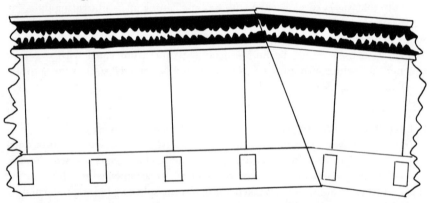

Figure. 7 Film damaged by creases. Prevention: *(1) Never step on film. (2) Use care in closing film can. (3) Secure leader to film with paper-holding strap. (4) Avoid spilling loose film on the floor.*

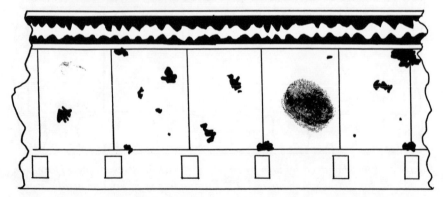

Figure 8. Film damaged by dirt. Prevention: *(1) Clean the projector frequently. (2) Store films in a clean location. (3) Rejuvenate and clean films at reasonable intervals. (4) Avoid manual handling of film surface.*

122

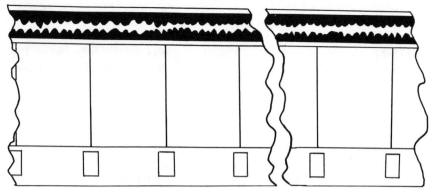

Figure 9. Film damaged by breaks. Prevention: (1) Check film splices for adequacy. (2) Make sure the film is properly set in the film channel. (3) Do not use bent reels which may catch and tear film. (4) Avoid sudden jerks by the take-up reel. (5) Make sure there is no loss of loop. (6) Avoid sharp bends or kinks in threading or rewinding.

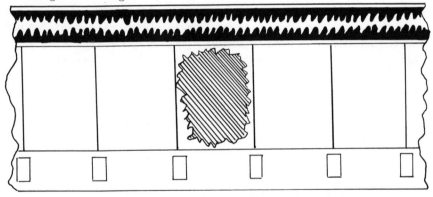

Figure 10. Film damaged by burn spots. Prevention: Inspect fire shutter for free movement. (2) Check running speed of projector. (3) Do not attempt single frame stop motion projection unless machine has provision for this.

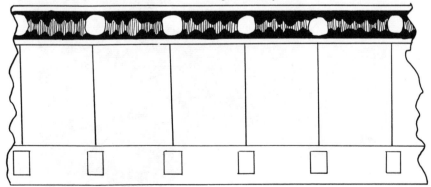

Figure 11. Film damaged by sprocket marks on film. Prevention: Make sure film is not reversed by checking the threading. (2) Check threading to ensure sprocket teeth engage film. (3) Inspect splicing to make certain the film matches the sprocket teeth.

Wet splicing is done by scraping a short portion of the film to be joined. Liquid cement is applied to the joint which has been scraped to approximate the regular film thickness. After allowing about 30 seconds for setting, the splice can be tested by gently pulling both sides of the film. Detailed instructions are given with each splicer; they are also available in books or pamphlets published by Kodak and other film manufacturers.

It is also possible to send films to labs for repair and rejuvenation, and in certain cases, this may be the only way to rescue a dry or brittle film. Costs of the treatment must be weighed against the economic and functional value of the film.

Electronic Inspection

Larger film libraries have electronic machines (see Figure 12) that perform the operations just described, along with a few more. They incorporate a film transport system, a defect-detecting device, and a cleaning facility for removing dust and loose dirt from the film. Depending on the type of defect detection system that is used, machines are capable of locating all of the structured defects and imperfections in a film. Running at fast speeds (between 500 and 600 feet per minute), they have the braking capacity to make an almost immediate stop when a flaw in the film passes the inspection device. A splice or other correction is made by the operator, the machine is restarted, and the processes continue. The range of features in such machines is very wide and makes their use most suitable for larger film libraries. The approximate cost of a single-loop (one-film) unit is $3,000–7,000 new and $2,000–4,000 used. The double-loop (two-film) unit runs $6,000–12,000 new and $3,000–6,000 used.

Figure 12. Electronic film cleaner and inspector.

CHAPTER 7
Designing
Film Programs

In a very broad sense, the showing of films may be said to have the same four functions that Charles R. Wright, in his book *Mass Communication*, attributes to the mass media: surveillance, prescription, education, and entertainment. Setting up four such broad classifications is a vulnerable act, but if it is remembered that a film can easily fulfill more than one function, the scheme becomes more acceptable. Certainly *The Hand* and *Why Man Creates* are entertainments, but they are educational as well, with some surveillance and prescription implied.

Once it is clear to the film user which of these functions he wishes to utilize, the goal of his film program becomes somewhat easier to formulate. While none of these functions is totally exclusive, usually one can be selected as the major reason for a program.

Are we going to describe the world today with a film such as *Future Shock* or *Hunger in America?* Then we are engaged mostly in surveillance, a description or examination of the world's condition—past and present. When we show *Smoking and You*, we are prescribing or offering suggestions for improving or correcting the world's condition. Education is the large category which in broad terms can be said to pass on the proven—and valuable—ideas, skills, and concepts of one culture to another. *Marvels of the Hive, A Dancer's World, Jackson Pollock,* and *The Eye of the Beholder* are obvious examples. The final function, entertainment, is provided by most feature films, cartoons, and experimental films, as well as by many other categories of films.

SINGLE AND SERIES PROGRAMS

A single program can be used to satisfy any of the functions. Examples can be found in the library, museum, school, and theatrical announcements in many newspapers. The range of topics is as wide as the number of film titles available.

The series program is more of a challenge to the designer. Not only must one consider the planning of each individual program, but one must also give attention to the overall structure, the sequential placement of the films, and a continuity from program to program. Again, the topics for a series are limitless, but a sampling of series titles may offer suggestions.

Popular Series Titles

The Animated Film	Masters of Horror and Fantasy
Bette Davis: Tribute to an Actress	Max Steiner and Film Music
The Cinema of Alfred Hitchcock	Midday Summer Cinema
Classic Film Series	Movies in the Parks
The Documentary Tradition	The New Yugoslav Cinema
Early Classics of Film Comedy	The Primitive Screen
Film Makers on Film	Prize-Winning Films
Film Previews for Professionals	Racial Stereotypes in Films
Films for a Summer Evening	A Salute to MGM
Films from Literature	Shakespeare on Film
Films on Environment	Sounds for Silent Films
Films—Too Good for Words	The Thalberg Years
A Foreign Film Festival	Tracy and Hepburn
Forgotten Films of the Thirties	Vacation Film Festival
Free Films for Kids	The Western Hero
It's a Small World	Women in Films
Karloff Meets Lugosi	The World on Film

The planning of a series program should be governed by a few basic concepts. Priority should be given to the totality of the program rather than to its individual elements. For example, if the series title is "Women in the Films of Alfred Hitchcock," it might be more appropriate to include *Marnie* or *Under Capricorn*—both of which were critical and popular failures—rather than a more successful Hitchcock feature. Selection of the elements should be based on the strength of their contribution to the major theme.

Attention should be given to the length and the time–day scheduling of the series. One that runs for too many sessions will encourage a fragmented, incomplete attendance. Whether the series is scheduled weekly, monthly, or semimonthly should be determined by some estimation of the size and interests of the probable audience. The accuracy of that estimation will depend on a knowledge gained by experience with that potential audience—its needs, pleasures, activities, habits, etc.

Arrangement of the films in the series should be determined by factors other than availability. Placement of film titles should be based on the development of the theme. Having a solid opening program is always an advantage, as is the building up to a strong film which provides an exciting summary/climax to the series.

The variety of film programs that can be presented is limited only by the creativity of those presenting the programs. The following discussion offers some general considerations to keep in mind when planning a program.

Aim of the Program

The initial step in any film program is a decision about its goal or aim. The rationale for presenting any film program should be determined and clearly understood by the sponsors and participants. Once the goal has been decided, an appropriate program can be planned.

Selection of the Films

Film selection will usually depend on the user's personal knowledge of film availability, or on the advice, ability, and cooperation of the film librarian. The films may include a short film, a theatrical feature, a government film, a sponsored film, or an amateur film. Selection sources and procedures are noted in Chapter 5.

Previewing the Films

Following selection, one or more previews of each film should be held for those conducting the program. They should feel at ease with the film and understand its role in the program.

Creating Audience Readiness

The next step is to create a readiness on the part of the audience for viewing the film. This can be accomplished by advance publicity, exhibits, film notes, or a short verbal introduction to the film. In most instances, the audience should know not only what they are seeing but also why they are seeing it.

Publicity

Perhaps one of the hardest initial tasks that a film user faces is assembling an audience. A film program given by an organization or a school provides a minimum audience which may be enlarged or not depending on the goal of the program. It is the recruitment of an audience for the general open-to-all showing that usually is the greatest challenge.

How to communicate with a potential audience is another statement of the problem. Possible methods are unlimited; however, no particular method will succeed all the time—probably because of the many variables that influence attendance—weather, time, day of the week, period of the year, television offerings, community counterattractions, etc.

The suggestions that follow may be considered as possibilities for establishing communication with a potential film program audience.

Within the Institution

Posters
Bulletin boards
Handouts, newsletters, bookmarks, etc.
Verbal invitations
Exhibits

Within the Community

Posters in stores, schools, libraries
Community activity notice in the newspaper

Paid advertisement in the newspaper
Delivered announcements to homes
Notices in school newspapers
Radio spot announcements
Cable television notice
Specific invitations—either written or spoken—to various organizations, clubs, societies
Mailed announcements

PREPARING PROGRAM NOTES

One of the easiest yet most effective ways of supplementing a film program is by the distribution of film notes. These notes can be one or more sheets of paper, a brochure, or a booklet. Most used is the single sheet—also called a handout, a throwaway, or a program. It contains material that will increase the viewer's appreciation and educational experience. The content is not rigid and a variety of approaches can be used. These include such elements as:

Production data, credits, cast
Critical quotes
Background information
Questions for thought or discussion
Actor and director biographies
Actor and director filmographies
Bibliographies
Critical essays
Original reviews

Most often the notes are given to the viewer as he enters, but occasionally the nature of the program will dictate a later distribution.

Sensitivity must be exercised in the preparation of the notes in order that the perception of the film by the viewer not be unduly influenced or predetermined. Composition of the notes can be an exciting creative activity. By using a preview of the film itself, published reviews, reference books, and general books on film, it is a relatively easy task to compile good film notes.

If time is short, certain introductory material can be presented via this format. It is wise to establish a permanent file of program notes, since they can be used again with future showings.

The notes can accomplish much—a creation of readiness, a saving of time, and an increase in film appreciation, among other things.

The following program notes (Example 13) were prepared for use with a college audience, some of whom were enrolled in a film appreciation course. The remainder of the group were invited guests. Emphasized is the "auteur" approach to film study, along with some other material that should facilitate any discussion which might follow the showing. The bibliography is offered as an aid for those who are interested in further information about the films and career of Alfred Hitchcock.

Example 13. Film Notes for a College Audience

FOREIGN CORRESPONDENT

Directed by Alfred Hitchcock, 1940

Alfred Hitchcock, a master in the art of making the suspense thriller, has directed or helped to create 49 films in his 40-year career. Often imitated, but never surpassed, his production career spans an era from the silent films and continues to the present day.

Hitchcock is a painstaking craftsman, who spends long periods of time in script preparation. Scripts are worked and reworked until every detail is perfect, and the motivation and action of each character is well understood. Long consultations with the art director will have insured that he has achieved what he wants in the way of setting. He rehearses his actors in conference, making sure that they understand every nuance of their parts. He is patient to the point of tediousness and careful of small details. He likes to use the same team on his pictures, because they are used to his methods of working and know what he wants. His method of filmmaking is thorough and is that of a perfectionist.

His camera technique is a combination of Murnau (moving camera) and Eisenstein (montage), and many techniques which Hitchcock originally introduced are still being used by avant-garde directors today. Light plays an important part in Hitchcock's distinctive personal style, especially the soft almost-grey indirect lighting which is used in immensely effective ways to increase tension or to distort reality. One finds recurrent themes or structures which appear in all of his films. Among these are:

1. Rigorous morality coupled with dark humor
2. Complacency eventually shaken
3. Confession
4. Unimpeachable normality contrasted with evil/extravagant abnormality
5. Nondialogue sound used instead of visual image
6. Cheerful brutality
7. Sexual innuendo
8. The intricate red herring
9. The double bluff
10. Eccentric humor
11. Exotic/gigantic backgrounds

A SELECTED HITCHCOCK BIBLIOGRAPHY

Geduld, Harry M. *Film Makers on Film Making.* Bloomington, Ind.: Indiana University Press, 1967.

Gessner, Robert. *The Moving Image.* New York: Dutton, 1968.

Knight, Arthur. *The Liveliest Art: A Panoramic History of the Movies.* New York: Macmillan, 1957.

Perry, George. *The Films of Alfred Hitchcock.* New York: Dutton/Vista, 1965.

Taylor, John Russell. *Cinema Eye, Cinema Ear.* New York: Hill & Wang, 1964.

Truffaut, François. *Hitchcock.* New York: Simon & Schuster, 1967.

In the following film notes (Example 14), which were prepared for a public library program by John Saylor, background material about the actor is offered. The content in this case was dictated by the fame of Lon Chaney as a creator of grotesques. He is the key element in the film and the reason for its lasting popularity. The notes stress biographical information since at the time of this showing there was no book available on Chaney. Since then *Faces, Forms, Films: The Artistry of Lon Chaney* by Robert G. Anderson has been published and mention of it in the notes would be appropriate.

Example 14. Film Notes for a Public Library Audience

Lon Chaney

in

THE PHANTOM OF THE OPERA

A Universal Picture—1925

Directed by Rupert Julian

Screenplay by Raymond Shrock and Elliot Clawson

Cast

Erik (The Phantom)	Lon Chaney
Christine Dare	Mary Philbin
Raul de Chagny	Norman Kerry
Florine Papillon	Snitz Edwards
Simon	Gibson Gowland

LON CHANEY

Born April 1, 1883, in Colorado Springs, Colorado, of parents who were both deaf-mutes, Lon Chaney spent much of his younger life taking care of his mother, who was left permanently helpless from an attack of inflammatory rheumatism. Out of necessity, he learned to express himself in pantomime. As a boy, he also spent much time watching the clowns in the town theater and later credited them not only for teaching him the basics of makeup, but also for inspiring some of his more sinister roles. Clowns, out of context, seem not only not funny but also project quite an eerie quality. At 17, he joined the theater as a stagehand and property boy and moved around the country picking up various stage experience until he reached Los Angeles, where he became involved in the movies as a director and actor in western "heavy roles". At this time, in order to keep working, he developed his special skill with the art of makeup. He carried a portable makeup kit and after checking the casting lists he was ready on the spot for any unusual part. From 1913 to 1919 he appeared in over 100 roles and directed and wrote scripts when he was not acting.

The Miracle Man (1919), in which he played the Frog, a pseudo cripple, brought him national attention. For his part he acquired the knack of throwing his shoulder out of joint which left him permanently lame in one shoulder. His first break into horror roles was in 1922 in *Blind Bargain*, playing the dual role of a mad scientist transformed into an ape-man. Stardom came with his portrayal of Quasimodo in *The Hunchback of Notre Dame* in 1923. For this role he wore a 70-lb. rubber hump and a harness which prevented him from standing erect. Chaney spent much time studying the relationship between psychological and physical horrors and combined the two, often with much physical pain, into his effective makeup. Unlike other horror stars, his mastery of makeup, his ability to project subtle emotions, and his unique versatility enabled him to elicit compassion and pity for even the most repulsive human creatures, whose acts of cruelty or horror most often came from their passionate need for love and kindness. Such was his portrayal of the Phantom of the Opera. The making of *The Phantom of the Opera* involved considerable secrecy and scandal. The film was shot and revised three times before release, due mainly to disagreements between Chaney and director Rupert Julian. As a result, another director, Edward Sedgwick, was summoned, but in the end Chaney directed many of the scenes himself. To build the character of the Phantom, Chaney lifted the top of his nose and expanded his nostrils with 3/8-inch rubber cigar holders, disfigured his cheekbones with special disks in his mouth, popped and dilated his eyes with chemicals, and elongated his skull with a matted wig. The unmasking of the Phantom (which in order to heighten suspense does not occur until the fifth reel) is the high point of horror as the camera switches in a montage of shots from Mary Philbin to Chaney and back until she unmasks him. The Phantom was a born freak gone mad and Chaney (aided by the beginning of Technicolor) developed a character so grotesque that people in the audience fainted at the sight.

He then combined his talents with Tod Browning at MGM, who also delved into horror and dreamed up impossible feats for Chaney to perform. In *London after Midnight* (1927) he wore thin wires in his eyes to make them bulge and a bridge of animal-like teeth which were so painful that he could wear them for only a short time.

Chaney was accused of relying solely on his makeup to portray a character, implying he could not act. But films such as *He Who Gets Slapped* (1924), *The Unholy Three* (1925), *Tell It to the Marines* (1927), and *While the City Sleeps* (1928), in which he used little makeup and exhibited his versatility and mastery of pantomime, proved otherwise. People finally realized that no amount of putty and false hair can create a believable character and saw that his best parts often involved no visual trickery.

Little is known about Chaney's private life because he did not allow personal interviews. He lived modestly, oblivious to his fame, and spent most of his time reading and studying his roles, makeup, and penology. Because of his private nature he was known as "the man of mystery." He wrote the section, "Make-Up," in the 14th edition of *Encyclopaedia Britannica*, and the preface for *The Art of Make-up for Stage and Screen* by Cecil Holland. He was married twice and had a son, Creighton (who later became known as Lon Chaney, Jr.), by his first wife.

Chaney's great versatility earned him the title "The Man of a Thousand Faces." He resisted the onslaught of the sound film because he felt that silent acting was the peculiar art of the cinema. Finally in 1930 (he and Chaplin were the last), he remade *The Unholy Three* into a talkie and exhibited such versatility with his voice that he was dubbed "The Man of a Thousand Voices." The smooth transition to sound film was cut short that year, however; he died on August 26, 1930, from a malignant throat tumor.

The film notes (Example 15) on *The Charge of the Light Brigade* were made for a high school English class studying the translation of literature into film. Attention is given to the film, the poem, and the historical incident that inspired it.

There are implications for further individualized study, and the notes should serve to create a readiness to study the film and the material upon which it was based. Published materials on this topic were nonexistent and the notes were written to satisfy a specific curriculum need.

Example 15. Film Notes for a High School Audience

THE CHARGE OF THE LIGHT BRIGADE

Warner Brothers—1936—115 Minutes—Black and White

Major Geoffrey Vickers	Errol Flynn
Elsa Campbell	Olivia de Havilland
Captain Perry Vickers	Patrick Knowles
Sir Charles Macefield	Henry Stephenson
Sir Benjamin Warrenton	Nigel Bruce
Colonel Campbell	Donald Crisp
Captain Randall	David Niven
Surat Khan	C. Henry Gordon
Producer	Hal B. Wallis
Director	Michael Curtiz
2nd Unit Director	B. Reeves Eason
Screenplay	Michel Jacoby
	Rowland Leigh
Music	Max Steiner
Photography	Sol Polito
	Tony Gaudio
Special Effects	Fred Jackman
	H.F. Koenekamp

BACKGROUND

While in China, a news correspondent named Michel Jacoby began collecting facts about the tragic charge and in 1934 wrote a story about it which he sold to Hollywood. Most of Jacoby's original material was discarded and a fictional narrative substituted.

The film took more than five months to make, with the "charge" itself requiring three full weeks to film. The filming took place in several locations: Lone Pine, California, supplied the background for some shots involving Arabs; Lasky Mesa served as the site for the British fort; and the San Fernando Valley was the site of the "charge." The second unit director is sometimes credited with the charge, but Curtiz participated fully in this section of the film, according to Flynn and others. 150 actors and actresses, 150 extra players, over 100 technicians, wardrobe men, makeup artists, and hairdressers were employed.

Obviously Curtiz used fewer than the historic 693 cavalrymen in filming the charge; it is the photography that gives us the illusion of several hundred.

Three railroad carloads of livestock, 50 trained military horses, four Brahman cows, a dozen fighting falcons, a carload of uniforms, and a carload of saddles and lances, complete with pennons, were used. To govern authenticity, Captain E. Rochfort-John, a former British officer, served as an advisor of military drills and tactics.

THE CHARGE OF THE LIGHT BRIGADE
by Alfred Lord Tennyson

Half a league, half a league,
Half a league onward,
All in the valley of Death
Rode the six hundred.
'Forward, the Light Brigade!
Charge for the guns!' he said:
Into the valley of Death
Rode the six hundred.

'Forward, the Light Brigade!'
Was there a man dismay'd?
Not tho' the soldier knew
Some one had blunder'd:
Their's not to make reply,
Their's not to reason why,
Their's but to do and die:
Into the valley of Death
Rode the six hundred.

Cannon to right of them,
Cannon to left of them,
Cannon in front of them
Volley'd and thunder'd;
Storm'd at with shot and shell,
Boldly they rode and well,
Into the jaws of Death,
Into the mouth of Hell
Rode the six hundred.

Flash'd all their sabres bare,
Flash'd as they turn'd in air,

Sabring the gunners there,
Charging an army, while
All the world wonder'd:
Plunged in the battery-smoke
Right thro' the line they broke;
Cossack and Russian
Reel'd from the sabre-stroke
Shatter'd and sunder'd.
Then they rode back, but not,
Not the six hundred.

Cannon to right of them.
Cannon to left of them,
Cannon behind them
Volley'd and thunder'd;
Storm'd at with shot and shell,
While horse and hero fell,
They that had fought so well
Came thro' the jaws of Death
Back from the mouth of Hell,
All that was left of them
Left of six hundred.

When can their glory fade?
O the wild charge they made!
All the world wonder'd.
Honour the charge they made
Honour the Light Brigade,
Noble six hundred!

HISTORY—THE CHARGE OF THE LIGHT BRIGADE

The charge was just one localized skirmish in the Crimean War, a war which was not wanted by any of the governments involved—Russia on the one hand and Turkey, England, France, and Sardinia in opposition. The conflict came about through Russia's desire for access to the Mediterranean Sea, a move which would upset the European balance of power and threaten Great Britain's sea power. An incident involving the Roman Catholic and the Greek Orthodox Churches gave Russia a superficial excuse to deliver an ultimatum. Turkey declared war on October 4, 1853, and on November 30, the Russian fleet destroyed the Turkish Black Sea fleet.

The British participation in this controversy is characterized by poor leadership, ineptitude, and blunders at every step of the campaign. The leaders of the British soldiers were not young men; most had not had any prior active military experience. Lord Raglan, commander-in-chief, was nearly 70; Lord Lucan, at 54, was commander of the cavalry division; Lord Cardigan, commander of the Light Brigade, was 57. Reconnaissance was not taken of the Crimean area before the landing. Good supply lines were not established. Cholera and other diseases ran rampant throughout the campaign, killing great numbers of men and horses.

Under these conditions, and with petty, bickering commanders, the order to charge was sent to the cavalry division. Lord Raglan, from his vantage point above the valley, saw the situation on the field much differently than his subordinate officers below. Thus he sent an order, ambiguous and obscure, to Lord Lucan, which led to the gallant but disastrous charge.

According to observers, the stately, majestic march of the Light Brigade directly into the Russian artillery and cannon fire ahead and beside them was a splendid sight to behold. Brightly and magnificently clothed, these horsemen were seemingly quite courageous and bold. They did not falter along the way. Yet, of the some 700 who charged that day, only 195 returned; 500 horses were killed.

The stubbornness, gallantry, and complete disregard for casualties served little purpose except to end Russia's dominant role in southeastern Europe. From this tragic war, only one positive result emerged—the work and the legacy of Florence Nightingale.

BIBLIOGRAPHY

Encyclopedia Americana, vols. 6 and 8 (1964 ed.).

Hamley, E.B. *War in the Crimea*. New York: Scribners, 1891 (3rd ed. Westport, Conn.: Greenwood Press, 1971).

Smith, Goldwin. *A History of England*. New York: Scribner's 1966.

Wallbank, Thomas W., Taylor, A.M., and Carson, G.B. *Civilization: Past and Present*, vol. 2. Chicago: Scott, Foresman, 1965.

Woodham-Smith, Cecil. *The Reason Why*. New York: McGraw-Hill, 1953.

FILM DISCUSSION AND STUDY GUIDES

One of the most valuable materials to the person using films is the discussion guide. It resembles in certain ways the lesson plans made by teachers who wish to structure to some extent the experience they are providing. A guide might include (1) *the data:* title, running time, color or black and white, year of release, producer or distributor, director, performers, audience level, and subject area; and (2) *the summary:* a synopsis of the film's plot stated objectively, the film's goals and concepts, questions for discussion, further activities, and at times, a bibliography.

The discussion guide for each film is unique, requiring different combinations of the elements above. Its purpose is to assist the person presenting the film to create a better total experience for the viewing audience. Most guides encourage the modification, change, addition, or deletion of discussion questions and supplementary activities; they offer a suggested base upon which the leader will build his or her presentation. Guides are available from several sources.

Film Distributors' Guides

As an added service, certain distributors offer guides with the purchase of individual films. They are enclosed with the film packaging and are meant to stay with the film. Unfortunately, they are often lost or misplaced with this method. An alternate method is for the library to file the original and enclose a copy of the guide with the film. Example 16 is representative of such a guide.

Some distributors publish books of study guides to accompany their films. Two interesting examples are *Dialogue with the World*, edited by Rev. G. William Jones, and *Film Utilization Catalog*, distributed by the Learning Corporation of America. The guide for the film *The Golden Fish* (Example 16) is taken from this catalog.

Example 16. Film Study Guide Prepared by an Educational Film Distributor

THE GOLDEN FISH

20 Minutes

Summary: Fate favors a boy's love for a goldfish in this film without dialogue from France, produced by Jacques-Yves Cousteau. One day, in his usual little-boy life, the hero stops at a street carnival. He is attracted to a tropical goldfish, the prize for winning a roulette game. An unspoken rivalry develops between him and a bearded man who tries unsuccessfully to win this golden prize. After accidentally breaking the hero's milk bottle, the man gives him money. The boy gambles immediately and wins his coveted prize. At home, the fish and a pet canary, each in his separate domain, play joyfully while the boy is out. No sooner does the goldfish accidentally jump out of his bowl onto the table than a sinister black cat enters the room through an open window. After menacing both of the golden delicacies, the cat tosses the fish back into its bowl and leaves. When the boy returns home with flowers for the fish bowl, his pets seem playfully unperturbed.

AIMS OF THE FILM

1. To tell, without words, a touching and suspenseful story of communication between a child and his pet.
2. To encourage children to use their imaginations in story telling.

QUESTIONS AND STORY TELLING

1. Why did the bearded man give the boy the money? How do you think he felt when the boy won the golden fish?
2. Why do you think the cat put the fish back in the bowl?

3. Do you think the story could really have happened? Why/Why not?
4. Do you own pets? How do you feel about them? How did you get them? Have you had any unusually good experiences with your pets? Tell a story about it.
5. Which scenes were true to life? Which were exaggerated? For example, consider when the fish dances in his bowl and the canary keeps twirling around his perch. Do you think pets really play in this way?
6. Can you think of other stories of children and animals in which amazing things happen? (e.g. Lassie, Black Beauty, The Three Bears, Bambi.)
7. Make up your own story about an amazing pet.
8. Try to tell the story of the film in sequences, putting in as many episodes as you remember and using colorful and detailed language.
9. Draw a series of pictures which "tell the story" of the film. Then ask another person in the class "to read" the story.
10. Did you notice the music? How did the music tell the story?

SUGGESTED READING

The Yearling—by Marjorie Rawlings; *The Red Pony*—by John Steinbeck; *National Velvet*—by Enid Bagnold; *So Dear To My Heart*—by Sterling North; *The Traveling Bird*—by Robert Burch; *Parakeetes & Peach Pies*—by Kay Smith; *Emett's Pig*—by Mary Stolz; *Nicholo's Favorite Pet*—by Inga Sandberg; *All the Lassies*—by Liso Skorpen.

Grade Levels: Elementary, General Audiences.

Subject Areas: Language Arts, Film Study.

(Study Guide prepared by: Laura Grossman, Film Instructor, 92nd Street YM/YWHA, New York, N.Y.)

Certain film companies produce and issue free study guides to films that are about to be shown commercially for the first time. Usually written by recognized experts, they are designed to correlate some classroom activities with a viewing of the film in a motion picture theater, often at a special student showing. When the film becomes available for direct rental by the school or is scheduled for a television showing, the guide can still be used. A most impressive study guide for the film *Patton* was prepared by Dr. Louis L. Snyder, a professor of history at the City College of the City University of New York. The guide is reprinted here as Example 17 in a slightly abridged version (illustrations and production staff not included) by permission of Twentieth-Century-Fox, the film's producer.

Example 17. Film Study Guide Prepared by a Commercial Film Distributor

PATTON: A SALUTE TO A REBEL
A Guide and Commentary for Classroom Discussion
By Louis L. Snyder, Ph.D.*

A DECALOGUE

These ten units deal with various phases of the career of General George S. Patton, Jr. as treated in 20th Century-Fox's film.

Each unit is designed for special research and discussion on topics from Patton's life.

For contemporary news reports on battles in which Patton took part in North Africa, Sicily, France and Germany, see the *New York Times* index for the years 1943–1945 and read the reports in the issues to which reference is made in the index.

Use Unit 10 for reference books to be read in conjunction with the film.

UNIT 1—THE BASIC THEME—WORLD WAR II

All civilized human beings agree on the horrors and bestiality of war and they hope that one day it will be regarded in the same light as cannibalism. Yet, it is easy to say that nothing justifies war on a mass scale, and that representatives of quarreling nations should sit down and adjust their differences peaceably without resorting to the bloody decisions of the battlefield. Perhaps that day will come.

Unfortunately World War II had to be fought. Appeasement of dictators Hitler and Mussolini and the Japanese war lords was completely ineffective. War could have been avoided by the simple expedient of accepting dictatorship, concentration camps, and genocide—the slaughter of an entire people—as a normal way of life. Decent human beings were faced with a choice of accepting slavery or fighting back.

World War I was different. Historians still debate the responsibility for that clash between the Central Powers and the Allies. But World War II was the direct outcome of aggression that could not be tolerated. In this sense it was an irrepressible conflict.

Questions for Research

1. Nationalism, imperialism, militarism, and international anarchy were the fundamental causes of World War II. How did each of these factors contribute to the outbreak of war?
2. The *fundamental* causes of both World War I and World War II were much the same, but the *immediate* cause was quite different. How did the assassination at Sarajevo on June 28, 1914 trigger World War I? How did Hitler's invasion of Poland on September 1, 1939 start World War II?
3. In what way did the Munich Conference of 1938 seek to appease dictators Hitler and Mussolini?

---

*Louis L. Snyder, Professor of History at The City College of New York, is an acknowledged expert on recent European history. A graduate of St. John's College, he took his doctorate at the University of Frankfurt am Main, Germany, and during World War II served as an officer in the U.S. Air Force. Dr. Snyder is the author of numerous books, as well as many articles and reviews.

4. How did the Hossbach meeting reveal Hitler's real plans? (Special research required.)
5. How did the pact between Hitler and Stalin pave the way for war?

UNIT 2—MEANING OF THIS FILM

A documentary film is composed of clips from the archives giving actual photographs of what happened. Such films, of course, have their value for students of history. *Patton* is not a documentary film but a *re-creation* of the role played by General George S. Patton, Jr. in World War II. It seeks historical accuracy in portraying Patton's personality and character, in re-enacting the drama of his career, and in showing the weapons and costumes used in the conflict. It is designed to give the viewer a fair picture of an unusual man—warts and all, a man who left an indelible impression on the history of his time.

This film is especially valuable for the student of history. It presents an objective view of a many-sided character. No attempt is made to show Patton as a hero-who-could-do-nothing-wrong or as a devilish militarist-who-could-do-nothing-right. The American general is revealed as a man of many moods, in swashbuckling arrogance, in soft hearted sentimentality, in infantile enthusiasm, and in Hamlet-like introspection.

From this film the student can absorb the stuff, the feel, and the smell of World War II. It is an unforgettable portrait of an extraordinary American fighting man. At the same time, far from glorifying or sentimentalizing war, the film depicts with great authority the utter brutality and horror of war on a mass scale—in this sense may be said to project the strongest of anti-war feelings.

Questions for Discussion

1. What is the difference between a documentary film on World War II and *Patton?*
2. On the basis of what you have seen in this film, how would you describe the personality and character of General Patton?
3. Is it reasonable to say that General Patton loved war for its own sake? Why?
4. Enumerate and describe the ways in which this film seeks to show both sides of General Patton's character.
5. Why is this film valuable for a student of history?

UNIT 3—THE PSYCHOLOGY OF LEADERSHIP

Great military leaders are unique, dazzling figures surrounded by an aura of charisma, masters of men, contemptuous of misfortune and death. From Alexander the Great to Napoleon they have been responsible for important changes in the course of history. Above all their success has been due to an understanding of the psychology of leadership. But each military commander approached the problem of leadership from a different angle.

Patton had definite ideas about the nature of leadership. He believed it to be more essential to be feared by his men than loved by them. In 1943, Eisenhower sent Patton to Tunisia to rejuvenate the American forces after the Kasserine Pass defeat by Rommel's veteran Afrika Korps. In *A Soldier's Story*, General of the Army Omar N. Bradley, USA tells how Patton set out deliberately to shock his troops into a realization that the easy-going days were over. "By the third day after his arrival, the II Corps staff was fighting mad—but at Patton, not at the Germans." After several months in combat, the Americans had begun to affect the British soldier's casual disregard for conventional field dress. When not under fire, they removed their heavy helmets and wore only the OD beanie issued for wear under the helmet. Patton issued an order prescribing the wearing of helmets, leggings, and neckties at all times in the corps sector. This included even doctors and nurses in hospital tents and mechanics in the ordnance pools. Patton himself went out to round up offenders in his "beanie campaign."

This was typical of Patton's concept of leadership. There was a job to be done and nothing would stand in the way. The troops were angered at their spit-and-polish commander—but signs of slovenliness disappeared. Patton was not popular, but he was respected and he left no doubt as to who was boss.

One of the secrets of Patton's success as a military commander was his willingness to commit himself to battle. In this respect he recalls the genius of Frederick the Great, the molder of modern Prussia-Germany. "War," said Frederick, "is decided only by battles and it is not decided except by them." He was always prepared to take risks which others would have regarded as suicidal. Placing primary emphasis upon mobility and firepower, the Prussian king drilled his troops to march fast and swing quickly from column to line. Often he fought on several fronts simultaneously. Skilled in basic strategy, he was also an able tactician, always seeking to obtain local superiority at one point and then moving to another.

Patton was a commander in the Frederician image. In American military history he ranks with Jeb Stuart, Nathan Bedford Forrest, Phil Sheridan, and Stonewall Jackson as a man of action.

Questions for Discussion

1. In your estimation what should be the qualities of an effective military commander?
2. What was the secret of Patton's great success as a combat leader?
3. The film shows Patton issuing an order against late morning breakfast for officers. What was his motive in insisting that good soldiers always got up before the sun?
4. What were Patton's main assets as a leader of men?
5. What were his faults as a military commander?

UNIT 4—THE SLAP HEARD AROUND THE WORLD

"George is pretty good at miracles. He never gets credit for the right things. You ask people about Patton twenty-five years from now and I bet they'll say, 'Oh yeah—he's the guy with the ivory-handled pistols who slapped that soldier.'"
—*General of the Army Omar N. Bradley*

It was, indeed, a slap heard around the world—in every Post Exchange where G.I.'s were eating hamburgers, in every foxhole where Willie and Joe were under fire, even in Adolf Hitler's headquarters.

The film accurately presents the slapping incident. During the campaign in Sicily, Patton, as was his custom, made a round of hospitals to cheer up the wounded men. Seeing an ambulatory patient, the general asked him why he was there. The enlisted man replied: "General, I guess it is my nerves. I can't stand the shelling any more."

Patton instantly went into a rage, screaming a torrent of abuse at the startled G.I. "Your nerves, hell, you're just a goddamned coward!" He accused the soldier of malingering, of cowardice, as unfit to be in the same hospital with wounded men. Nearby doctors and nurses, helpless and embarrassed, could not say anything.

Patton lost control of himself altogether. He swung at the G.I.'s head, knocking off his helmet. "Shut up," he shouted, "I won't have these brave men here who've been shot see a yellow bastard crying!" Fuming, he stormed out of the hospital, shouting imprecations about psychoneurotics and cowards."

It was a shocking, brutal performance. The story soon spread through the battle units and back to the United States. When a news commentator revealed the incident over the radio, a great public clamor arose for Patton's dismissal.

Eisenhower reprimanded Patton sharply and ordered him to apologize to the slapped G.I. Moreoever, he required Patton to appear before officers and enlisted men "to assure them that he had given way to impulse and respected their positions as fighting soldiers of a democratic nation."

Ordinarily, the incident would have been dismissed as an unimportant and unfortunate display of temper. But it became a major event in Patton's career. Although he went on to lead one of the most dashing campaigns of the war, he never quite lived down the ignominy of his bizarre behavior in that hospital in Sicily.

Perhaps Patton's erratic behavior was due in part to terrific strain and to the sights and suffering he had seen among the wounded in the hospital. Bradley explains Patton's act without condoning it, suggesting that Patton did not understand that men could break under the intense emotional strain of battle. To him it was axiomatic that those who did not fight were just cowards. He reasoned that if one could shame a coward, one might help him gain self-respect. Years later, Bradley wrote, "I cannot believe that George Was intentionally brutal . . . Patton simply sought to purge that soldier of 'cowardice' by shaming him . . . I shall go on believing . . . the private whose face he slapped . . . did more to win the war in Europe than any other private in the army."

Questions for Discussion

1. Why does the film pay so much attention to the slapping incident?
2. What does the term "psychoneurosis" mean to you?
3. Why did Eisenhower, despite Patton's reprehensible conduct, decide not to relieve him immediately of his command?
4. Are you satisfied with Bradley's explanation? Why?
5. How did the slapping incident affect Patton's later career?

UNIT 5—THE MOUTH THAT ROARED

Some great military leaders have also been remarkable administrators and diplomats. Among them were Julius Caesar, George Washington, Frederick the Great, Napoleon, and Eisenhower. But Patton's talent was limited to the military. As a child he was fascinated by toy soldiers, as an adult he studied military history and the lives of all the great commanders of the past. Throughout his life he retained his love for the soldier's career, which he deemed to be a noble profession. As the film shows, he was fascinated by the great battles of history.

Outside his profession, Patton was like a fish out of water. He had a weakness for heading into trouble by speaking on matters he little understood. The slapping incident was only one example of his habit of saying the wrong thing at the wrong time. In March 1944, before the invasion of the Continent, he was stationed in the British Midlands. He was called upon to dedicate an Allied service club in Knutsford, a nearby town. Instead of limiting his speech to Anglo-American friendship, he made this dangerous remark: "The idea of these clubs could not be better because undoubtedly it is our destiny to rule the world."

This was a prize example of Patton's genuine ability to put his foot into his mouth. Reporters were waiting and they deemed the remark as a slur against the Russians. Patton's unthinking comment exploded into a world crisis when it reached the press wires. With many allies the United States was at war to prevent Hitler from ruling the world, and here an obtuse American General was speaking of "our destiny" to take over leadership of the globe. The United States Senate quickly tabled Patton's nomination for promotion to permanent major general.

Once again Eisenhower was embarrassed and angry. "I'm just about fed up," he told Bradley. "If I have to apologize publicly for George once more, I'm going to have to let him go, valuable as he is. I'm getting sick and tired of having to protect him. Life's much too short to put up with any more of it."

Fifteen months later, Patton was in trouble again. This time, as commander of the Third Army on an occupation mission, he was told that it was official policy not to employ former Nazis. He paid no attention to the order. He was quoted as saying the ordinary run of Nazis weren't much different than Democrats and Republicans back home . . . and that if we did not move to take Russia now, we'd only have to do it in 25 years . . .

This foolish, indeed almost stupid, remark, was too much for Eisenhower. Patton was relieved from command of the Third Army and exiled to an obscure "paper" staff of the Fifteenth Army. Unable to understand the gravity of his comments, Patton never got over Eisenhower's "ingratitude." Ironically, not long after, on December 21, 1945, Patton died in Luxembourg of injuries received when a truck collided into his staff car near the German city of Mannheim.

Questions for Discussion

1. What did the German intelligence officer mean when he described Patton as a "pure warrior"—"an anachronism . . ?"
2. Why did Eisenhower bail out Patton twice when he could easily and justifiably have dropped him?
3. What were the differences between the Nazis and the Democrats and Republicans that Patton refused to recognize?
4. What is meant by the phrase "discretion is the better part of valor?"

UNIT 6—AUTHENTICITY: PATTON AND BRADLEY

The producer of *Patton* was most fortunate in obtaining the services of General of the Army Omar N. Bradley, USA as Senior Military Advisor. An eyewitness of General Bradley's stature meant much for the authenticity of the film. Many hours of consultation with the famed American general helped to insure accuracy within the dramatic framework of the production.

Bradley is the only one of the senior American military commanders of World War II in the European Theatre now alive. During the war General of the Army George C. Marshall, Chief of the U.S. Army General Staff, converted the American Army into a vast and mobile machine. He chose its top three commanders for field service in Europe. Eisenhower became the coordinator, Bradley the thinking machine, and Patton the special combat fighter.

During the conquest of Sicily, Bradley was a corps commander subordinate to Patton in the Seventh Army. In January 1944 he was selected by Eisenhower to lead the ground forces in Operation Overlord, the invasion of Europe. The roles were reversed—Bradley now became Patton's superior officer. Throughout the Normandy fighting, Bradley commanded the U.S. Twelfth Army Group, which in August was made independent of the British Twenty-first Army Group under Montgomery. In this way Bradley and Montgomery were given equal status.

Bradley, a calm, steady officer, was not only a brilliant military strategist but also a gifted leader of men and an attractive human being. Called by some "the Quiet American" and by war correspondent Ernie Pyle "the G.I.'s General," Bradley was respected by all who knew him. Even the temperamental Patton was willing to serve under him.

Bradley had some reservations about Patton, although he was aware of Patton's intuition, "which made him a great field commander." "Had Eisenhower asked for my opinion, I would have counseled against the selection . . . I seriously doubted the wisdom of forcing Patton to stomach the reversal of roles in command." Eisenhower assured him that Patton would submit without rancor.

Once again Eisenhower was right. Bradley later reported that in August 1944 Patton came to him eagerly and as a friend without pique or grievance. "My years' association with him in Europe remains one of the brightest remembrances of my military career."

Questions for Discussion

1. In what way did General Bradley, as Senior Military Advisor, give authenticity to this film?
2. What was the result of the reversal of roles of command in the case of Generals Bradley and Patton?
3. Point out elements in George C. Scott's remarkable portrayal of Patton that reflect an actor's research and study in preparing for such a part.
4. What impression of Bradley do you get from Karl Malden's characterization?
5. What reservations did Bradley have about Patton being in his command? Why did he change his mind?

UNIT 7—RIVALRY: PATTON AND MONTGOMERY

General (later Field Marshal) Bernard Law Montgomery was one of the outstanding field commanders of World War II. Under his leadership the British Eighth Army won one of the most brilliant victories in the history of the British Army at El Alamein (October 23–November 7, 1942), where he routed the mixed Axis forces of General Erwin Rommel, the German Desert Fox. Montgomery completed the conquest of Italy's African Empire, and again in March 1943 defeated Rommel's reinforced army at the battle of the El Mareth Line. In the summer of 1944 he was one of the Allied commanders who won the great victory of the Battle of Normandy. He led the 21st Army Group across the Rhine to the Elbe River. It was a record of which the British and the Allies could be proud.

Yet underneath the smiles of cooperation among the Allied commanders were some deep-seated rivalries. Strong men in all professions are apt to succumb to envy of their peers: such rivalries were especially strong among the top officers of the Allied forces. Indeed, one of Eisenhower's greatest talents was his ability to resolve the differences among spirited American and British commanders serving under him.

This film reveals one of these highly personal conflicts. Both Patton and Montgomery were fine combat leaders, but they were toally unlike each other in temperament and personality. Montgomery was the slow, careful planner who insisted upon waiting until he was thoroughly equipped and ready to take on the enemy. Patton, always too restless to wait, was like a caged tiger. Counting on dash and verve, he struck fast, moved quickly, and halted only when his tanks ran out of fuel. Montgomery was the apotheosis of the conservative leaders; Patton—Blood and Guts—was ever the general-in-a-hurry.

A complicating factor was that Patton had an unconcealed dislike for his British colleague. Until the day he died, Patton never ceased to believe that had priority in supply been given to him instead of to Montgomery after the Normandy campaign, his Third Army would have moved even more speedily through the German defenses. He was also irked by Montgomery's proposal that the Third Army be halted permanently on the Moselle while he, Montgomery, moved on to Berlin. Patton had only contempt for this type of thinking which assigned to him a secondary role to a British commander.

Questions for Discussion

1. What part did General Montgomery play in the history of World War II?
2. What differences were there in the combat styles of Patton and Montgomery?
3. Do you feel that this film goes too far in the direction of underestimating the significance of Montgomery in the war? Why?
4. How was Eisenhower able to get British and American commanders to work together for the common good?
5. What were the respective roles played by Patton and Montgomery in the final campaign of the war?

UNIT 8—GENERALSHIP: RELIEF OF BASTOGNE

The Battle of the Bulge was Hitler's last gamble, the final attack of the Nazi war machine, and a dangerous challenge to the Allies, especially the Americans. In December 1944, at a time when Germany seemed to be on the verge of collapse, her armies pushed back from France almost to the Rhine, she suddenly launched a tremendously powerful counterattack. In stunning surprise, just as in 1940 they had overrun France, the Germans struck again. The same General von Rundstedt was in command, the same area—the Ardennes—was the locale of the attempted breakthrough.

The Germans repeatedly sought for weak points along the 400-mile Allied front. Eisenhower was faced once again with a critical decision: How could he stop the spearhead of the German attack and turn it from the west? His eyes were on Bastogne, a little market town which was the hub of a seven-fold road network. Here an American force was trapped.

What then happened was one of the most astonishing feats of generalship in the American campaign. Patton was at Third Army headquarters preparing his Saar campaign. Bradley telephoned him (the Americans had a magnificent communications system) and ordered him to halt units of the Third Army and move them immediately to the hard pressed 8th Corp some 90 miles to the north. In a classic swift-moving maneuver, he led his men from their bridgehead on the Saar to the snow-covered Ardennes front within a matter of days in weather that was the worst in 38 years.

At Bastogne, General Anthony C. McAuliffe and his 101st Airborne Division had withstood a seven-day siege at the cost of 482 killed and 2,449 wounded—

against three German divisions. Called upon by the Germans to surrender, he replied with a famous single-word rejection: "Nuts!"

The film shows these dramatic events as Patton and his troops executed their classical rescue. The siege of Bastogne was finally lifted on December 26, 1944 after the garrison had been supplied from the air and had beaten off heavy German attacks.

This was exactly what Eisenhower had planned: the Germans were now forced to turn their great counterattack from the west and the northwest to the south. The instant the Germans made this decision the whole impact of their offensive was blunted. Von Rundstedt had counted on a quick triumph, only to be thwarted by Patton's remarkable move.

Questions for Discussion

1. What was the aim of Hitler's great counterattack in the Ardennes?
2. Why was Bastogne a critical spot?
3. Why was the "speed" factor of enormous importance in this battle?
4. What was the role of General McAuliffe in the Bastogne story?
5. What was the importance of the relief of Bastogne in the final outcome of the war?

UNIT 9—PATTON'S PLACE IN HISTORY

Despite his contradictions in character, Patton takes a place as one of the outstanding American commanders of World War II. "History has reached out and embraced General George Patton. His place is secure. He will be ranked in the forefront of America's great military leaders." (*New York Times*, December 22, 1945.)

Students of history are interested primarily in facts. Patton accomplished the following in the defeat of the Axis:

1. Battle of El Guettar: In late March 1943, while Montgomery was pouring his Eighth Army through the French-built Mareth Line defense, Patton pushed beyond Gafsa to El Guettar. When the Germans tried frantically to shake the Americans off their flank, Patton stopped them with a concentration of firepower.

2. Invasion of Sicily: The Allied conquest of Sicily took just 38 days. While Montgomery moved around Mount Etna north to Messina, Patton's Seventh Army swarmed through the hub to the north and then along the coast road, reaching Messina on August 17, 1943.

3. Breakthrough in Normandy: After the invasion of Normandy (Overlord, June 1944), Patton's Third Army cut off the peninsula of Brittany, and then thrust on to Paris, the German frontier, and the Siegfried Line. His tanks moved so fast that they outstripped their supply lines.

4. Relief of Bastogne: This was Patton's most striking military achievement. *(See Unit 8.)*

5. Advance to Prague: In the closing days of the war, Patton moved swiftly into Czechoslovakia. He was less than 60 miles from Prague, but for political reasons he was not allowed to occupy it. His advance was halted at Pilsen in April 1945.

Questions for Discussion

1. What did Patton accomplish at El Guettar?
2. What was the strategic purpose of the invasion of Sicily and what was Patton's role there?

3. What part did Patton's advance across France and Germany play in Allied victory?
4. Why was the relief of Bastogne a classic military maneuver?
5. What were the political considerations impelling Eisenhower to stop Patton before Prague?

UNIT 10—RECOMMENDED FOR FURTHER READING

Following is a reading list of basic books for research, writing of themes and essays, and discussion of *Patton*.

Allen, Robert S., *Lucky Forward: The History of Patton's Third U.S. Army* (Vanguard Press: New York, 1947).

Army Times, Warrior: The Story of General George S. Patton, by the editors of the *Army Times* (Putnam: New York, 1967).

Ayer, Fred, Jr., *Before the Colors Fade: Portrait of a Soldier, George S. Patton, Jr.* (Houghton Mifflin: Boston, 1964).

Bradley, Omar N., *A Soldier's Story* (Henry Holt: New York, 1951).

Eisenhower, Dwight D., *Crusade in Europe* (Doubleday: New York, 1948).

Farago, Ladislas, *Patton: Ordeal and Triumph* (Ivan Obolonsky: New York, 1964).

Hatch, Alden, *George Patton: General in Spurs* (Messner: New York, 1950).

Marshall, S.L.A., *Bastogne: The First Eight Days* (Infantry Journal Press: Washington, 1946).

Nobecourt, Jacques, *Hitler's Last Gamble: The Battle of the Bulge*, trans. from the French by R.H. Barry (Schocken Books: New York, 1967).

Patton, George S., Jr., *War as I Knew It* (Houghton Mifflin: Boston, 1947).

Semmes, Harry H., *Portrait of Patton* (Paperbook Library: New York, 1970), original edition 1955.

Snyder, Louis L., *The War: A Concise History, 1939-1945* (Messner: New York, 1960). Paperback, Dell, Laurel edition, No. 9393, 1964.

Toland, John W., *Battle: The Story of the Bulge* (Random House: New York, 1959).

Wellard, James H., *General George S. Patton, Jr.: Man under Mars* (Dodd Mead: New York, 1946).

The Cast

General George S. Patton, Jr.	George C. Scott
General Omar N. Bradley	Karl Malden
Captain Chester B. Hansen	Stephen Young
Brigadier General Hobart Carver	Michael Strong
General Bradley's Driver	Cary Loftin
Captain Richard N. Jenson	Morgan Paull
Field Marshal Erwin Rommel	Karl Michael Vogler
General Patton's Driver	Bill Hickman
First Lieutenant Alexander Stiller	Patrick J. Zurica
Sergeant William George Meeks	James Edwards
Colonel Gaston Bell	Lawrence Dobkin
Air Vice-Marshal Sir Arthur Coningham	John Barrie

Colonel General Alfred Jodl	Richard Muench
Field Marshal Sir Bernard Law Montgomery	
	Michael Bates
Lieutenant Colonel Charles R. Codman	Paul Stevens
Major General Walter Bedell Smith	Edward Binns
Third Army Chaplain	Lionel Murton
Major General Lucian K. Truscott	John Doucette
Soldier Who Gets Slapped	Tim Considine
Willy	Abraxas Aaran
Tank Captain	Clint Ritchie

Credits

Producer	Frank McCarthy
Director	Franklin J. Schaffner
Screen Story and Screenplay by	Francis Ford Coppola & Edmund H. North
Based on Factual Material from "Patton: Ordeal and Triumph" by	Ladislas Farago
and	
"A Soldier's Story" by	Omar N. Bradley

Photographed in Dimension 150®
Color by De Luxe—170 Minutes

Teachers may obtain additional copies of this Guide by writing to 20th Century-Fox Film Corporation, 444 W. 56 St., New York, N.Y. 10019, attention Mr. Hal Sherman. Portions may be quoted for purposes of educational or editorial comments.

Books

Certain book publishers have issued individual books on specific classic films. Each can serve as a detailed study guide to the film. Outstanding series of this type include the "Focus on" series, published by Prentice-Hall (Englewood Cliffs, N.J.), which includes among its titles *The Birth of a Nation*, *Blow-Up*, *Bonnie and Clyde*, *Citizen Kane*, *Rashomon*, *The Seventh Seal*, and *Shoot the Piano Player*. The "Filmguide to" series is published by Indiana University Press (Bloomington, Ind.) and includes *The Battle of Algiers*, *The General*, *The Grapes of Wrath*, *Henry V*, *La Passion de Jeanne d'Arc*, *Psycho*, *The Rules of the Game*, and *2001: A Space Odyssey*. The "From Fiction to Film" series published by the Dickenson Publishing Company (Encino, Calif.) features the classic *An Occurrence at Owl Creek Bridge* and *Silent Snow, Secret Snow*.

Other book publishers have issued collections of study guides. Among the more outstanding are *Discovery in Film* by Robert Heyer and Anthony Meyer, *Films in Depth* by Paul Schreivogel, *A Guide to Short Films for Religious Education Programs I, II* by Patrick J. McCaffrey, *Media in Value Education* by Jeffrey Schrank, *Themes: Short Films for Discussion* by William Kuhns, and *101 Films for Character Growth* by Jane Cushing. These books, along with other titles, are annotated in Appendix 3. A film guide for *The String Bean* taken from *101 Films for Character Growth* is included here as Example 18.

Example 18. Film Study Guide from a Book

THE STRING BEAN (LE HARICOT)

Rating: Excellent

Topic: Old age needs the encouragement of a selfless purpose in life

Synopsis: This film tells with tenderness and dignity the story of an old woman who cultivates a potted string bean plant with a loving devotion. Sunning and watering her thriving green friend is her sole diversion in her tiny Paris lodging where she sews handbags for her livelihood. When her plant becomes too large she surreptitiously plants it in the Tuileries garden and visits it daily, until the gardener discovers it. She moves her plant and begins again. Her faith and optimism form the slender narrative of a wordless film poem. Sechau, writer and director, is hailed as the French poet laureate of the screen. (17 minutes)

Age Level: Junior high school–adult

Questions for Discussion
1. What feeling or mood is yours after viewing this film?
2. Is such a situation as portrayed here a common one in life around us?
3. What important feelings did the care of the plant evoke in the old woman?
4. React to the conclusion of the film.
5. What personality traits of the old woman are displayed in this film?
6. Is there significance in the choice of a string bean plant rather than a tulip or some more appealing plant? What is it?
7. Discuss the absence of dialogue and the use of background music.
8. How would you rank this film in reference to others you have seen?

Individual study guides may be purchased from certain film organizations and distributors. A few that offer guides at a modest cost are the American Federation of Film Societies, Mass Media Ministries, National Catholic Office for Motion Pictures, New York State Council on the Arts, St. Clement's Film Association, Teaching Film Custodians, Universal Education and Visual Arts, and Walter Reade 16.

Homemade Guides

By using the structure of published film discussion guides as a model, the creative person will soon be able to fashion original ones by using program notes, articles, reviews, and, of course, personal viewings of films.

The study guides for the 1946 feature film *Humoresque* (Example 19) and the 1965 feature film *The Servant* (Example 20), which follow, show such local productions designed for use with an adult audience.

Example 19. Film Study Guide Prepared by a Librarian

HUMORESQUE

1946—125 Minutes—Black and White

Cast

Helen Wright	Joan Crawford
Paul Boray	John Garfield
Sid Jeffers	Oscar Levant

Rudy Boray	J. Carrol Naish
Gina	Joan Chandler
Phil Boray	Tom D'Andrea
Florence	Peggy Knudsen
Esther Boray	Ruth Nelson
Monte Loeffler	Craig Stevens
Victor Wright	Paul Cavanaugh
Baver	Richard Gaines
Rozner	John Abbott
Paul Boray (as a boy)	Bobby Blake
Phil (as a boy)	Tommy Cook
Eddie	Don McGuire
Hagerstrom	Fritz Leiber
Club Singer	Peg La Centra
Teddy	Richard Walsh

Credits

Studio	Warner Brothers
Producer	Jerry Wald
Director	Jean Negulesco
Screenplay	Clifford Odets
	Zachary Gold
Original Story	Fannie Hurst
Photography	Ernest Haller
Art Direction	Hugh Reticker
Music Conductor	Franz Waxman
Musical Director	Leo F. Forbstein
Music Advisor	Isaac Stern
Editing	Rudi Fehr

COMMENTS

All talents combine to make a glossy, stylish film that we no longer see today. Acting, direction, camera work, and music overcome the banal Fannie Hurst story that had been filmed several times prior to this version. The climax is famous for attempting the impossible in film melodrama. How well it succeeds has been a topic of discussion since the film was released.

QUESTIONS FOR DISCUSSION

1. Man's isolation and the difficulties involved in loving and being loved have been themes found in every art form through the ages. Does this film add anything to one's understanding of them? Does it seek to?
2. Comment on the scene at Helen Wright's house, during which Paul Boray first meets his future patroness. What elements of their characters are first portrayed here?
3. Do you think that Helen's music ("I Guess I'll Have to Change My Plans"; "What Is This Thing Called Love?"; "You Do Something to Me"; "Embraceable You") speaks for her as Paul's music did for him?
4. Discuss the significance of the following sequences:
   a. Paul playing nervously with the window shade pull while conversing with Sid.

b. The restaurant scene with Sid and Gina: the broken wine glass; the circles on the table from Sid's wine glass; Gina's blowing out the match.

c. The lighting of Helen's cigarettes in scenes where her relationships with Paul and other men are involved.

d. The man and the dog on the beach during the suicide scene.

5. Do you think there is anything symbolic about Helen's being nearsighted?

6. What is the significance of the following remarks:

a. "Let me alone, Paul. I'm a lost crusade."

b. "She's as complex as a Bach fugue."

c. ". . . We don't laugh enough."

d. "Some people want to get there fast and don't want to pay for the ride."

e. "Bad manners are a sign of talent."

f. "Your playing needs restraint; it's too brash."

7. There are several scenes in the film where height is emphasized. Can you recall any? What is the significance of the height? Does the perspective of height change? If so, why?

8. Does this film demonstrate that love often plays "second fiddle" to other needs, emotions, etc.? Explain.

9. "Kitsch" is a word used to describe certain films. Its dictionary definition is "artistic or literary material held to be of low quality, often produced to appeal to popular taste and marked especially by sentimentalism, sensationalism, and slickness. Can *Humoresque* be described as kitsch?

10. A humoresque is defined as "a musical composition typically whimsical or fanciful in character." Why such a title, then, for this film?

Example 20. Film Study Guide Prepared by a Librarian

THE SERVANT

1963—115 Minutes—Black and White

Directed by Joseph Losey

Produced by Joseph Losey and Norman Priggen

Screenplay by Harold Pinter based
on the novel by Robin Maugham

Released by Warner-Pathé

Cast

Barrett	Dirk Bogarde
Tony	James Fox
Vera	Sarah Miles
Susan	Wendy Craig

BACKGROUND

The Servant is one of Losey's best known and most complex films. Externally it deals with a struggle for possession of a wealthy weakling. The changing relationships between the leading characters is shown by Losey's visual style—moving camera, symbolic decor, deep focus, actor placement, etc. Dialogue by Pinter and Maugham also accentuates this direct exploration of personalities and this implied account of the class structure of England.

QUESTIONS FOR DISCUSSION

1. In the film, what is the significance of the:
   a. Mirror
   b. Flowers
   c. "By Appointment" sign
   d. House
   e. Staircase
   f. Dripping faucet
   g. Stair railing
   h. Workmen in the house
   i. Home of Susan's parents
   j. Divider partition in the bar
2. Consider the relationship(s) of Tony and Barrett. Can you cite a specific scene in the film where they were acting as:
   a. Master and servant
   b. Homosexual couple
   c. Husband and wife
   d. Playmate and pal
   e. Son and mother
   f. Sadomasochistic pair
   g. Nanny and ward
   h. Boss and worker
3. What do you think is Losey's meaning in the:
   a. Interview scene?
   b. Restaurant scene?
   c. Hide-and-seek scene?
4. *The Servant* may be considered to be a study of relationships which involve servility and exploitation rather than cooperation and collaboration. With this in mind, discuss briefly the relationship of:
   a. Tony and Barrett
   b. Vera and Tony
   c. Vera and Barrett
   d. Susan and Barrett
   e. Susan and Tony

PRESENTING THE FILM

Although the professional level of theatrical projection is hard to achieve in an institutional setting, some steps can be taken to make certain that the presentation of the film is optimum under the existing conditions. Nine activities are listed which should occupy the programmer's attention before, during, and after the film presentation.

1. Set up the room and the projector before the audience arrives. After the projector is positioned, check the following (Figure 13 provides a diagram):

Amplifier switch should be in the off position.

Power cord should be connected to a power supply.

External loudspeaker cable should be connected to the projector.

Rewind mechanism should be disengaged.

Spring belts should be in place around the appropriate wheels or pulleys.

Film speed control should be set for the desired speed, sound or silent.

Film direction indicator should be set to forward.

Magnetic or optical sound switch should be set to the desired sound format.

2. Test the projector, the image, and the sound before the audience arrives. The following checks may be made in order to obtain a smoother presentation:

Tone control should be set at neutral and, if necessary, adjusted after the showing begins.

Amplifier switch should be set to the on position.

Volume control should be set at a moderate level—just loud enough to produce a hum. It will probably have to be adjusted upward when the audience is seated. The

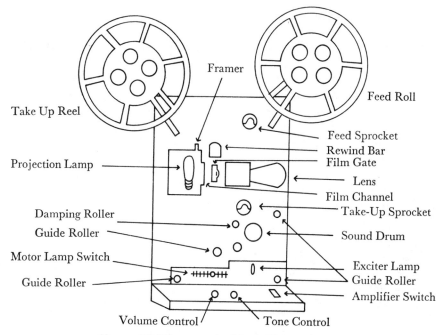

Take Up Reel

Framer

Feed Roll

Projection Lamp

Feed Sprocket
Rewind Bar
Film Gate
Lens
Film Channel
Take-Up Sprocket

Damping Roller
Guide Roller
Sound Drum

Motor Lamp Switch
Exciter Lamp
Guide Roller
Guide Roller
Amplifier Switch

Volume Control
Tone Control

Figure 13. Diagram of a 16mm film projector.

physical presence of the audience will soften the quality and lower the level of the sound, due to the absorption and interruption of sound waves.

Motor switch should be turned to the on position to allow the motor to run for five seconds. Avoid jumping immediately to the lamp position; rather, ease into it.

Lamp switch should be turned to the on position, thus lighting the screens.

Focus the lens by loosening or simply turning the screw until the corners of the screen image are in sharp focus.

Sound system: Test it by moving a thin paper card between the sound lens and the sound drum; a thumping sound should be heard on the loudspeaker.

Motor and amplifier switches should be turned to the off positions.

Take up reel should be secured to the take-up arm, not just placed in position.

Feed reel (the reel with the film) should be placed on the upper feed spindle and secured in place. The film is then threaded in accordance with the machine being used. See Figure 4 for a typical threading diagram.

Amplifier and motor switches are turned to the on positions; after a five-second wait the lamp switch is turned on.

Framer: Image is adjusted so that the complete frame is shown.

Volume control is adjusted if necessary.

Volume, lamp and motor controls are turned off.

Reverse motor switch: Select the rewind position; by reverse action start motor and return to beginning of film. Turn motor off at the appropriate point. Return the direction switch to the forward position.

The projector has now been tested and threaded and the operator's attention should be given to the physical qualities of the room.

3. Arrange the screen, seats, and projector so that viewing is maximized for all. Avoid extreme side seats. A suggested arrangement is shown in Figure 14.

4. Make every attempt to darken the room as much as possible. If some light is necessary, it should be arranged so that it does not fall on the screen. Compliance with safety laws with regard to exits is necessary but some exit signs are excessively bright and can interfere with the quality of the projected image. Check to see if a bulb of lower wattage can be substituted.

5. Remove or conceal any distracting signs or objects adjacent to the screen area. The screen should be isolated so that it receives the complete attention of the viewers.

6. Provide adequate ventilation. If smoking is allowed, have ashtrays available. If possible, designate a separate section for smokers. Whatever the rules on smoking may be, the audience should be informed officially of them and not be forced into assumptions.

7. After the audience has arrived, the projectionist has several responsibilities during the actual showing:

Set the amplifier switch to the on position a few moments before starting the film.

Darken the room.

Place the motor switch in the on position; wait five seconds; then place the lamp switch in the on position.

Adjust the volume and tone controls after checking the sound quality at a distance from the projector.

During the showing, it may become necessary, in order to eliminate jumping and unsynchronized sound, to use the loop setter to readjust the loop size.

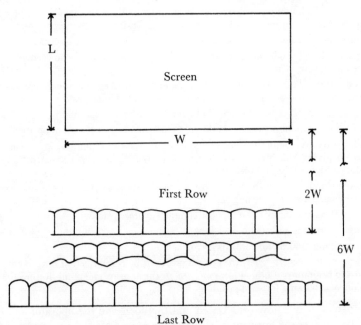

Figure 14. Screen size and seating.

8. The projectionist stays by the machine throughout the program, making any necessary adjustments. The goal is to provide a smooth, uninterrupted showing of the film.

9. Rewinding films is not always necessary, since some film companies use the rewinding process as an inspection check. The wishes of any company in this regard should be clearly noted on their containers, boxes, and printed materials.

Emergencies

It is wise to have a box of replacement parts at hand for use in emergencies. Included should be some spare projector lamps, exciter bulbs, rewind cables, masking tape, soft artist's paintbrushes, extension cords, reels, and any other items that may be needed for adequate projection. A second projector should always be available for emergency use. Another recommended precaution is to *inspect the film in advance.* It takes only a short time and that preliminary is repaid if an interruption or mishap is avoided.

Should the film break during the actual showing, stop the projector and rethread it after rewinding enough film on the take-up reel to provide pulling leverage. Any attempt to splice the film immediately consumes too much time and a hasty job tends to be unsatisfactory. If the film is rented, the permanent splice can be made when the film is rewound by the distributor. However, make sure that the distributor of the film is informed about the film break in order that he can repair it properly.

IMPROVING PROGRAMS

The following suggestions are general and are usually applicable. There are always exceptions and only by experimentation and trial can expertise in programming be gained.

Watch the timing carefully. If the audience is exhausted by the length of any one element, they will not be able to participate fully in the other portions of the program. Most programs that last more than two hours lose some of their potential effectiveness (and some of their audience). Since most feature films are from 90 to 120 minutes in length, the implication for their use is clear. Do as much as possible to introduce the feature by using film notes and save any available time for either a short introduction or a final discussion. It would probably be a disservice to an audience to attempt more. When shorter films are used, anywhere from 30 to 90 minutes is a satisfactory time period for the complete program.

It is not always necessary to show a complete film. At times a section or sequence can be most effective for the program's purpose. It is also possible to break up certain films into sequences or "acts" and have short discussions after each one. If the latter procedure is followed, care must be taken to limit the number of interruptions. The point at which the film is to be stopped should be exact and clearly understood by the projectionist.

A summary rule of timing can be found in the show business adage "Always leave 'em wanting more." It is better to have a shorter program than one that is exhausting in its length.

Communicate with the participants. If the program actively involves the audience, they should be informed what is expected of them: to listen with care to what is said by others; to think before speaking; to avoid interrupting others; to contribute, but not monopolize; to ask for clarification when necessary; to respect differing opinions; to reject the role of missionary; and to be succinct and to the point when speaking.

Prepare the leader of the program. The responsibilities of the program leader are mostly concerned with procedures rather than with specific knowledge. The latter need can be filled by a resource person when necessary. The tasks of the leader include:

Expressing appreciation of all comments.

Remembering that his role is one of guiding rather than informing.

Speaking in moderation—the leader should not talk too much.

Keeping the program moving.

Encouraging participation by the greatest number of audience members.

Defining issues and offering clarification when requested.

Offering interim and final summaries.

There are other things a leader might do to make the program successful.

Act as a host or greeter as the audience arrives.

Be flexible in handling the discussion. Although some framework is necessary, a rigid outline of points to cover should be avoided.

Remain in the room while the film is being projected. The leaders's absence is interpreted by some individuals as a measure of his interest in the program.

Observe the viewers: their entry, their responses to the film, and their general behavior. Each audience is unique and challenging. The alert leader recognizes audience characteristics and uses them to create a better program.

Vary the program methodology. Try to be somewhat unpredictable in the choice of methodology that is used in any series presentation. Often the techniques used are determined by the setting in which the program is presented. Some examples of possible techniques for use in programs are given in the next section.

Program Techniques

An introduction is almost always necessary. It should be very brief, with an explanation of what is to be shown and why it was chosen. Some mention might be made at this point of the individual viewer's role in the program and how the program differs from other film showing situations.

Advice on "what to look for" should be avoided, as should any subjective comments that might influence the viewer's perception of the film. Plot or content should not be disclosed.

Large group discussion is usually held after a viewing and allows some, rather than all, of the audience to participate. Diversified views are expressed and relating them to the general theme may be difficult. This format is flexible and free in structure, which presents a challenge to the leader, who must deal democratically with numerous personalities who may be unknown to him. It is possible to break a large group up into smaller units, with a leader appointed for each ahead of time. These leaders should have been present at previews, and should be acquainted with any study guides, plans, etc.

Small group discussion is ideal when the audience numbers from 10 to 15. Obtaining participation is easier, and it is possible to get to know the personalities involved. A more discernible result is usually possible with this size group.

Communication between the *guest speaker* and those presenting the program must be as complete as possible. The speaker should be familiar with the program purpose, the time allotted to him, the film to be shown, etc. A format incorporating a guest speaker is more structured but may still allow for audience participation in a final question-and-answer session with the guest.

A panel of speakers may be used when diversity of opinion is desired or when several reactions to a film are sought. Individual statements may be made, followed by a discussion among panel members and the moderator. A common procedure is to conclude with questions from the audience addressed to specific panel members.

The *"buzz session"* can allow for more individual participation, with the audience broken up into groups of three, four, or five persons. The groups are sometimes asked to discuss specific questions and are given a short period—perhaps 15 minutes—in which to do so. Later the audience reassembles and the conclusions, decisions, or comments of each group are reported by its spokesman to the entire assembly.

Arrangements for these programs may vary as in Figure 15.

Many other forms and arrangements are possible, but the overriding principle in any methodology is to provide the optimum setting for the actual film presentation. In most cases the audience has been attracted primarily by the film and did not come to hear long introductory presentations. Allow the major program time for viewing and audience participation.

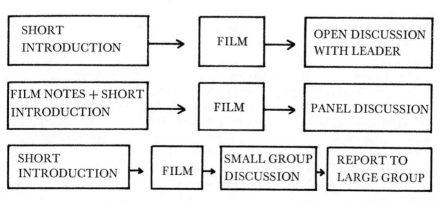

Figure 15. Discussion arrangements flow chart.

Discussion Problems

Certain problems native to discussion programs can be minimized by recognizing them beforehand. Some suggestions for handling these problems are dealt with here.

The Too-Quick Beginning. Audiences need a few moments to compose themselves after viewing a film. The entire film including any end credits should be shown, and then lights put on gradually once the screen blacks out. A few introductory sentences by the discussion leader will usually allow enough time for audience readjustment.

The Slow Discussion. If the group is not willing or ready to participate, try to frame a general provocative question. Dogmatic statements should be avoided. Ask the viewers to think about the question for a moment. After they have focused their thoughts, ask for opinion or reaction to the question. Follow up with a related question. The leader should save personal comments until the discussion is well under way.

Personalities in the Audience

People problems demand tact and care:

The reluctant participant. It is not necessary for everyone to participate. What is essential is that anyone who wants to speak have the opportunity to do so.

The overzealous participant. Basic rules should be announced with diplomacy at the start: the person who monopolizes, digresses, or talks at great length will be politely discouraged. It may even be necessary to interrupt or ignore an audience member, but this is the leader's right and often his responsibility if a comment is rambling and verbose. The best service the leader can perform for the group is to identify the substance of a comment by a short succinct summary.

The rude participant. At times comments from an audience member may offer offense to others. The statements may be intentional or not. The leader should try to soften or explain the comment, or even use it for group exploration. No individual should even be exposed to ridicule, sarcasm, or criticism from another audience member. The leader must be most sensitive to the feelings of each audience member. However, healthy interaction between audience members can often be encouraged by the leader. He can withdraw momentarily and allow the dialogue to take place on the floor, reasserting his leadership when he deems it appropriate.

The "far-out" participant. Every large audience usually has at least one member who puts an entirely different and irrelevant interpretation on the program's content. Each contribution by him seems remote from the path the discussion has been following, and it may take considerable effort by the leader to get back to the original track.

The ideal participants. At times the leader will discover and favor audience members who have views sympathetic with his own. A closed dialogue may ensue. The tendency to rely on one or more persons for comment, corroboration, or support should be avoided. The leader should try to have all viewpoints expressed and his summaries should include opinions that may not be his own.

EVALUATION OF THE PROGRAM

Two aspects of evaluation must be considered. First, the program as a totality should be examined by the presenters, the participants, and the audience. Evaluation can be verbal or written, formal or informal, but there should be some feedback about the effectiveness of the program. Although it is not always possible to obtain this information immediately, it is generally agreed that the further removed in time the evaluator becomes, the less reliable are his comments.

Some direction should be forthcoming for subsequent programs and any experimentation in technique, arrangement, etc., can be developed further or discontinued.

Second, the film portion of the program should be evaluated as an individual element. Criteria about audience reaction, stimulation, response, motivation, and challenge may be used in some cases, while a simple scale can be employed in others.

However it is accomplished, there should be some tangible evaluation of any film program. The necessity for this continual evaluation cannot be overemphasized, since the effectiveness of films depends upon the film itself and how it is used. In many instances the film is only as good as the person using it. A film by itself offers much less to the general viewer than does the film that is placed in a program context. It is much more difficult to arrange this frame in which to present the film, but ultimately, the viewer's experience is also much more rewarding.

Opinion can always be requested from the audience in either oral or written form. However, the more detailed evaluation should come from the program organizers, sponsors, and participants. These general thoughts may guide the evaluation: Were the purposes met? How could the program be improved? What techniques should be used again? What procedures should be avoided? Evaluate all the elements of the program: introduction, film, discussion, speaker, etc.

FILM IN THE COMMUNITY

Most communities have organizations whose members meet on a fairly regular basis because of a mutuality of interest among the members. Found in many communities are organizations such as:

PTAs	Volunteer firemen
Dad's clubs	Rescue squads
Elks	Ethnic groups
Rotary clubs	Social centers
Chambers of Commerce	Service clubs
Senior citizen groups	
Boy Scouts	Hospitals
Girl Scouts	Nursing homes
Church groups	Public service groups
Gardening clubs	Political groups
Bridge clubs	Art councils
Bowling clubs	
Art clubs	

The showing of films pertinent to the activities of each of these community groups is not only a logical activity but a most desired and profitable one. To bring training films, discussion films, entertainment films, etc., to these organizations is certainly offering a community service.

One ideal situation is to have a room within the library, school, or institution set aside for meetings. In some instances there is an auditorium available, whereas in others it is necessary to "assemble" a room for this purpose. However it is arranged, the use of such a facility by groups within the community will undoubtedly generate good will toward the host institution. In the case of schools and libraries, the ultimate value of such cooperation with community groups is obvious.

If additional service, such as program advisement, film selection, workshops in discussion leadership, and training in projector operation, can be offered, the effect upon the organizations within the community will be most noticeable.

Community Film Societies

The rationale for a film society is the desire of a group of people to view, discuss, and study films that are not available in theaters or on television. In the latter case, the presentation of a film on television is *not* the same as a film showing. Many people object to the editing, the commercial interruptions, and the small image, which diminishes the effect of most films. The closing of neighborhood theaters, the high admission prices of those still operating, antiquated booking policies, and the general low quality of recent films are factors that dismay the serious filmgoer.

The function or aim of a film society is obvious: to show films of high quality that are not generally available and, by those showings, to encourage the study and appreciation of film as an art form.

Film societies begin as a result of the energy, enthusiasm, and dedication of a few individuals, who in turn seek out similar persons. The search can take place in any community: a small town, a college campus, or a large urban setting. A group is formed that has clearly defined goals which involve films and film programs. Much of what has been written elsewhere in this volume is pertinent to film societies and their programs.

Finance is one factor that plays a large part in the successful operation of a film society. The films that are booked usually command relatively high rental costs, which must be met in some fashion. Possible arrangements include admission fees, memberships, subscriptions, and subsidies.

As with other community groups, the interaction between the film society and the library or school can be a mutually beneficial arrangement. If the plant, equipment, and expertise on film (availability, rental costs, procurement, evaluation, etc.) reside in the host institution, the use of that institution is justified in yet another way. In these years of accountability, this is an important consideration.

Scheduling Film Showings

Film showings held in unusual locations are becoming more frequent. In an effort to reach more people, sponsors have scheduled film programs in parking lots, playgrounds, stores, closed-off streets, at fairs, and at other nontypical places in communities. Sometimes regular electric power is brought to the projector by extension cords, whereas at others the power supply is housed in a van or vehicle specifically designed for bringing services to the community. Problems, including controlling light or securing and managing space, can usually be handled with a minimum of difficulty. It would be erroneous to assume that film showings can take place only within an institution; they can be held on many other sites within the community.

Examples of scheduling film programs to groups within the community are numerous:

Neighborhoods in early evening shows during summer vacations

Nursing homes in the early afternoon hours

Hospitals, where the time of showing can vary

Community organizations for evening meetings

Fairs or 4-H meetings held during the day

To these examples many more innovative ideas may be added.

School Film Societies

The general characteristics of organization and operation of a community film society can apply to a school society. Its major activity is the screening of good films for pupils—usually outside of school time. When feature films are shown on school premises without a profit motive, many distributors offer impressive reductions in rental fees. If the school media specialist is able to assist in selecting and helping to obtain the films at a minimum cost (including free films, of course), the quality of the societies' programs should be high.

School societies should begin slowly and plan a few programs each year rather than many. The time for the program will vary with individual schools and may depend on the scheduling within each school. Much theoretical discussion has taken place about flexible scheduling but in reality, school time tends to be rigidly structured and any accommodation is difficult to arrange. Lunch hours, assembly period, activity periods, after school, split sessions, Saturdays, early evenings are all possible times.

Costs can be covered in a variety of ways. Admission may be charged under certain conditions. The program may be sponsored by student associations, the PTA, or the school. Members of the society may earn the costs by conducting other fund-raising activities.

The selection of the program is most important. Efforts to educate the student viewers by exposing them to heavy silent film classics or arty/message shorts should be resisted. The proven plan is that followed by movie theaters for their Saturday matinees: open with a curtain raiser—a cartoon or a good two-reel sound comedy. A feature film that is not overly familiar should be the main event.

The challenge here is to find a film of high quality that is suitable and unfamiliar to the audience. Foreign films may be used from time to time but again the selection is of prime importance.

The sections on publicity, program notes, discussion techniques, evaluation, etc., in this chapter can all be adapted for use by school film societies. For example, the discussion need not be held immediately after the viewing; it can be postponed until a later meeting of the society.

CHAPTER 8
Equipment Selection, Evaluation, and Use

PROJECTORS

There are two major types of hardware used in a nontheatrical projection—the 16mm sound projector and the 8mm silent projector. General variations of each type exist and are noted below.

16mm Sound Projectors

The manufacture of these projectors is limited to only a few companies. Some of the largest are listed in Table 8 along with some recent models; their full addresses are given in Appendix 7. It is emphasized that models change almost each year, and the ones cited in the table serve only as examples. For the latest data on projectors, the best source is *The Audio-Visual Equipment Directory* published yearly by the National Audio-Visual Association. The 1974–1975 edition was the twentieth of this most valuable reference, which gives detailed information about each machine. Listed in Table 8, in addition to current model numbers, are the sound formats (optical, magnetic, or optical–magnetic), reel capacities, and weights. Only those projectors designed for school and/or library use were considered. Prices for this group range from $450 to $1,200 after typical discounts are applied. Figure 16 shows a typical 16mm projector.

It is possible to identify two kinds of 16mm projectors by their method of film threading:

1. *Manual Threading.* With this projector, the operator puts the film into the projector by hand, following a path that is indicated somewhere on the machine. Usual places for this diagrammatic path are on a lower inside flap which lays flat when the machine is in operating position, or on the various elements of the machinery itself.

Figure 4 shows a general schema of the threading process. Since the sound track is printed ahead of its corresponding visual, it follows that the film is threaded through the illumination-lens system of the projector first and then through the sound system. Briefly, the threading goes from the feed or supply reel to the projection lens to the sound system and out to the take-up reel.

Many operators prefer the manual threading method, since it allows adjustment of several factors during projection without an interruption in the showing. The projectionist has more control here than with an automatic threading system.

2. *Automatic Threading.* With this type of machine, the operator makes sure that the film end is regular rather than jagged by making a perpendicular cut across the width of the film. With some models, a lever adjustment must precede the feeding of the film into the machine. The machine is started, and the film is

Table 8. Comparative Physical Descriptions of 16mm Sound Projectors

Manufacturer and Model Number	Sound Format	Reel Capacity (ft.)	Weight (lb.)
Bell & Howell Co.			
Filmo Sound 566T	Optical	2000	38
Filmo Sound 8302L	Opt–Mag	2000	33
Filmo Sound 1500 Series	Optical	2000	37
Eastman Kodak Co.			
Pageant AV-126 Series	Optical	2000	36
Pageant AV-256 Series	Optical	2000	38
Pageant AV-12M6	Opt–Mag	2000	38
Pageant AV-12E6	Optical	2000	36
Pageant Arc	Optical	2000	41
Singer Education Systems			
Graflex 16-1000 Series	Optical	2000	39
Graflex 16-1100 Series	Optical	2000	39
Graflex 16- 900 Series	Magnetic	2000	39
Honeywell, Inc.			
F-16 Series	Optical	2000	42
F-16A Series	Opt–Mag	2000	35
International Audio Visual, Inc.			
M Series	Opt, Opt–Mag	2200	34
ST Series	Opt, Opt–Mag	2200	34
Kalart Victor Corp.			
75 Series	Optical	2000	40
80 Series	Optical	2000	40
82-25 MPR	Opt–Mag	2000	40
90-12	Optical	2000	38
Viewflex, Inc.			
Jan Series	Opt, Opt–Mag	2200	48
M Series	Optical	2200	36

Figure 16. A 16mm sound film projector.

placed at the entrance to the threading path. Mechanical claws guide the film by its sprockets along the threading path and even onto the take-up reel.

This method is preferred by the uncertain user, since it is automatic. Two major reservations should be noted here. First, the control of the projectionist over the film is limited. Second, if any difficulty occurs within the machine, correction may necessitate stopping the machine for comparatively long periods. Other difficulties with automatic threading include possible destruction of film and difficulty in showing selected portions of a film (i.e., the middle 10 minutes of a 30-minute film). If the machine is a new one or in excellent repair, *and* if the film used is in excellent condition, then good results can probably be obtained with these machines. But combine an older projector with a poor film print and a nervous projectionist, and the result may be disastrous.

In addition to the threading procedure, there are other characteristics that purchasers of 16mm projectors may want to consider.

Illumination. The intensity of a light source in a 16mm projector should be determined by the use for which the projector is intended. Large audiences, big auditoriums, a long projection throw, poor darkening conditions—all these factors may suggest a larger illumination source. Popular choices run from 500 watts to 2,000 watts. Higher wattage will increase initial projector price and later bulb replacement costs.

Lenses. Most projectors come with a standard 2-inch focal length projection lens. Departure from that size may be necessitated by the room in which the projector is to be used most often. A shorter focal length is used in a small room with a short projection throw, whereas a longer focal length may be used in a long narrow room where the projection throw is considerable. (Care should be taken to protect the projector lens from theft—they are expensive and can be removed easily. When projectors are not in use, they should be stored securely.)

Take-up reel capacity. Most machines will accommodate 2,000-foot reels. If it is necessary to use reels of a greater capacity, a machine with longer supply arms and take-up arms may be needed. Fortunately most films are packaged on 2,000-foot or smaller reels.

Sound. Two types of sound systems are available: optical and magnetic. With the optical system, the sound track is photographically printed on the film. The track is decoded by changing light impulses into varying electrical impulses which are then amplified and sent to the speaker. The magnetic sound track uses a magnetized coating placed near the film's edge. This sound reproduction system resembles that found in audio magnetic tape reproduction. A reading head translates the magnetized tape into electrical impulses which are amplified and sent to the speakers.

Magnetic recording facilities are useful in a projector when original sound tracks are to be produced. It is possible to have existing film coated magnetically and then replace the existing optical track with a locally produced magnetic one. In other cases, an original sound track can be added to either silent films or locally produced films.

Evaluation and Selection

The evaluation and selection of 16mm projectors can be based on a number of factors: sales appeals, demonstrations, word-of-mouth recommendations of associates, etc. There are very few agencies that actually test projectors and report results. One is Educational Products Information Exchange (EPIE; 463 West St., New York, N.Y. 10014). They have given permission to reprint the articles in Examples 21, 22, and 23, which appeared in the September 1972 issue of *Tel-A-B.I.T*, a publication of the Bureau of Instructional Technology of the New Jersey State Department of Education. Although the articles are addressed to a school audience, they present many general considerations on projector selection, evaluation, and use that are of value to any user of 16mm equipment.

Example 21. 16mm Projectors—What Do Users Look For?

In the late winter of 1971–1972, some 24 elementary and secondary school teachers, and ten "student aides" from grades five through eight, spent a bit of time setting up, operating, and answering questions from EPIE about several models of 16mm projectors.

The major purpose of this field trial was to see which features of projectors users think are particularly important. Of course the teachers and students had very limited experience with each machine, so they could not judge every factor which might make a projector good or bad for their purposes. Trends in their answers do occur, however, and school people who are thinking of buying 16mm equipment may find it useful to know what some teachers and student operators looked for.

We can say that these 34 people seem to consider efficient operation *before* they do quality of picture and sound—or perhaps manufacturers have licked picture and sound problems but not mechanical and design ones. Questions five and six in the questionnaire asked what they would say to colleagues who are considering buying a projector—what are this projector's strengths and weaknesses? For all the projectors (six were included) the weakness most frequently mentioned was heaviness. Only three of 34 respondents mentioned sound or picture quality.

The question of heaviness—the most often repeated comment, pro or con, of all—is curious, since these six projectors are very close to the lowest end of the weight continuum for 16mm projectors, which runs from about 30 to 300 pounds. Yet even the projectors called "compact" as a strength by some were called "heavy" as a weakness by others. There is a message here, for producers who may be able to lighten the load, and for school officials who must make arrangements for easy, efficient, non-problematic use of projectors. Some means for easy transport seems desirable.

A surprised and happy teacher said of one of the projectors, "I was able to work it without breaking it! [It's] possible to load it without much difficulty." Of course ease of operation, the most popular "plus," is not so simple a matter as weight. Some respondents mentioned ease of assembly, others ease of adjustment of sound and focus. More than anything, however, they seemed to be grateful for having the burden of threading film lifted from their shoulders, whether by a simplified system for manual threading or by an automatic threading system. Unfortunately here it was that directions failed. "Once you locate the proper place," said one teacher, "it is easy to thread—automatic." Student aides in particular were apprehensive about operating problems. As a weak feature important enough to call to prospective buyers' attention one student wrote, "Well, if you make a little mistake when you set it up, a lot can happen." About the same projector another said, "You need a lot of practice to work it," and a third said ominously, "It chews the film apart until you practice many many many times."

Problems with directions and with finding the significant parts of the operating system were frequently mentioned. "Only problem is deciphering the operating directions," said a teacher about a projector which she found easy to operate, clear as to sound, and sharp as to focus. On one projector, otherwise very favorably regarded, difficulty in finding the lever to engage the film and with deciphering case markings seemed to cause real frustration.

A few valuable features were mentioned once or twice—quiet operation, long cord, built-in splicer, sturdiness, etc. Isolated dissatisfactions occurred as well, with a plastic case, awkwardly placed reel and cord storage places, slow rewind, etc. Whether built-in speakers are a pro or a con is evidently a question of taste—or a function of the room in which the respondent envisages the projector in use. For whatever reason, some praised them, some knocked them.

One question asked of all respondents was whether they would buy the projector they were trying. Even in view of the very small number of respondents it seems safe to report that all of them, students and teachers alike, who worked with the Bell and Howell 1545 projector said "yes." Such unanimity did not occur for other machines.

Once other considerations—notably the setting in which the projector will be used and picture and sound quality—have been taken into account, school decision-makers will be well advised to look into ease of operation and clarity of directions. Projectors must suit the users as well as show good pictures.

Projectors included in field trial of user questionnaire:

Bell and Howell Model 1545
Bell and Howell Model 1550
Kalart-Victor Model 7515
International Audio Visual Autoload ST-OH
Singer-Graflex Instaload 16
(RCA) Viewlex AT-20X

Example 22. Tests on Three 16mm Projectors

In 1969 the Department of the Army made a wide variety of performance tests on eight 16mm projectors, three of which are still on the market. Selected test data for those three are reported here. Included are results of tests which concern the major operational features which EPIE considers particularly important to efficient projector operation.*

The Department of the Army compared the projectors with Joint Army–Navy (JAN) specifications and with one another. In examining the data one should keep in mind that JAN requirements are very rigorous, perhaps more rigorous than the school situation may require.

The projectors are:

Projector 1—Eastman Kodak AV 126TR-R (with transistorized amplifiers, silent and sound speeds)
Projector 2—(RCA) Viewlex 1600 (with zoom projector lens, automatic threading, transistorized amplifiers, silent and sound speeds)
Projector 3—Kalart-Victor 70-25 (with silent and sound speeds)

A. Light output

JAN specifications require that illumination on the screen be free from objectionable bands and that the average illumination at the four corners be not less than 70% of the illumination at the center.

(Measurements are in foot lamberts. EPIE recommends an average of 16 ±2 foot lamberts for satisfactory viewing.)

Projector 1—tested 22 feet from screen; 750 watt lamp
Center screen illumination—27.5
Average corner illumination—22.4 (81%)
Average overall illumination—24.9
Projector 2—tested 26 feet from screen; 1000 watt lamp
Center screen illumination—25.8
Average corner illumination—14.9 (58%)
Average overall illumination—19.6
Projector 3—tested 22 feet from screen; 750 watt lamp
Center screen illumination—14.5
Average corner illumination—9.8 (68%)
Average overall illumination—12.2

---

*See *EPIE Report* Number 45, "16mm Motion Picture Projectors."

JAN specifications also require that the flux on the screen be not less than 350 lumens with a 750 watt lamp, 520 lumens with a 1000 watt lamp. None of the projectors meet the standard; projector 1 ranked best on this standard, projector 3 least well. (Actual lumen ratings are not reported.)

B. Projector noise

JAN specifications require that noise of the projector mechanism not be greater than 60 decibels (db) above a given reference point.

Projector 1—64.0 db; room ambient level 32.5 db = 31.5 db extraneous

Projector 2—64.75 db; room ambient level 34.0 db = 30.75 db extraneous

Projector 3—63.0 db; room ambient level 32.5 = 30.5 extraneous

(EPIE recommends that 44 to 53 extraneous db be considered high, over 53 excessive.)

C. Audio reproduction

a. *Power output and distortion, amplifier:* JAN specifications require that the amplifier deliver an output of at least 7½ watts with a total harmonic distortion of no more than 2% of any frequency from 100 Hz to 7000 Hz.

Projector 1—9.3 watts, 1.11% distortion

Projector 2—6.0 watts, 1.11% distortion

Projector 3—30.0 watts, 15.6% distortion at 50 Hz, 6.9% at 100 Hz

b. *Frequency response, amplifier:* JAN specifications require that frequency response of amplifier not exceed the range of ±2 db from 50 Hz to 8000 Hz. Projectors 1 and 2 meet the JAN specification; projector 3 does not.

c. *Qualitative listening tests, speaker:*

Projector 1—good; meets JAN standards for frequency response and distortion

Projector 2—fair; fails to meet JAN standards for frequency response and distortion

Projector 3—good to excellent; meets JAN standards for frequency response and distortion.

D. Image

a. *Travel ghost (vertical blur)*

Projector 1—none

Projector 2—slight

Projector 3—none

b. *Picture jitter (film registration):* JAN standard is no more than 0.2% of image height or width. All three projectors meet the standard.

c. *Image focus:* JAN standard is equal sharpness of focus of the four corners of the projected image of the film passing through the gate of the projector. Projectors 1 and 3 meet the specification; the image in projector 2 is blurred on the edges.

E. Heat

EPIE recommends investigation of projector heat output, for operator safety, film safety, and comfort. The Department of the Army did not test heat output.

F. Operation

The Department of the Army reports all three projectors "reasonably convenient to operate." Projector 3 is somewhat difficult to thread, and the automatic threading mechanism on projector 2 is less efficient than the investigators felt it should be.

Principal Manufacturers of 16mm Projectors for School Use

Audiovisual Division, Bell and Howell, 7100 McCormick Rd., Chicago, Ill. 60645

Eastman Kodak Co., 343 State St., Rochester, N.Y. 14650

Graflex, Inc., 3750 Monroe Ave., Pittsford, N.Y. 14534

Honeywell Photographic Products, 4800 East Dry Creek Rd., Denver, Colo. 80217

International Audio Visual, Inc., 119 Blanchard St., Seattle, Wash. 98121

Kalart-Victor, Hultenius St., Plainville, Conn. 06062

Paillard, Inc. (Bolex projectors), 1900 Lower Rd., Linden, N.J. 07036

Viewlex, Inc., Broadway Ave., Holbrook, N.Y. 11741

Example 23. 16mm Projectors—How Many Projectors Are Enough Projectors?

It would be ideal, in the abstract, to have "one projector and one screen for every classroom." But that may overfill your needs. Here are factors which will help the classroom teacher make film a part of his teaching strategy even though he hasn't his "own" projector.

1 — There is a projector stored near his classroom which can easily be transported and which he must share with comparatively few other teachers.

This is an easy requirement to meet if classrooms near one another are very much alike, so that the same equipment can be used in them. A good plan is to have the projector on a rollable stand with lockable wheels. Then it is easy to move and is protected from jarrings and falls, and the person moving it can transport all the accessories (except the screen) in one trip.

2 — The projector is easy to use and in good operating condition.

Ease of operation is something one must investigate by trying, or by hearing from someone who has tried—see another article in this newsletter. Whether a projector is in good operating condition (*most* of the time) can depend to some extent on ease of operation, but even more it is a function of how well the people who use it regularly have been instructed in its use. Certainly the teachers who share the projector must know the machine well, and they must know just where to go for help if it is needed.

3 — The projector was selected with his classroom in mind.

Here we come to the crux of the matter. Most 16mm projectors will work—they have been around long enough to give manufacturers time to "debug" them. Different projectors have different features, however. It is unlikely that the same projector can be used effectively in two rooms which are very different in size, shape, measures for excluding light, provisions for ventilation if curtains must be drawn, acoustics, ambient noise level, adequacy of wiring, placement of electrical outlets, and other such mundane characteristics. "Effective use" means that students are able to see and hear film presentations from comfortable seats (preferably the ones they normally occupy), unbothered by noise, ventilation problems, or glare. It means that students at the sides see substantially what students in the center see, and that students far from the screen need not strain for detail. To achieve it, carefully chosen screens and projectors must be properly placed.

For instance, in a room that has more space in front than in back, it may be best to use a portable rear screen projection set-up, with speakers built into the projector, instead of the more usual projector at the back, speakers and screen at the front. Rear screen projection helps, too, if room darkening means bad air—pulling the shades and then shutting the windows to keep them from flapping. Rear screen projection requires darkness only near the screen.

If rear screen projection will not work in a hard-to-darken room, a special screen—metalized or lenticular—will help. Because they reflect more of the projector light than conventional screens do, they require darkening only in the screen area.

These comments merely touch on the problems which may arise when classrooms share projectors. Poor acoustics, immovable seating, antiquated wiring, all can cause trouble. Some problems may mean more projectors—there may be no way to adjust either the equipment or the rooms to permit sharing. Once you have decided just what the problems are in your school, you may want to see what specialists have to say about the matter. In addition to *EPIE Report* Number 45, mentioned elsewhere, you are referred to:

Audiovisual Projection, Pamphlet S-3. Eastman Kodak Co., Rochester, N.Y., 1966.

Green, Alan C. (ed.), *Educational Facilities with New Media,* Department of Audiovisual Instruction, National Education Association, Washington, 1966.

Pulman, Robert R. E., "A Review of the Fundamental Aspects of Motion Picture Presentation," *SMPTE Journal,* 78:559, July 1969.

Vlahos, Petro, "Selection and Specification of Rear-Projection Screens," *SMPTE Journal,* 70:89, February 1961.

8mm Projectors

8mm Silent Projectors

Confusion has existed with this size film for more than a decade because of two major types of film available on the market. The older is called regular 8mm film and at one time was obtained by splitting a roll of 16mm film in two. The sprocket holes were the same size as those on 16mm film; it was not necessary to have this large size sprocket and corresponding gear tooth to convey the smaller lighter film through cameras and projectors, but the hardware was determined by the split 16mm process. Later a new system was designed using small sprocket holes and providing a greater visual area. Since it increased the visual area by about 50 percent, this film was called Super-8mm. However, it required an entirely new set of cameras and projectors.

This, then, is the current situation with regard to narrow gauge film. There are two types, with corresponding hardware for each. The older regular 8mm has not faded because of financial investments made in the development and purchase of cameras, projectors, and commercially produced softwear. For example, nearly all of Blackhawk's silent classic films are available on 8mm, whereas Super-8mm versions are not as numerous. A discernible trend in amateur filmmaking is toward the increased use of Super-8mm raw film, which provides a larger image and is now more widely available than the regular 8mm.

Prospective users of this narrow gauge format should consider the dual system. If the use of regular 8mm is not forseeable, then a Super-8mm projector should be chosen.

The general comments made about 16mm projectors with regard to threading, lenses, illumination, etc. apply here also. The question of 8mm hardware is not much of a problem as one might imagine. It is possible to purchase 8mm projectors, Super-8mm projectors, and dual projectors (which will handle both formats). Some of the companies manufacturing these projectors are listed below. For the latest data, however, the reader is again referred to *The Audio-Visual Equipment Directory* published by the National Audio-Visual Association.

Allied Impex Corp.	Eastman Kodak Co.
A.V. Systems, Inc.	Media Systems Corp.
A.V.E. Corp.	Minolta Corp.
Bell & Howell	North American Philips Co.
Brumberger Co.	Paillard Inc. –Bolex & Hasselblad
A. B. Dick Co.	Ponder & Best, Inc.
DuKane Corp.	Producers Service Corp.
GAF Corp.	Purpose Film Center
Karl Heitz, Inc.	Retention Communication Systems
Information Handling Services	Riker Communications
Jayark Instruments Corp.	Viewlex, Inc.
Keystone	

Addresses for these companies are noted in Appendix 7.

8mm Silent Cartridge Projectors

A specialized kind of projector uses film encased in a plastic container, which eliminates any threading procedure. The cartridge is simply placed into the machine, which is then turned on for projection. The most popular model of this machine is made by Technicolor and requires a cartridge that is not compatible with any other machine. The Technicolor cartridge offers a running time from 30 seconds to approximately 8 minutes, with the film arranged in a continuous loop. Thus the film keeps repeating until the machine is turned off and the cartridge removed. The software is often called "a single-concept loop," since the time format enables only one or two concepts to be developed visually.

Projectors and cartridges are available for both regular 8mm and Super-8mm film but here again the trend is toward using Super-8mm. Other silent cartridge projectors are available but these are used mostly by commercial organizations in training or sales. The film cartridges used in these machines run for much longer periods and are larger in size. All of these formats are noncompatible and therefore of little interest to schools, libraries, colleges, etc.

8mm Sound Projectors

The added dimension of sound can be obtained in the silent projectors described above. Three systems are obtainable: optical, magnetic, or a combination of optical and magnetic.

Provision of the sound facility will increase the cost of the machine by a factor of approximately 3. Instead of $125 for a silent machine, the sound version will cost about $350. Software prices increase proportionately, too. When the prices for both software and hardware begin to approach their equivalents in 16mm, the choice is obvious: forget 8mm sound in favor of the 16mm format.

Summary

At this writing, the most efficient, economical, and useful systems are 16mm sound projectors, the 8mm–Super-8mm dual silent projector, and the Super-8mm silent loop projector. Forthcoming changes in technology may bring the videotape, disc, or card into widespread use, thus making these systems obsolete. At this point video developments are experimental and we must depend on what exists now.

PROJECTOR INFORMATION SOURCES

Books

Books that deal with information about film projectors are few and concentrate on giving directions for operating and maintaining projectors. Several audiovisual texts have short sections of this kind. A sampling would include such titles as *Application and Operation of Audiovisual Equipment* by Fred J. Pula; *Audiovisual Equipment Self-Instruction Manual*, 2nd ed., by Stanton C. Oates; *Audiovisual Machines* by Raymond L. Davidson; *AV Instruction: Technology, Media and Methods*, 4th ed., by James Brown, Richard Lewis, and Frederick Harcleroad; *AV Instructional Technology Manual for Independent Study*, 4th ed., by James Brown and Richard Lewis; *Mediaware—Selection, Operation, and Maintenance* by Raymond Wyman; *Operating Audiovisual Equipment*, 2nd ed., by Sidney Eboch and George W. Cochern; and *Projectionist's Manual*, Nav. Pers. 91983-A.

Periodicals

Descriptive information about film projectors can be found on occasion in many periodicals. The following are some periodicals that contain such information on a fairly regular basis: *American School and University, Audio-Visual Communications, Audiovisual Instruction, Business Screen, Educational Screen and AV Guide, Educational Technology, Film News, Filmmakers Newsletter, Industrial Photography, The Instructor, Photo Methods for Industry, Previews, School Management, School Product News, Today's Filmmaker,* and *Training in Business and Industry.*

The information in these periodicals is mostly descriptive and in many cases announces either new projectors or modifications of existing ones. Evaluations are conspicuously absent—probably because of the high cost of testing and the displeasure of the manufacturers at any comparisons or negative comments. Since most of the periodicals survive by advertising, they avoid alienating their clients.

Manufacturer's Catalogs

One of the best sources of general information about projectors is the literature put out by the manufacturers of such equipment. The advertising booklets, brochures, and catalogs describe—in positive and glowing terms—the qualities, characteristics, and capabilities of the machines. A good source of specific information is the manual that accompanies each machine when it is initially sold. These booklets, available from a few manufacturers on request, should be kept on file and used as a permanent reference.

Evaluation Sources

As indicated previously, evaluations of projectors are difficult to find. Occasionally periodicals such as *Consumer Reports* or *Consumers' Research Magazine* will test and evaluate Super-8mm projectors but their audience is the at-home user and the models they consider may not be appropriate for institutional use. Other periodicals avoid this area for fear of offending advertisers.

There are some services which do testing of educational hardware that are worthy of mention as pioneer or primitive attempts in a neglected area of educational accountability.

EPIE Institute (Educational Products Information Exchange, 463 West St., New York, N.Y. 10014) will undertake certain tests, comparisons, and evaluations and publish the findings. The reports are more decisive in the software field but they do make some attempts in the hardware field. Current service is available by subscription and past reports can be purchased. The organization will also undertake contract work for institutions and organizations.

ALA Technology Reports (ALA, 50 E. Huron St., Chicago, Ill. 60611) undertakes the evaluation of various pieces of hardware but treats each one individually rather than comparatively. Advantages, disadvantages, limitations, clumsy features, etc., are noted.

Government Reports. Although the information is hard to obtain, tests made by government agencies (such as the armed forces) are most valuable. State departments may be able to obtain this information more easily than other institutions. The obvious implication here is that any such evaluation is public information and should be accessible.

State departments, along with large city organizations, may initiate hardware studies. The difficulty here once again is the dissemination of such information.

Previews (R. R. Bowker, 1180 Ave. of the Americas, New York, N. Y. 10036). This periodical, which has been devoted to reviews of software, has announced a section called "Hardware Reviews." By an arrangement with Kent State, new hardware will be subjected to controlled tests and to everyday use in an institutional setting and the results will be published in *Previews*.

Conferences

The annual conferences held by such national organizations as the American Management Association, the Association for Educational Communications and Technology (AECT), and the National Audio-Visual Association (NAVA), as well as by regional and state groups, can provide a source of information on hardware. Not only is much printed material available at these conferences, but the chance to see the hardware and talk to a knowledgeable sales representative is often rewarding. Other organizations of interest are listed in Appendix 5.

PROJECTION SCREENS

Two classifications of screens can be noted—those used for front projection and those for rear projection. Front projection is the most common usage and can be described as the placement of an image on the viewing surface, which is usually coated with a particular light-reflecting material. (See Figure 14 for an example of front projection.) The four major types of screens used for front projection are compared in Table 9.

Table 9. A Comparison of Front Projection Screens

Type	Bright-ness	Image Accuracy	Color Trans-mission	Side Viewings	General Comments
Beaded	VG	G	VG	G	Beads fall off with use. Good for narrow rooms
Matte	G	E	E	VG	Requires greater darkness. Good for wide rooms
Lenticular	VG	G	VG	VG	Generally most adapt-able to all situations & use
Super Bright (Aluminum)	E	G	G	F	Can be used in semilight locations

The type of screen purchased should depend upon factors unique to each situation—the intended utilization, budget, physical setting, etc. Here are some general suggestions concerning screens.

Screen Width. The width should be approximated as one sixth the distance of the farthest viewer from the screen. If the last row is 30 feet from the screen location, the screen should be about 60 inches wide. Width should also be one half the distance between the first row and the screen. If the first row is 12 feet from the screen, its width should be about 72 inches.

Screen Illumination. The width of the screen gives an approximation of the illumination necessary for a good clear image. With beaded and lenticular screens, the illumination necessary can be stated as the product of 10 times the width. Thus a 50-inch-wide screen needs a 500-watt lamp. For matte screens, a factor of 12 should be used, while super bright screens need a factor of 8.

Screen Storage. When not in use, screens should be rolled up. Portable screens should be stored in cool dry clean places. An inexpensive plastic covering will prolong screen life considerably.

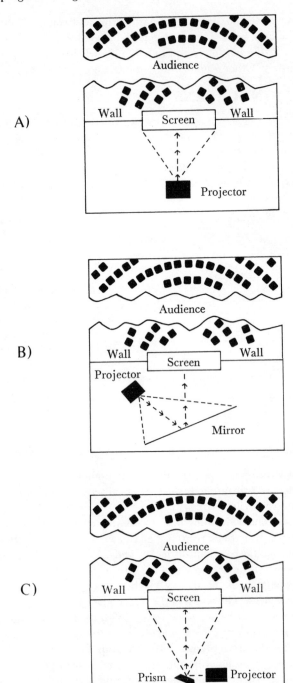

Figure 17. Rear projection systems. A: *Direct rear projection;* B: *Rear projection via mirrors;* C: *Rear projection via prisms.*

Rear projection screens have become quite popular recently and range in size from small 8mm single-concept loop screens to auditorium installations. See Figure 17 for examples of this system. With this type of projection, the image is placed on the rear surface of a screen made of special material that allows the passage of light through it. The usual rear projection system employs mirrors, which reverse the image so that the viewer sees it the way it was intended rather than backward. Screens for rear projection are of three major types. *Glass* is used in large permanent installations. It offers efficient noise reduction, and is easy to maintain. *Plexi-acrylic* is also used in larger permanent installations. It is lighter and more resistant to breakage than glass but does not provide as efficient sound proofing. *Flexible plastic materials* are used in smaller permanent installations and in portable units. They are lightweight but present more problems in maintenance than the other types.

A few of the companies that manufacture projection screens are:

Brewster Corp.	Hudson Photographic Industries, Inc.
Brumberger Co.	Knox Manufacturing Co.
Da-Lite Screen Co., Inc.	Charles Mayer Studios, Inc.
Draper Shade and Screen Co.	Radiant Manufacturing Co.
Eastman Kodak Co.	Singer Education Systems
R. Friedman Associates	Wilcox-Lange, Inc.

Addresses for these companies are given in Appendix 7. Additional companies are listed in *The Audio-Visual Equipment Directory* published yearly by the National Audio-Visual Association.

CHAPTER 9
Film Service—
Today and Tomorrow

THE PROBLEMS

Throughout this book various problems, difficulties, and obstacles in providing film service have been mentioned. This chapter is a summary of these major issues.

Attitudes, Education, and Film Characteristics

There is a lack of basic understanding of film. Film is the art form of the twentieth century and although not a universal language, it is probably the most popular mass communication medium the world has ever known. Film is unique unto itself and must be respected as a totality. It cannot and should not be thought of as an auxiliary medium to be used to capture an audience for some less popular medium or service. Film can be used *with* many other communication forms but should never be used solely *in the service* of those forms.

Films should not be treated as come-ons for books; inducements to visit libraries, schools, churches, etc.; baby-sitters; time-fillers; opening acts to warm up an audience for speeches to follow; or pleasant, nonintellectual pastimes to be taken lightly. They are an art form to be used, studied, discussed, and, most of all, enjoyed.

Films are different from other media, such as print or recordings, and that difference initiates problems in selection, evaluation, acquisition, cataloging, storage, use, and circulation. New procedures must be learned or created for each of these functions, and the additional responsibility often is accepted by librarians reluctantly.

Film information needs standardization through guides and indexes similar to those existing for books. Consider, for example, evaluations of films, which are now scattered throughout hundreds of publications. Although the situation

177

improved noticeably during the early seventies, the organization of film reviews and evaluations still has a long way to go. When the number of films reviewed each year is compared to the vast number of films produced, the percentage is small indeed. The viewing of films by a local evaluation committee is an expensive, time-consuming activity; at best, the committee members can consider only a small number of films each year. What is needed is an agency similar to the NICEM operation but one that will not merely provide descriptive annotation but will offer evaluations as well. Certainly the appearance of *Film Review Index, Multi-Media Index,* and other indexes of reviews is most encouraging.

Film availability is variable and must be improved. Because of film's high price, popularity, and general availability only through rental, the procurement of films can often be a formidable problem. Rental from the less expensive agencies sometimes requires advance notice to them of almost a year. The same is true of certain popular free films, which are not available via purchase or rental. Distributors of feature films have difficulty supplying classic films, whose showing in schools and colleges usually takes place during the same few weeks of a film history course.

It should be noted that feature film availability has increased in direct proportion to the decline of the large/urban movie theater. In their search for continuing revenue, producers are making films available in the 16mm format earlier and in greater quantity than ever before. Films Incorporated has gone the furthest in publishing a full catalog of feature films which can now be leased for a five-year period. A few years ago, the idea of leasing quality features to institutions was unthinkable to film owners.

The future should see the release of most films in a new form—on videodiscs, videocassettes, or videocards—which will solve the problem of availability to some extent. In the interim, obtaining films on specific subjects at the exact time when they are needed is a problem worthy of industry and professional attention.

Film cost is high. It can be shown that film cost can be amortized by dividing the film cost by the total number of viewers during the life of a print. A short film costing $200 shown 200 times to an average audience of 20 comes to five cents a circulation or viewer.

Prices will decrease considerably as films are mass produced in one of the forthcoming video formats and it is probable that eventually they will cost the same as a book or recording. Whatever forms they eventually appear in, the implications for libraries, schools, and other institutions are great.

Film service and use need more investigation. The literature that deals with the use of film is scant indeed. A vital need is the collection and organization of past research that is applicable to this area. Such a collection would indicate that most research studies, whether current or from the past, deal primarily with film's effectiveness in accomplishing certain educational objectives. Often comparisons with other methodologies are made. There seems to be little investigation of methodology in the use of film alone. Similarly, professional journals in the educational and library fields emphasize what was done rather than how and why it was done and with what results.

There is a need for formal, structured studies in the area of film usage, presentation, and service. (The few that do exist are vulnerable when seen from the perspective of the seventies.) More current research is needed.

A survey of the doctoral dissertations accepted by library schools shows only one study in the period 1960–1972 that concerned itself with film services in libraries. The attitude of those in charge of doctoral programs may be a factor in this lack of attention to a vital area.

Increased and improved training for film librarians is necessary. Although courses dealing with the total area of nonprint materials have increased in number in library schools, there are few offerings that deal with film exclusively. Usually it is handled as one topic in the general audiovisual course or as a subtopic in courses on building collections.

The courses that deal with film emphasize film history or filmmaking procedures. Rare is the course that treats the many topics considered in this volume which would seem to be basic for film librarianship. As one example, how many schools have students prepare, use, and evaluate a study guide with actual audience experience in film presentation? Yet, if there is one speciality that will be needed in the libraries of the future, it is that of film librarian. Much of the content of libraries will be in some audiovisual format and the person in charge of this material will have to have considerable expertise in handling the reservoir of existing films *and* the flood of new material that will appear. Film materials seemingly do not have as high an obsolescence rate as books. Many films that are 30 or 40 years old still enjoy mass popularity and audiences seemingly do not tire of repeated viewings.

Films are a prime target for censorship. Because of the enormous power of films to affect people, they are feared by certain individuals. No discussion of censorship will be provided here. Suffice it to say that the easy availability of film in a miniaturized format will bring about a much louder cry from those few individuals who wish to govern what their fellow citizens see and hear. It is absolutely necessary that the Supreme Court rid this nation of the evils of local censorship by supporting laws that reinforce two concepts: freedom of choice for adults and protection of the young.

Circulation of Film

Films should be loaned to all users who can benefit from seeing them. This statement or philosophy puts to rest the question of public libraries' loaning of films to schools. The problem here is financial rather than philosophical, and its solution will depend on proper allocation of community funds. Relationships between libraries might be examined to determine what is best for the user population, and some rearrangement of both institutions might occur.

There should be a standardized method of reporting and maintaining circulation figures for films. There should be agreement or consistency in resolving these questions:

Is one circulation equal to one showing? One borrowing?

When three films are shown to 60 people, is the attendance 60? Is the attendance 180?

When a film is borrowed but not shown, is it one circulation? No circulation?
When a film is shown by others in addition to the borrower, is it one circulation? Several?
When four films are shown to a varying attendance of 10, 15, 20, and 30 people, is the audience size 10? 15? 20? 30? 19?

The booking of films often presents problems. With rentals and with circuit use, the booking of films can be a frustrating experience. Because of a tight booking situation, films may have to be ordered far in advance. To try for flexibility in film choice becomes impossible, since the commitment has been set by the advance booking.

There is little opportunity to say, "I am trying to do a program on prejudice with my group tomorrow; what films do you have that I might use?" Then, too, confirmations are given months ahead of time, and in the interim, the film may be lost or severely damaged just prior to the scheduled showing date. In such situations it is not unusual to have to accept a sixth or seventh choice substitute rather than have no film at all.

The time of a film loan is almost always too short for previewing, showing, and reviewing. As indicated elsewhere, the mass production of films in miniaturized form will alleviate much of this problem.

The attitude of librarians toward nonprint is not always receptive. Although there is unanimous agreement by professional organizations concerning the presence of nonprint materials in library collections, there is still reluctance and some outright refusal by certain librarians to include these materials. The feeling is "It's fine for the other fellow but it's not for me." Such a self-serving attitude may stem from fear, inexperience, and even ignorance concerning audiovisual materials. Since film alone as an example of one of these materials is a complex complete subject unto itself, the reluctance to take on more material is understandable in part.

Some librarians fear film use and avoid participation as much as they can. Based on the evaluations reported in Appendix 1, librarians *do not* discuss the films they show. Unlike other groups, which welcome exchange of opinion and even controversy, they seem to hide from it. The operation of the projector, which is a relatively simple mechanical procedure, frightens them so that this responsibility is usually delegated to a custodian, page, or aide. Not only is there a general refusal to man the machine, but librarians often do not stay for the showing.

All these actions represent an attitude toward film in particular and nonprint materials in general. It is not necessary to reiterate the dangers to librarianship and libraries that result from this attitude. Adequate film service is only one of several innovative ideas facing libraries today. It is essential for practicing librarians to refresh themselves continually by both in-service education and informal self-instruction via professional books and journals.

The lack of acceptance of nonprint takes other forms. Consigning the nonprint service to a separate isolated corner of a building where no one else can see it is a typical example. Lack of attention in publicity releases and other informational or public relations vehicles can relegate nonprint services to a minimal role. Another method is to provide little financial support for the service, so that the personnel are on a part-time assignment and the collection stagnates.

Adequate film service requires space. In addition to financial support for personnel, hardware, software, and operation, film service requires space within an institution. Storage, inspection, and record-keeping activities demand a distinct unit-type location and cannot be superimposed on existing print services. Many older facilities simply do not have any available areas for this service and new construction or remodeling may be economically prohibitive.

Costs for film service are too high. While circuits, pools, and centralized collections are partial solutions to the high cost of film service, it is hoped that more direct ways will be found to lower costs. This will occur with the new technology that promises mass production of film (software) for both home and institutional use. The substitution of plastic for metal and miniaturization by using transistors, printed circuit boards, and other tiny electronic devices will eventually lower hardware prices. Other elements of the new technology that will eventually lower film service costs are cable television, videocassette, videodisc, and videocard.

The cry for additional funds for supporting services in libraries is so often repeated, it is cliché. Nevertheless, *the Federal government must provide a larger share of economic support for all libraries.* The argument for this is obvious. In most American communities, the local sources for raising revenues are exhausted, and since the largest amount of tax dollars is paid to the Federal government, it is the obvious source for funding library operations, which include film service. What is necessary is a reordering of priorities by the Federal government, urged, if necessary, by a combined pressure or lobby group made up of the National Education Association with all its affiliate organizations, the American Library Association, and all other concerned groups.

A centralized clearinghouse for film use, service, and information is needed. The historical chronology at the beginning of this book indicated several attempts to organize such a service. All (with the exception of EFLA) failed because of a lack or discontinuance of financial support. While EFLA's goals and purposes are most praiseworthy, the audience it serves is much smaller than merited. Since it is a self-supporting organization, the range and scope of its activities are determined by a limited budget. Financial support and security are essential for any organization or center designed to serve a mass audience.

It is not inconceivable that the establishment of a center at a university might succeed in today's world. The Educational Resources Information Centers (ERIC) act as such clearinghouses and seem to be surviving. With guaranteed government funding and an independent operation, a film center would have a potential for useful national service. Its role would be simple but most valuable— the collection of information about film, including production, research, evaluations, use, service, etc. Information gathered could be made available in microfiche, books, periodicals, or any other form that would enable wide dissemination at low cost.

A redefinition of the library and its audience is necessary. Is the library a book repository? A storehouse? An archive? Or is it a flexible organization that can exist in many forms to deliver diverse services? Can certain—not all—institutions change into community information centers? Can school libraries and public libraries consolidate or at least work together? All these questions need examination, for they affect film service in communities.

Should libraries continue to pursue in vain that great majority of nonusers in the community? Should they be satisfied with only that small percentage of the faithful who approve of the library as it now exists?

If a broader audience for service is sought, what types of service will appeal, be of value, and be accepted? Today's potential audience is made up of persons who are far different from the turn-of-the-century library user. If libraries are to survive, they must study their audiences as carefully as the teacher does his student and the doctor his patient. In one sense, that is what is meant by the word "professional."

THE POTENTIAL

We are on the eve of another act in the continuing drama of our time—the communications revolution. The "shock" or "massage" that the new communication form will supply will be greater than that experienced thus far. To examine its implications, it is necessary to look at what we have now and what the future promises.

Film use presently exists as a relic from an age recently past. The projector, film availability, film cost, restricted use, contracts, high rental fees—all are legacies from the golden age of commercial films. During the thirties and forties, filmgoing was the most popular mass recreation and film itself the most popular mass medium. The profits from participation in the film industry were enormous, and easy for owners to come by, since the studios, the distributors, and the exhibitors were a monopoly. In a large sense, they controlled film use.

That era has passed and each home now has a form of movie theater in its television set. A television set today resembles the movie theater during the days of block booking or circuit theaters, when the number of films available to the theater operator was limited. Television programming presently is restricted to the number of channels a particular home can receive clearly using the antenna system. But cable television can multiply that number by a factor of 4–10 in most cases.

CABLE TELEVISION

Cable television (CATV) is sometimes known as community antenna television, since its original purpose was to improve television signal reception. In communities located at some distance from the sending TV station, very tall antennas were constructed. For a monthly fee, homes were connected by coaxial cable to the master antenna, thus enabling the connected or wired homes to pick up an increased number of signals, with much greater clarity in each instance.

The CATV of the future will evolve from this simple technical improvement in signal reception to a system that can supply clear signals on 40 to perhaps 80 channels, along with two-way communication. A portion of these available channels might be devoted to community or neighborhood matters.

Later developments might include the attachment of electrostatic printing devices to the set, which then could deliver various printouts—the newspaper, bibliographies, local information, etc. The two-way communication would facilitate shopping, research polling, information retrieval, etc. An experiment in two-way cable tried in Irving, Texas placed in each home a console with four buttons which could be punched in different combinations to provide up to 15 different responses to questions posed by the TV set.

Eventually all cable will probably be linked together into a network, similar in certain ways to the telephone system as it now exists in the United States.

With such a potential economic, social, and political force on the horizon, it is not surprising to find activity on the part of certain commercial organizations at fever pitch. Motion picture companies, the television networks, sports promoters, the telephone companies, the music composers' organizations, newspaper chains, etc. all want a piece of the action.

An examination of a small cable company might be helpful. Consider the Island Cable Company, which services Long Beach Island in New Jersey. After a franchise was granted to the company in 1964, they erected a 170-foot tower to receive signals. By 1971 they had installed 96 miles of cable that now services some 6,500 subscribers. Their programs come from New York (Channels 2, 4, 5, 7, 9, 11) and Philadelphia (Channels 3, 6, 10, 12, 17, 29, 43). The signals are picked up by the master tower antenna, then amplified, combined, and put on the cable. At every 3,000 feet in the cable, amplifiers are placed to boost the signals.

It should be remembered that it is the franchise granted to the Island Cable Company which is all important. It represents, among other things, the license to conduct a most profitable business. Assume, for example, that the charge for cable service on Long Beach is the average one—$6 per month. At a cost of $72 each year, the 6,500 homes would provide a yearly income of $468,000 to the Island Cable Company.

In 1971 the New Jersey Assembly approved a one-year moratorium on the awarding of local CATV franchises within the state. Charges of extortion and bribery in securing the francishes caused this action and the state needed time to formulate rules governing the awarding of the franchises. Lacking state regulations, each of New Jersey's 567 municipalities had the power to negotiate their own franchises. About 150 municipalities did this—sometimes without public bidding or advertisement. Similar abuses of franchise assignment, such as rate overcharge, cream-skimming (failure to extend service to all possible households in an area), or trafficking (reselling franchises), have motivated other states to set up CATV Commissions which will regulate the CATV industry within those states.

The moratorium against CATV franchises in New Jersey was lifted in April 1973. In mid 1974 there were 25 CATV firms in operation, with 64 more franchised by municipalities. Approximately 110 applications for CATV franchises were still pending.

To gain more information about CATV and franchise assignment, The RAND Corporation in 1971 made a study in the Dayton, Ohio, area. Twelve political subdivisions of this geographic area cooperated. A model franchise was developed by a representative local government committee and then was sent to the CATV companies for reaction and suggestion. An account of the findings of the nine-month study was presented on January 25 and 26, 1972, at the Policymaker's Conference on Urban Cable Communication in Dayton. The study and the Conference were funded by the Kettering and Ford Foundations. Naturally, the conference was attended by those who have a large economic stake in CATV: hardware manufacturers, film distributors, government representatives, legal consultants, etc. The model franchise considered such matters as consumer rate charges, profit limitations, franchise costs and fees, ownership, term of the franchise, geographic-area coverage, and locally originated programs.

Another major event in CATV history was the publication in late 1971 of the Sloan Report. In preparation since June 1970, the Report was based on research and interviews held with many persons concerned in some way with CATV. Once again, this study was funded by the Alfred P. Sloan Foundation and its findings were published in a book entitled *On the Cable—The Television of Abundance*. A few of the general recommendations were:

1. To approve pay TV via the cable.
2. To remove restrictions on bringing in distant signals.
3. To pay royalties to the producers of programs.
4. To waive the "Fairness Doctrine."
5. To waive the "Equal Time" provision.
6. To allow public TV stations to operate CATV.
7. To grant CATV franchise preference to neighborhood groups.
8. To limit cable franchises to a 20-year period.
9. To limit the number of subscribers served by one CATV system.
10. To allow local newspapers and TV stations to operate CATV.
11. To bar networks from owning/operating CATV.

Although state and local governments may set regional regulations, it is the Federal government as represented by the Federal Communications Commission (FCC) which exercises primary control over CATV. Some of its rulings have been:

1. A CATV system must carry the local community station in addition to any others that it may offer.

2. A program imported from a distant station cannot be shown on the same day that the local station shows that program.

3. In the top 100 market area (90% of the TV audience) any existing or proposed television station may object to a CATV plan to import distant signals. It is then mandatory (and almost impossible) for the CATV system to prove that such importation will not harm the existing/proposed station. This ruling is responsible in part for the nondevelopment of CATV in major market areas.

4. Every cable system of more than 3,500 subscribers must initiate its own shows by April 1, 1971.

5. One channel may be used for pay TV—but under severe restrictive rules.

The question of certain copyrighted material such as films has recently been settled by an agreement between the cable industry and the Motion Picture Association. Revision of the existing copyright law rests with Congress and not with the FCC. This is an example of two industries making a mutual agreement that will be beneficial to both without having to wait for Congress to pass a law which will define certain aspects of their operation.

As CATV strains to grow, more complex rulings are being issued by the FCC. Recent revisions of the 100 market rule, including the enumeration of the number and type of signals that can serve, along with a definition of "a distant signal," have been announced. Still pending are such important aspects as channels for public access and channels for two-way capability.

CATV is a complex new medium that undoubtedly will provide the next shake-up or massage of the American people. At present it is surrounded by economic opportunists, existing power structures, three levels of governmental regulation/abuse, and finally, a few concerned individuals and groups.

Responsibility for an informed public falls to these concerned individuals and groups. Cable television must not be thought of as simply "more of the same but a lot clearer," but rather as a new medium with unexplored capabilities and potentials. With this concept in mind, community leaders might:

> Form citizen groups whose function should be the gathering, assimilating, formulation, and dissemination of information about cable television. Educators, teachers, administrators, librarians, and media specialists must assume leadership roles in these groups.
>
> Work to delay the granting of franchises until the public are aware of their rights and interests and have an opportunity to express themselves.
>
> Provide continual surveillance if a franchise has already been granted. Questions pertaining to use, discrimination, fees, service, programming, etc. are within the province of a supervisory committee composed of local citizens.

THE VIDEOCASSETTE*

Another technological development, the videocassette, has even greater implications for film use and service. For the past few years there have been many articles appearing in the mass periodicals with titles such as "TV Cassettes Are Coming!" or "Here Come the Video Cartridges!!" and so on. More specialized magazines such as *Forbes* or *Fortune*, which cater to the business community, have also featured numerous reports about the videocassette. Unfortunately the attention of the journals of the education and library professions has been spasmodic and quite casual. Once again those persons directly affected by the newest communications medium are among the last to participate in its evolution and planning.

---

*Recent developments indicate an initial prominence of the videodisc. All comments in this section are applicable to that format, and the term videocassette should be interpreted in an all-inclusive sense.

In its simplest terms the videocassette is a container which houses a ribbon of material on which are transcribed both sound and picture symbols. The industry's term for the combination of container and ribbon is "software." The containers are of two general types: the cartridge, which consists of one smaller reel mounted over another in a concentric arrangement, and the cassette, which is a miniaturized version of a reel-to-reel system. Material housed within the container may be magnetic tape, videotape, photographic film, holographic tape, or any other material which is capable of accepting and storing symbols which can later be decoded. There is also a possibility of plastic discs similar to LP's being used. The logical name "hardware" is given to the instrument or machine that is used for the decoding process.

The total hardware necessary for a videocassette system consists of two pieces. The first is a unit whose purpose is to decode the symbols stored in the videocassette and translate them into signals suitable for reception by a television receiver or monitor, which is the second hardware piece. Since 95% of United States households already contain television sets, a strong foothold has already been established in the American home.

More than 40 manufacturers have announced systems that are variations of the general one described above. The reasons for such competition is obvious: rewards to the winner of this "Battle in the Marketplace" will be enormous. Each of the giant manufacturers hopes that this system will be the successful one and, thus, we have had CBS (EVR), Sony (Videocassettes), Avco (Cartrivision), Ampex (Instavision), RCA (Selectavision), Telefunken (Teldec), and others all proposing their own unique, noncompatible hardware and software.

As an approach toward a professional standard, perhaps a system could be described which would incorporate the best features of the many individual systems. This ideal system might include the ability to:

1. Play back a prerecorded cassette.
2. Record programs off the air.
3. Record personal programs by camera.
4. Stop a single frame for an extended period.
5. Provide for slow motion.
6. Operate from both house current and batteries.
7. Be portable/lightweight.
8. Furnish a picture of high definition.
9. Be available at a reasonable cost (both hardware and software). Estimates for the cost of the basic hardware in 1972 ranged from $200 to $1,000 for the recorder/playback unit. Television receivers cost $100 to $500. Accessories such as cameras, portable power packs, etc. were not included in these estimates and will increase the figures appreciably.

Estimates of software prices range widely. Blank cassette costs have been mentioned as $25 for 2 hours, $17 for 1 hour, $13 for 30 minutes, and $10 for 15 minutes. Single showing rentals of feature films are quoted from $3 to $9, depending on title. Outright purchase of *Citizen Kane*, for example, is $495. Another type of comparison of price structure can be made with Saul Bass's popular film, *Why Man Creates*. In 16mm format its cost is $270, while the Time-Life Video Library sells it in videocassette form for $150.

The amount of activity surrounding the imminent birth of the new medium has been enormous. Producers, actors, writers, manufacturers, distributors, attorneys, and government representatives have been involved. The three traditional phases of the motion picture industry may be used to indicate and describe their concerns.

Production

All the creative and craft people, actors, writers, musicians, producers, etc., want a share of the potentially enormous profits accruing from the sale of the software. Financial participation is usually requested in the form of royalties rather than a straight fee arrangement. Piracy and copyright violations are concerns of these groups. Every problem of copyright infringement is inherent in the videocassette, be it literary, musical, or dramatic. The translation of any material into videocassette form without copyright clearance is clearly a violation.

Nevertheless, in spite of all the barriers to reproduction, it should be noted that most of the currently existing video material has already been optioned for reproduction in the videocassette format. This includes existing libraries of feature motion pictures, educational films, syndicated television programs, etc. The older media once again become the content of the new medium, as McLuhan predicted.

Much speculation has been made as to new material developed specifically for the videocassette. Probably pop style material, narrative film stories, and pornography will be the important entertainment categories. Educational topics might include the garden, skiing, industrial training, medical procedures, religious sermons, fashions, cooking, travel, etc.; the possibilities are limitless.

Unlike television, large audiences are not necessary. In certain cases the sale of a single edition of 2,000 videocassettes may be economically sound and profitable. Current network television costs of $50,000 a minute are not unusual and have precluded specialized audience programming for small groups.

Distribution

Many agencies have been announced as distributors of the videocassette. They include department stores, book stores, movie theaters, drug stores, gas stations, and even the local milkman. Not surprisingly, the videocassette-of-the-month club has already been announced. There has been little mention of the school or library in this connection.

Patterns of distribution mentioned most often are rental and outright sale. The possibility of free loan has been ignored.

Exhibition

The home learning center of the future becomes one step nearer actuality with the videocassette system. It is this market which has caused the most activity and interest in videocassettes. The industrial market and the school market, both of which will probably develop before the home market, may be considered as evolutionary phases of the videocassette. In all three instances the exhibition is private rather than public. One possible exception is the use of videocassettes on cable television. By having large collections of videocassettes available for exhibition via CATV, the problem of providing content for the many channels may be partially solved.

The videocassette provides individualized choice in both education and entertainment—the program you want when you want it. It puts the owner-investor of a TV set back in control, after the 20-year domination of the TV industry. Anything that can be read, heard, and/or seen is potential content. It has been called, "the paperback of the television industry," but it is much more than that. Its potential is unlimited and its effect on society can only be imagined at this time. Corporation obstinacy, organizational greed, and a complete dedication to self-interest are the current recognizable barriers to its ultimate realization.

The role of institutions with respect to these new media is almost unlimited. Libraries can circulate the software as another element in their collections. Using a library channel on cable television, which should be a part of every franchise, professionals can program films in endless variety. The combination of cable television and the videocassette can give the library an entry into every community home with a much expanded potential for service. Schools, colleges, and universities will have available to them a most potent method for education. The videocassette can be considered as a form of textbook that shows and tells simultaneously. Its appeal and use with a wide range of students should earn it quick acceptance.

Churches are in a position similar to both libraries and schools. As a means of increasing and broadening audiences or as a religious education medium, the videocassette should have great effect.

In summary, nearly all of what has been put forth in this volume has transfer, meaning, and application to the new technology of the videocassette. True, it is a new medium; but it closely resembles the film used by schools, libraries, colleges, and churches during the past two decades.

Institutions must compete for the attention of today's audience. In a very broad sense, this can be accomplished with the fulfillment of two conditions: (1) by giving an audience something it needs or wants that cannot be obtained elsewhere with ease; and (2) by offering this service with as much excellence and quality as possible.

Consider a film program designed for discussion to be given in the local public library. That institution is giving the following things that are not easy to find elsewhere:

Film material not usually shown on television

A better image and sound than home television can provide

A chance for sociable interaction with people who have just shared a controlled common experience

A proximity to materials which will enrich, enlarge, and enhance the viewing and the discussion

There are other values, of course, but the entire program will be a futile exercise if the second condition is not fulfilled. Effort, thought, and creativity must be put into the program. These elements, along with the film, determine the quality of the program.

The same criteria for success in film use apply to other institutions. Churches, schools, and colleges should offer unique film programs of high quality. This book's intent has been to identify and discuss the factors that contribute to such programs.

APPENDIX 1
Evaluations of Library Film Programs

As part of their experience in the film courses I teach at the Graduate School of Library Service at Rutgers University, my students are asked to attend, observe, and evaluate film programs in libraries. Some of the evaluations are presented in this appendix to illustrate what is actually happening in the field. I include first selected excerpts taken from long reports and then some observations by Helen Ransky, which are perceptive, informed, critical, and often humorous. Although all names have been eliminated, these evaluations cover situations in New Jersey, New York City, Long Island, and Pennsylvania. Some editorial rearrangement was necessary, but in all cases an attempt was made to retain the original opinion, feeling, or evaluation.

In certain ways the evaluations tell more about current film use than several chapters of text and they reflect oversights in current practice. Hopefully they will lead students to consider the challenge of film service and the many problems to be tackled in providing good film programs and service.

SELECTED SHORT EXCERPTS FROM FILM PROGRAM EVALUATIONS

I began to suspect the library was not too well prepared when I heard one librarian, ten minutes before the program was to begin, ask another if the films had arrived, and just who was supposed to handle the program. It turned out that the questioner was the one in charge!

The audience settled down: four Hispanic kids, an East Indian mother and her little boy, one old man who wandered in from the Bowery, and me. No introduction. Lights out. Film starts. No leader. No title. From time to time the machine and the picture would start to chatter—probably some of the sprocket holes had been stripped during a previous showing and the films had not been subsequently inspected and repaired.

* * *

The programs were held in the library's meeting room, a large attractive room in the basement with handsome draperies and large potted plants. At the foot of the stairs in the entrance hall there was a table with a coffee and tea setup, cups, napkins, etc. (a ten-cent charge), and a member of the library staff acting as hostess. The room itself was set with card tables and chairs for anyone who had brought his lunch and pleasant music was playing in the background. However, when I called the library two weeks earlier to inquire about a possible scheduled film program, the staff member neglected to tell me to bring my lunch, so I had to be satisfied with a cup of coffee.

* * *

The actual program was well-organized and started on time. It lasted from 8:30 to 10:00. There were 40 people in attendance (the librarian said this was average). The audience was mostly young adults, but there were a few adults with children. Everyone was attentive and seemed to enjoy the showing. One reference librarian was present. He introduced the program by naming the film. A library page ran the projectors.

* * *

The film was shown in a basement room that was attractively decorated with bright orange curtains and chairs with orange seats. The room was well-ventilated although when the door was closed, I experienced a feeling of confinement.

There was no warm-up for the film. The librarian simply closed the door, turned out the lights, and said, "O.K. Everybody ready?" The audience replied affirmatively and she responded with, "O.K. Let's go." During the program, the audience was well behaved and attentive. When it was time for a reel change, they groaned and took the opportunity to get a drink of water or go to the bathroom.

* * *

The film showing was very smoothly organized. When people stopped drifting in, the lights were cut off and the movie was begun. The picture was sharp and clear, and the film itself was of good quality. The sound was audible and one could see the screen very well. Of course there was a wide choice of seats. Two projectors were used and the transition was performed with ease. The projectors were somewhat noisy and it is unfortunate that they did not have a larger screen.

* * *

Films are viewed on Sunday afternoon in the assembly room. Before the program began, it was clear that the showing would not go smoothly. The room is not wired properly for sound, so loose wires ran from the projector in the back of the room down the center aisle to some hidden speakers in the front of the room. Another problem was the use of a single projector which was in poor operating condition. After it had run about 10 minutes of each reel, the film sprockets began to slip, and the projectionist had to stop and make adjustments. The program was introduced by a woman totally uninformed about the film. Right before the program was to begin, she quickly ran to the projectionist and asked what she was to introduce. Then she went to the front of the room and announced, "Today we are to see *Waterfront*, a film for which Marlon Brando won an Academy Award."

* * *

Approximately 7–15 people viewed the films at one time or another during the evening. At eight o'clock when the program was scheduled to begin, six people other than myself were present. Four of these were children, so that the first film, an animated cartoon, was received fairly well. The librarian in charge of the program introduced the films and added a brief preface to explain the purpose of this night's programming. After one false start, the librarian was able to run the projector correctly and the showing went smoothly.

* * *

The only introduction was the announcement over the loudspeaker that the film was going to be shown, given about 10 minutes before it was begun. No special preparation was made in the room other than the provision of chairs. After the showing there was no presentation or discussion of any kind. At the beginning of the film there were about 20 people in the audience although there was room for more than 100. The audience, made up largely of Chinese-Americans, talked and laughed often, but did not actually cause much of a distraction due to the loud sound track. Some left during the film but at least as many new people came in during the showing; everyone took care not to obstruct the projection or get in each other's way.

* * *

The library usually has about 150 people for their regular showings but this time only about 50 persons attended. The reason for this low attendance was the lack of publicity outside of the library. The film was obtained from a commercial distributor who does not allow outside publicity about his films. There were no support materials apparent to change the room environment. Only one small poster announcing this film was on the wall over the charging desk.

* * *

The woman in charge gave a brief introduction describing each film and pointed out that the teenage filmmaker of one of the films to be shown was sitting in the audience and would be willing to answer any questions after the showing. Sound and projection were excellent. The young viewers were surprisingly attentive and reacted most vocally to the animated cartoon.

One distraction of the program was the continual switching-on of the lights after each film and the wait as the new reel was placed on the projector. While the program director flipped the lights on and off, her assistants were preparing the reels. Another projector could have eased this problem.

* * *

Both film showings at the library were pleasant. As you enter, there is always a poster advertising the film to be shown. The staff made me feel right at home even though I was the only one in the audience. We waited a few minutes before starting the show to be sure no other viewers were going to come. There was no printed program or planned discussion, but the projectionist, janitor, and I had a good time talking about the film during the reel changes.

* * *

The head of the Film Festival tried to give an introduction but she had no microphone and could not be heard over the milling crowd of 250 small children, so the program was begun without it. The first three films had been written, filmed, directed, and performed by local high school boys. Although the films were very well done, they could not hold the attention of so many little children for long. The sound was not loud enough and at times it was completely obscured by the screaming children. Even after scores of children were ejected from the auditorium, chaos reigned—especially after it was discovered that one could make shadows on the screen by placing various parts of the anatomy in front of the 8mm projector. No attempt was made at a final discussion as the hundreds of children and a few adults filed from the hot and noisy auditorium.

* * *

The film showing was held in the library meeting room. There was a poster on the outside door of the library and a small announcement in the local paper about the films. Everyone was invited to bring sandwiches, as coffee would be served. About half of the audience did bring their lunch. Everyone helped themselves to coffee while waiting for the film to begin.

Before the start of the film, an apology was made to the audience about the condition of the films. They were old and worn and there was a potential of program interruption. After a few initial difficulties, the films ran smoothly. They were about the Amish people in Pennsylvania.

The reference librarian talked between films. He admitted that he knew nothing about the Amish people. Even though he is originally from the midwest, he *is* the reference librarian and books on the subject were on display. If he had become familiar with the subject, the discussion would have been better.

* * *

The program was late in starting. After a half-hour wait, 29 people sat down for the showing. There was no preparation of any kind for the viewing. The room is an attractive, accessible, and conveniently sized place for film showings. There would be plenty of space to set up a small display of library materials relating to the evening program. However, no attempt was made to utilize this avenue of library public relations even though the library does have a fine collection of film materials. Other than the late start, the mechanics of the film program went smoothly. The chairs were properly placed so that everyone could see and hear. The heating and the ventilation were quite comfortable. No cords were exposed for people to trip over. The main door should be oiled so that there is no annoying squeak as people enter or leave during the program.

In a most unfortunate allocation of personnel, the film librarian—although working Wednesday nights—is assigned to the reference desk for the evening.

Thus, the one person in the system most qualified to provide supervision and lead discussion is on duty elsewhere in the building.

* * *

Since other sections of the library were still functioning, we had only partial darkness; light rays from the adult area came over the stacks and cut across the top third of the screen. Right behind the viewing area there must have been an office—the door was slightly ajar and typing could be heard during the entire program. Because the entrance to the library was also in the children's area, you were often disturbed by people coming and going and there was a low undertone of conversation from the adult section.

* * *

The film showing was prefaced by an origami demonstration by one of the children's librarians present. The children then were encouraged to try paper folding themselves. This exercise was used to introduce the film *Clay*. All of the children were remarkably well behaved—possibly because the majority of them were from the invited classes who were from a local Catholic grammar school and were escorted by their teachers. I should mention also that there was exceptionally good school–library communication concerning this program. In class the week before the showing, the children were instructed in making their own creations of clay models or figures which were brought to the showing and displayed by the librarian.

* * *

This is a large one-room library that is fairly new. Several films on dance were to be shown in the children's section, divided from the main library room only by a 7-foot bookcase. The library was open, extremely crowded, and noisy, and lighting was barely dimmed for the showing of the films. Conditions were very poor, the main problem being the distraction caused by the noise of the patrons.

The program seemed to embody everything that is poor in a film presentation. The environment was very bad, with poor lighting, noise, and patrons moving about. The projector was simply turned on at 7:30 and the films began. There was no introduction or conclusion. The potential for developing the theme of the performing arts was lost. After the showing I examined their collections. They had ample print material to support the showing as well as a good assortment of pertinent recordings.

* * *

Approximately 70 people attended, including about 40 students on a class trip. The director of the library spoke briefly on National Library Week and introduced the guest speaker, Mr. _____, a local resident who has traveled extensively in India and Tibet. Following the film he conducted a question and answer period, speaking briefly about Tibetan art, culture, history, and religion. The program was well run and Mr. _____ seemed very qualified to discuss the subject. The audience responded favorably to his format. The travelog and documentary genre was most suitable for this library presentation.

* * *

As we entered the room, we were greeted by a hostess and handed an annotated program. About 25 persons including about 10 children viewed the films. Seating arrangements were satisfactory. There were no external or internal disturbances.

Prior to the start of the program, music was played through the speaker system. The hostess welcomed the guests and spoke briefly about each film. The projector had to be threaded twice and a wall served as the screen. As one entered and left the room, it was necessary to go around the projection cart and step over electrical cords. There was no theme or connection between the films.

* * *

The library is small and crowded. The librarian set up her projector in the children's's section, which is a long narrow area separated by stacks from the adult collection. Projection qualities were poor, with the librarian losing the loop five times in the first few minutes of the showing. No introduction was given. From conversation with the librarian, I gathered that she knew nothing about the films. She did offer the opinion that perhaps the program was too intellectual. Inadequate promotion, poor facilities and projection, tolerance of intrusions, absence of an introduction, lack of focus or theme, and a consistent crudity made for an inferior viewing experience.

* * *

Approximately 10 children, the library custodian, one bored mother, and myself were present. The large meeting room used was well suited to the showing of films. In addition to its size, it was well ventilated; the chairs were arranged so that everyone could see and no one would be sitting on top of the next person (there were many more chairs set up than were necessary). The projector was located in the back, away from the door, and wires were not run where they would be tripped over. Picture image was large and clear, and the sound was easily audible without being deafening. Outside noises were minimal. The only drawback to the physical environment was the size of the screen. Although the one used was large enough for this audience, the image ran off at both sides. If a larger screen was not available, it would have been better to adjust the position of the projector.

Just prior to the showing, a librarian entered and had a brief conversation with the custodian. She said nothing to the group and remained only for the first 10 minutes of the film.

* * *

When we arrived at 7:05, the librarian asked if we were there for the film program. When we replied affirmatively, she turned off the right side lights and began the film. Another librarian came out of the back room and told the first one not to show the films until 7:30. The first librarian asked us if we could wait until then. In this library two people must seem like an audience. By 7:30 four more people joined us.

Larger chairs are needed for adult programs. The small chairs brought one's knees uncomfortably close to one's chin. The library does not seem to have another room for a film program and wants to keep the adult side of the room open for use during the films. Therefore a means of blocking the light which streamed onto the screen is needed. There were about two people using the adult section while the films were on. The light on the screen did cause the picture to fade considerably.

* * *

Three ushers were present to handle the audience, which consisted mainly of elderly people with a small sprinking of other adults. The library is located in a business and shopping district and the program arrangement of several short films allowed for people to come and go without creating a disturbance. A leaflet briefly listing the films was handed out but there was no introduction or conclusion material presented. Perhaps this was because much of the audience was not present for the whole program; nevertheless a short discussion might have made the atmosphere a little more welcoming for the others.

OBSERVATIONS IN DETAIL

KOVACS!

Presented by the Free Public Library and the *Times* Newspaper

Convenient parking on newspaper's property. Not far to walk to the interesting entrance to the Community Room—you have to pass by the composing room of the newspaper which has viewing windows set into the walls.

The Community Room is a small auditorium complete with stage. The screen was hung from the stage ceiling. Comfortable seating—individual padded card table chairs with armrests. Convenient floor ashtrays. The room painted in pleasant colors. Poster along the walls advertising various *Times* newspaper columnists.

Good mixture of young (no children) and old. Relaxed, talkative. Large turnout, even though film had been shown twice the previous year, and once the night before. Many people knew each other, whether personally, or because they have attended other presentations together, is not known. Mood of audience indicated that they came prepared to laugh—their guffaws often overpowered the narrator of the film.

No print materials. Twenty-five minutes before scheduled movie showing, at 7:35 P.M., a *Times* employee and an editor of the *Times* introduced themselves. The program became an informal combination of question and answer period, running commentary, discussion, and reminiscence, among the two MC's and members of the audience. They discussed Ernie Kovacs as a person and discussed his talent. The audience, which was already relaxed, became even more so, enjoying high good humor. The MC's asked questions of each other also, to keep the dialogue going and to bring out more information.

The two MC's also gave periodic time checks—sort of a count-down toward the main feature. (The movie started at exactly 8 P.M.) About five minutes before the film started, the MC's gave a brief description of Kovacs's life, his rise to fame, and a sort of eulogy. They then thanked the audience for coming, for bearing with the 25-minute discussion, repeated a request for no smoking, made announcement of the next week's program, and wished everyone a good time. The house lights dimmed and the film began.

Only one film. Started on time after a 25-minute discussion period. No discussion or wrap-up after the film.

When I first entered the room, I felt ambivalent about people smoking. I don't mind smoking, but the air was very smoggy. Windows were open to alleviate the situation, but, since it was cold outside, this made people sitting close to them uncomfortable. When the MC's began the discussion period at 7:35, they asked the people, in a nice way, to please stop smoking for the rest of the evening. The people complied with the request.

There was a "standing room only" audience. Some found seats by sitting on the windowsills. Others were invited, courteously, by the MC's to come to the front of the room and sit on the floor, if they wished.

Train tracks ran right by the *Times* building. Once during the film, a train, with whistle blowing, went by, shaking the building and drowning out the film sound.

The only real flaw in the program, to me, was that there was no representative from the Library to explain where the film came from, how it was made, etc. Since there were no credits at the beginning or end of the film, I never knew the narrator's name, or the actors' names (except for Kovacs and his wife, Edie Adams). The only explanation of the film that the MC's gave, was that it was a series of Kovac's videotapes and that the film could be shown only because of the *Times'* association with the Library. They explained that Ernie Kovac's estate has access to materials that it will not release if profit is involved, i.e., this film cannot be shown commercially. The only other place it could possibly be shown would be on public television.

THE BOSTON TEA PARTY
THE SHOT HEART (*sic*) ROUND THE WORLD

After driving five miles out of the way, looking for the headquarters of the ——— Library system, which I erroneously assumed would be housed in its own building on its own grounds, I finally found it set back in a shopping center where it would be difficult for anyone unaware of its location to find it, especially at night. It occupies several store areas and is identified by a black and white unlit sign.

Entering the library, I asked at the desk if there was a film showing, as there were no signs, posters, etc. "That room over there" was indicated. Looking around, I found a door open behind bulletin boards and display tables. It led to a panelled and painted room, partitioned off from the main library by walls built only three quarters of the way to the ceiling. This meant that when the lights were out, and the film started, the lights in the main library brightened the room enough to fade out some of the picture. (After the film had been running a while, one librarian went out to the main library and shut off two ceiling lights, which darkened the room a little more.)

The seating was fairly comfortable. A piece of rug was placed in the aisle for informal seating. (The loudspeaker cord also ran under this rug.) There was a portable screen with a loudspeaker underneath it at the entrance end of the room. The projector was on a cart at the other end.

When I entered the room, the ratio of children to adults was about 5 to 1 and didn't change as more people came: 50–60 altogether. Many of the children were quite young, 3–4 years old; most were well behaved; others ran in and out constantly (even during the films), slamming the door, playing with balloons, cards, and toys, and screaming. Since there was an Investment Club meeting in the library, and stores surrounding it, I had the distinct impression that the film program was actually a babysitting service. (Perhaps I should have been forewarned by the 7 p.m. starting time.)

The program started on time. The only introduction by one of the librarians (there were two) was: "This is the *Boston Tea Party*, the first one." During the program, there were unending sources of distraction—people opening and closing the door (and since the screen was at the entrance end of the room, this meant that light from the main library shone directly on the screen every time the door was opened); greetings between children entering and leaving; main door of the library shutting with a "bump-bump" every time someone came in or went out and which could be heard distinctly in the film room. The loudspeaker was turned on about five minutes before the film and the static hum was awful. The projector was noisy and had to be adjusted while the film was running—half of the picture was off the screen at the start, then the picture frame was lopsided on the screen throughout the entire showing. The sound was static at first, then loud and not too clear. The room was warm and got warmer. At one crucial point in the film, the film stopped and the screen went blank. Apparently the librarian, who was new and not familiar with the projector, had pushed the wrong switch.

After the first film, there was an intermission while the second film was threaded on the projector. Then, "All right, we're ready for the next one now."

I had assumed, by their titles (again wrongly), that the two films were educational documentaries about the Revolutionary War. It turned out they were two sequences of a Walt Disney film, *Johnny Tremain*. I couldn't understand why they had split the film into two parts, under two different titles, until I realized they had probably been two segments of a TV show for *The Wonderful World of Disney*.

In any case, the prints were poor; no beginning or ending credits, (it was annoying to recognize actors' faces and not know their names); in many places the sound and the picture were not synchronized; the film would often jump as if it had been spliced in too many places, too close together; and the film ended before the sound.

My "baby-sitting" theory seemed to be confirmed when, during the last half of the second film, parents began poking their heads in and calling out children. The remaining children gave a round of applause at the end of the second film, which had featured a lot of shooting and killing, and the program was over.

Nothing much can be done about structural defects, or the heat either, as there is probably one control for the entire library.

The projectionist, being new, should have had a little more practice using the projector, and should have made sure that it was adjusted correctly so that the film was on the screen.

I also wondered how much of the sound (which was loud) could be heard in the main library over the three-quarter walls and if it was distracting. Also, what affect did it have on patrons in the main library when the librarian went out and turned off two ceiling lights so it would be dimmer in our room?

However, the major problem that concerned me was the placement of the screen right next to the entry door. Since this branch of the library offers a film program almost every week, I would think they would have this problem solved by now, unless they don't consider it a problem. All they would have to do, is reverse the screen and projector positions, so that people entering the room would not have to walk in front of, or behind, the screen, and light from the opening door would not shine directly on the screen.

WHITE MANE
THE BLUE DASHIKI
MOOD OF ZEN

Attending ——— Library's Free Monthly Movies Program, I entered the library and found a poster made of yellow paper, decorated with black paper "reels" and "film" announcing the film showing. There was also a small booklet, part of the library's announcement materials, next to the poster, listing dates, times, and descriptions of the film programs for February through May.

I took a booklet. Then, as the poster did not indicate where the films were being shown, I asked at the desk. I was sent upstairs to the meeting room. At the head of the stairs, I found another poster, identical to the first, announcing the film showing, but still not indicating where. This was a problem, as there were rows of doors along this upper gallery, as well as a hallway. Fortunately, I was able to ask a lady, who was coming along the hall, the location of the meeting room.

It was a nice large room, decorated with white paint and blonde wood panelling. There was fairly comfortable seating. An oval rug was placed on the floor in front of the seating area. The wall at the front of the room was fitted with a counter and cabinets along the lower part, while the upper part was painted white and served as the screen. Two loudspeakers were placed on the counter at either side of the front wall.

The projector was located on a cart directly inside the entrance to the room. If you walked to one side of it, you had a clear walkway; on the other side, you had to step over extension cords leading to outlets and a stereo console at the side of the room. Classical music was being played softly when I entered at 7:50 P.M.

I had the embarrassed feeling that I would be the only person in the audience, as I was the first person in the room. However, at 7:55, fourteen other people came in, the majority of them in late middle age, or elderly. Since they seemed to enter as a group, I assumed they had been in the library already for other purposes, and an announcement had been made, calling them together.

At 8:02 P.M., the lady who had directed me to the meeting room welcomed us to "Movies at 8." She explained that these film programs were one of the services the library provided. The aim of the programs was to show the shorter 16mm films that have been popular during the past five years. She also stressed that they liked to present a wide variety of these films during one program. She announced that a special program would be presented during the next week—for Library Week—a 1 1/2-hour film about Gertrude Stein.

Then the lights were turned off—sudden darkness, which was startling—and the program started.

The program certainly was diverse. It didn't much matter in what order the films were shown, as none related to each other, or to any theme.

The first film, *White Mane* (B&W, 35 min.), was substituted for *Stained Glass—A Photographic Essay* and *Trinidad and Tobago*, two films which had not arrived in time for the program. *White Mane*, a French film, reminded me slightly of *Dream of Wild Horses*, because of its theme and some of its photography. In the main, though, it was a French "wild horse–cowboy–boy–tames-horse" picture with a mystical ending. The other films were *The Blue Dashiki* (Color, 14 min.), which showed how a young black boy earned enough money to buy a dashiki that he saw in an African import store; and *Mood of Zen* (Color, 14 min.), which explained the Zen philosophy of cooperative harmony of nature and man.

The first film was not focused until halfway through the picture. The lights remained off during the entire program, even while the projectionist threaded each film on the machine, which was very efficiently done.

After the program, we were all routed down the back stairs, as the library was closed.

Except for the poor focus during the first film, there were no particular technical problems. Personally, I think the major problem was the choice of films—I thought I was going to fall asleep during the first one. Thinking that perhaps it was just the films shown for this program, I looked over the titles and annotations of films shown in other months, but none of them struck me as being too stimulating.

CANCER—THE EMBATTLED CELL (Film-lecture)

Since I felt that the last film program I attended at this library (March 8) was more of a children's program, I decided to see what an adult program was like.

The library was quieter this night, not as many people, probably because the surrounding stores were closed. Posters were placed around the walls, on the stacks, and on an easel in the main room of the library, announcing the film and lecture.

Again, I was one of the first ones to arrive, so I took some time to look around the library itself. I was interested to see posters announcing, "If you have a report to do, see us and you'll have more." I found myself wondering who this applied to—businessmen, college students, high school students—or all of them.

Entering the screening room, I found the screen in the same place as before, right by the door. This night, the walls were covered with children's drawings, and a mobile made out of cans was suspended from the ceiling, the efforts of the Weekday Nursery Class, held at the library.

For a while I was the only member of the audience. Then two older ladies entered, discussing their ailments and the doctors they went to; followed by a middle-aged man. One of the two librarians that I had seen on my last visit came in to set up the film on the projector.

When the program started at 7:30, there were four in the audience, the two ladies, the man, and myself. Also in attendance were two librarians, one to run the projector, the other to introduce the program, and the lecturer.

One librarian started the program by saying, "I want to thank you all for coming. Mrs. B. will be the guest lecturer. We'll start with the film the Cancer Society sent." Then she left the room. The lights went out and the film started.

Again, no credits, we just leapt right into the film. This time, the frame was centered on the screen, but it was still lopsided. (After the program was over, I went back and checked the projector. I found its legs were not even, so it stood "tipsily" on its stand.)

After the film started, a stray child walked in and out of the room three separate times. Then we were able to settle down and watch the picture.

I don't want to get into film criticism, since my main concern is film programs, but I must make the passing comment that this was a very poor film considering the wealth of material about cancer that could be presented visually. In fact, the only mention made of cancer itself was that it was a rapid, uncontrolled growth of cells. No mention was made of warning signs, treatments, what cancer looks like, where it can be found, tests, etc. Also, it was an old film, judging by the style of clothes worn by the actors. Instead of a little shock therapy to motivate people to get check-ups, it was just an advertisement for the Cancer Society—bland and inoffensive.

After the film Mrs. B., a volunteer for the local branch of the American Cancer Society, said she didn't know what to say because there was such a "big crowd" (aren't four saved better than none?) and she didn't know what to add, because the film was "so beautiful" (are films about cancer supposed to be "beautiful"?). So she explained the purposes of the Cancer Society and mentioned some of the programs and clinics they've sponsored. The entire program, film and "lecture," lasted 25 minutes.

The librarian went out of the room to get literature and to photocopy material about cancer tests from the lecturer's one brochure. She came back with two photocopies, said she would get two more, but was apparently waylaid somewhere as we never saw her again. Meanwhile, the librarian who had left before the film program started returned.

There was a more informal discussion, after the "formal" lecture, among the ladies, the man, the lecturer, and the remaining librarian—mostly personal reminiscences about their own operations, or those of friends and relatives. Apparently the appeal of this film program had reached those who were already aware of the dangers of cancer, rather than those who needed to know.

I imagine several factors contributed to the small attendance, one probably being the depressing theme, a topic people usually don't want to hear or talk about. Another reason was the fact that it was a nonshopping night and people didn't need a baby-sitter for their children. Another might have been that it was a cold evening.

THE CREATION
THE GIFT OF LIFE
THE DEAD BIRD

I chose to attend a film program at the Cultural Center because (1) I felt a museum is something like a library, and (2) not many libraries have adult film programs, and I wanted to see as great a variety as I could.

Room 22, where the program was held, was on the first floor—or basement floor, depending on which entrance you use—of the Museum. There were guards everywhere, who were helpful, so it was no problem to find the room, although it would be easy to miss if you were not directed to it.

The room was small, capacity about 66 (I counted the chairs while I was waiting). The museum brochure states that seating is on a "first come, first served" basis, but since I was early, I had no trouble. I also found out from this brochure that I was attending a children's showing of the films, although no mention of this was made in the newspaper advertisement. The same films are shown again at 4:00 P.M. Sunday afternoon, when no children are allowed to attend without an adult.

The room was carpeted, panelled, and had a country-style decor; deer heads on the wall, old-fashioned farming utensils (harrow, pitchfork, etc.) standing around or leaning against the walls. Seating was comfortable; armrests on chairs, padded vinyl, ashtrays fastened to the backs of the chairs.

The projector was on a cart in a closet in the back of the room. There was a raised platform-stage at the front with a podium at either side. The screen was ceiling mounted and pulled down in the middle of the front wall.

The audience was made up of a pack of Cub Scouts, with five Scout leaders and three of their wives. Another pack of nine Scouts, with one leader and a little girl, entered shortly after. Other than myself, there were only four members of the audience who were not with a group. The children were restless and many did not want to see the movies—"Who wants to see a movie?" (kids); "*Sit down*" (Scout leader); "Hey, look at the old lady" (yelled by a Scout about one of the members of the audience)—were some of the comments heard.

A young man was the projectionist. The program started when a guard came in and said, "Smoking is not permitted in this room" (despite the ashtrays on the backs of the chairs), shut off the lights, left the room, and closed the door.

The three films were all spliced together, so there was no intermission for rewinding and rethreading.

Considering the types of films shown, the children were well behaved, although they got a little restless toward the end.

The program itself confused me. The first film was a poetry reading about the creation of the world. The second started out with a pregnant woman sitting in a chair and a heartbeat as the background "music." As the film developed, showing the woman being rushed to the hospital, I began to be a little alarmed for the Cub Scouts, as it very definitely looked as if we were going to see a graphic depiction of childbirth. I could sense the restlessness of the Scout leaders, also. However, just at "the good part" as we used to say, the film switched to show an old, old person who was dying, and became, from then on, a sentimental and very religious treatise on "as one is born, one dies." In fact, it became *so* religious, with quotes from the Bible and little sermonettes, that I seriously questioned whether or not the Museum was going into the church business. The only excuse I could see for this film, was that it was shown on the day before Palm Sunday and that it was probably part of an Easter program.

Both films needed to be picketed by Women's Lib organizations—there were endless little quotes about men loving their wives as the "weaker sex"; that God created "man" (never went on to tell about "woman"); and so on.

The third film was unexpected, as it had not been announced, and everyone was already preparing to get up and leave when it flashed on the screen. It was *The Dead Bird*, a children's story in film form, and it re-attracted the Scouts' attention, which had been wandering. In fact, after it was over, one Scout called, "Hey Mom, that was the best one."

At the end of the program, the lights came on and we all filed out—I, to return home—the Scouts, to go to the next activity on the day's agenda.

Thinking it over, I felt there may have been *some* rationale behind the selections—The Creation, Life and Death, and Death. I was interested in knowing if the program would be handled in any different way for the adults on Sunday, but I was not interested enough to go back and sit through those films again!

THE ARK
ARETHA FRANKLIN, SOUL SINGER

I made this excursion into the Pennsylvania countryside, one hour from home, because I felt that here, at last, I was going to see a contemporary film that would certainly draw a crowd of teenagers. This program, and the reaction to it, would surely be helpful to me in my school library work.

Fortunately, the lights were on in the library, illuminating the stacks of books that could be seen through the windows, or I would have missed it completely. The only sign in front of a building that looked like an old, converted wooden army barracks, announced that this was the "Civic Center—Little League." It was located in a rural area, on a two-lane highway between two towns. Two boys were playing ball in the parking lot as I pulled in.

There was a poster inside the door of the library building announcing the film programs for the month. I later found out that this had been the *only* month they'd had film programs. The poster was cleverly done in black and white.

"Join Us for Family Film Nights" was the heading, with each of the four film programs written on drawings of projection screens. This night's showing was to be *Aretha Franklin, Soul Singer* and Rudolph Valentino in *The Sheik*. The rationale behind that combination escaped me.

Opposite the poster, was a pleasant librarian, seated at a desk, who told me that the film would start at 7:30, but that I couldn't go "back there" now, as it was still dark.

I spent the waiting time in the library. You could tell how small it was by looking at the card catalog drawers which were labeled from A to Z, just a single letter on each drawer—one for A, one for B, etc.—and which were divided into Adult and Juvenile. The library was pleasant and clean; tiles on the floor, well lit, with furnishings that looked as if they had been donated—sofas, chairs, end tables, etc.

The only other person in the library, besides the three librarians, was a middle-aged man. As I was browsing through the books, the two boys from the parking lot came in, chewing gum wildly, and started playing checkers at a corner table set up for that purpose. The librarian passed by and asked if anyone was there for film night. I said, "yes," and the boys, who hadn't known about it, became excited and ran to call their parents to ask if they could stay for the program.

About 7:30, while in a front corner of the library, I heard a faint call, "Film time," from the back of the building. In the time it took me to close the book I was looking at, replace it on the shelf, and walk to the back of the library, the lights in the film room had been turned out (if they had ever been on) and the first film had started.

I had to "feel" my way in total darkness down a narrow corridor leading through a plastic-covered stacks storage area, stepping over and around obstacles as I encountered them, until I reached a musty, damp, back storeroom. The light from the screen and movie projector gave me enough illumination to find a seat on one of the folding chairs that had been placed in a haphazard grouping.

In the faint light, I could see that we were in an unfinished (or decaying) part of the building; no curtains or blinds on the windows, holes in the ceilings and walls, and patches of ceiling hanging and ready to fall. All over the room were boxes of books which, I found out later, were there for a spring book sale. The projector was on a cart behind the chairs. The screen was portable and set up right in front of the first grouping of chairs.

The starting audience was composed of the librarian running the projector; a girl, about 13 years old, who I assumed to be the librarian's daughter, as she helped out with the program and sat by her; the two boys, about 9 or 10 years old, who popped their bubble gum loudly throughout; three little girls, about 6 or 7 years old; and myself. During the first film, the little girls left. One returned a short while later with her father. They left when the film about Aretha Franklin started, as did the gum-chewing boys. I then became the sole audience for this film.

I stood (or sat?) my ground and stayed for the entire showing.

After the first film, since I had missed the opening credits, I asked the librarian its title. She told me, *The Ark,* and explained that it had been sent in place of *The Sheik,* which had been unavailable at the last minute. *The Ark* was a futuristic type, antipollution, message film. Her comment about it was, "Well, that was rather bleak, wasn't it?"

After the entire program was over, the librarian's daughter turned on the lights and I got up to leave. The librarian's comments about the film wanting to make you dance—and the fact that I was the only person to see it—opened up a chance to talk to her.

I found out that this month's attempts were the first by the library at running film programs. Before, they had had to borrow or rent equipment, which made it impractical, but this year they had purchased a new projector, cart, and screen. This night's showing was the last of four film programs. It had to be the last, because the days were getting longer and they had no blinds to keep out the light.

The librarian had a rather apologetic air as she spoke to me, embarrassed because there had been no audience. She said the first two programs had drawn a large crowd, the third had attracted a few people (and the fourth was just me). She remembered me from my phone call, earlier in the day. She lamented because she didn't understand why more people hadn't come out, she had even put posters in the community college. "Maybe *The Sheik* scared them off." I commiserated with her and commented on the fact that it had been the very first warm spring day, people had probably done things outdoors. Also the Shenyang acrobats were on a "special" on TV that night and might have given her some competition; carefully avoiding mention of the fact that the surroundings for seeing her films were most depressing and uncomfortable.

She said, "Oh well . . . (pause) . . . , thank you for coming. I hope you enjoyed it." I thanked her and left.

"THE GREAT FLICKS OF YESTERYEAR"

WILL ROGERS
SLAPSTICK
STORY OF THE SERIALS

Presented by the Free Public Library and the *Times* Newspaper

Compared to my other library visits, each progressively worse than the preceding one, the *Times* program had seemed to be the most successful, so I decided to revisit it to see if its first success (*Kovacs*) would be repeated.

I arrived at 7:50 P.M. on a rainy evening. There were fewer people gathered in the Community Room; it was about half full when I entered. Again, there were many that knew each other and there was a good deal of greeting and chatting. Also, again, there was a good mixture of young and old. This time there were many more parents (mostly fathers) with young children.

Last time, the room had been warm. This time, to de-humidify it, the air conditioner was on and it was cool.

Without a crowd of "standees" to block my view, I had a chance to survey the scene and count the chairs—there was seating for 132. There were two projectors at the back of the room, mounted on a high, scaffold-type stand at one side of the entry door.

While we were waiting, a maintenance man threaded one machine and started it to focus the film, check whether or not it was centered on the screen, and check the sound level. It was a film that the *Times* produces for the local schools. Just as I was getting interested in it, he shut off the lamp but let the film run. A little while later, he turned the lamp on again. It was a riot, as he did this several times before he rewound it, all the while shouting at a gray-haired maintenance lady, who was sitting in the back corner, about the focus, the sound, etc. Finally the lady left, but the man kept fiddling with the film.

It was so funny, and so much was happening, that I was turned three-quarters of the way around in my chair, looking towards the back (I was sitting in the first row) and writing away like mad on my pad. Each time I looked up to see what was going on with the projectionist, I was confronted with a sea of faces, looking at me, and probably wondering what I was writing about! It was unnerving.

At 8 P.M., starting time, there was a sudden influx of people. At 8:05, the place was about three-quarters full. The maintenance man had given up on one projector and was now threading film on the second one. The obnoxious man was still expounding his views to his boy and the friend he had met. I was becoming embarrassed for him.

Finally, at 8:10, one of the MC's that had introduced the last film program stopped talking to a young lady at the back of the room and came forward.

He bade us welcome. He also asked us to forgive the delay, but explained that they always like to start the program 10 minutes past the published starting time unless they had a full house. He said they expected to have a full house the following Wednesday, when they were holding their second program about acupuncture. He then explained a little about that.

Also, the following Thursday would find them having another film program about the "Wyeth Phenomenon." In addition to the Wyeth film, there was going to be a travel film—not the first one they had planned, since the library was unable to secure it, but another, which the library assured him was even better—about Vancouver. Also on the agenda was a children's film, *White Mane*, "a story about a child's love for his horse." (This film, which I had never heard of before, has been haunting me since I first saw it. I was bored by it, yet it keeps cropping up in all the literature I've been reading as an example of a great children's film—and here it was again!)

After his announcements of coming attractions, the MC went on to say that there was no need to introduce this night's films, as everyone had come to see them because they knew what they were. He concluded by saying, "Our projectionist tonight, as on all nights, is ———, one of our great friends."

The lights dimmed as the MC went out the back door, but it was still bright enough for me to see the notes I was taking as the first film flashed on the screen. A little while later, someone closed the doors to the hall, blocking out the light and it got darker.

We saw the three films. Since each was part of a series about the history of motion pictures, each time a new film started we had the same introduction over again. It got a little wearing by the third time. (By this time, the projectionist had gotten the second projector working, and after the second film started he rewound the first, creating a terrific squealing noise. That was the only real annoyance during the program, except for the man who kept talking and explaining through the whole thing.)

Everyone enjoyed the films—I guess slapstick is perennial—and gave a round of applause at the end. The lights came on and the program was over. Going out, I overheard a lady ask the projectionist where the films came from. He told her, the library. She wondered if a private individual could borrow them and a man with her said, "Sure, if it's from the library." I was heartened, as it seemed that the program *had* stimulated interest and the lady would now be directed to the library.

APPENDIX 2
Selected Materials for Film Study

Perhaps the most rewarding experience that teaching provides is the opportunity for the instructor to learn from the pupil. Such was the case when David Brown appeared one day in my class. With formal training and a long career as a religious educator, David had a deep interest in the use of films in the communication of ideas, values, and information. During the year that we worked together, David often discussed his experiences in using films with religious groups. This willingness to share is further evidenced by his permission to use his paper in this appendix.

The reader should note that the annotated titles included here offer David's point of view on using the materials in one special context. Many of these titles also appear in Appendix 3, where complete bibliographic details are supplied.

SELECTED MATERIALS FOR FILM STUDY
by David Brown

Ten years ago, I was completing a pastorate in Powder River County, Montana. The parish covered over 3,000 square miles in the high plains southeast corner of the state: mostly wheat, sheep and cattle ranches. Roads were primitive, often impassible. REA had arrived recently and could not yet guarantee service; power outages of up to three days were common. Telephones and CATV were found only in Broadus, the county seat. Broadus also boasted the county's only motion picture theater, open on weekends.

As the only Protestant pastor in the county, I had gone out into the country and gathered eight small congregations which met in schools, dance halls and ranch homes. I was also responsible for a church of some 200 people in Broadus. The people in town expected a traditional religious service each week, but this practice made little sense in the out-lying locations. It hadn't taken me long to realize that these sturdy ranchers and their families didn't come to services to hear me preach. They were looking for human contact, and the monologue of preaching didn't give them much of that. Yet some sort of proclamation of good news was necessary. What should I do?

After a few experiments, I began to load the old Victor 16mm projector into the back of my car and hope it survived another 120-mile round trip to one of the now combined supper-service-family nights. The machine was perhaps 20 years old when I got to use it (a hand-me-down from a church in Rockville Center, N.Y.). It finally fell apart during the second reel of Louis de Rochemont's *Martin Luther*. Up to that point, I had managed to get some fairly good free films: *The Long Stride, Overture/UN, The Red Balloon,* etc. I didn't show anything I couldn't justify risking the projector for! The films were not fully utilized, since I was a novice, but certainly most were well received. They brought isolated, lonely people a sense of belonging to a common humanity, some compassion for people who lived very different lives, and perhaps even some joy.

About that time, I came across a comment attributed to William Blake. I sometimes used it to explain myself to officials of the Board for Homeland Ministries and other people who thought I should stay with the time-tested routine of three hymns, long prayer, and sermon. Blake said, "If the doors of perception were cleansed, everything would appear to man as it is, infinite." I don't suppose that this helped me win any arguments, but I liked it. It did help me feel even more right about what I was doing.

I've come a long way in using films since my Montana days. The experiments of a decade or more ago led to the development years later of some fairly complicated film programs. One of these was designed for the Champlain Association of the Vermont Conference of the United Church of Christ, a council of representatives from two dozen small Congregational churches that meets twice annually for fellowship, mutual encouragement, and consideration of issues important to the churches.

My program for May 1970 was built around the film *Where the People Are,* a cinéma vérité report of the honest anguish of a smalltown boy from upstate New York who went to Princeton Seminary and then to New York for further training. As the result of involvement in the peace movement, he turned in his draft card and was deeply embarrassed by the lack of courage and usefulness of the church. The film was shown to a group of 200 or so, with the request that each viewer role-play being a member of a committee charged with responsibility for selecting a candidate to recommend to their fellow church members as their next pastor. After the film, the people met in small "committees" and decided, on the basis of what they had seen, whether or not to consider the young man any further. The main purpose of this exercise was to let the people discover the way the pastoral placement process works in the United Church of Christ. A second purpose was to bring into the open the growing split between the church leadership (mainly liberal) and constituency (mainly conservative). A third and related purpose was to be aware of some of the valid criticism being directed at the church.

One clergyman in the Association had been a classmate of the protagonist's. He joined a panel which included the local denominational official who is the equivalent of a "bishop" (i.e., responsible for seeing that churches have pastors of some sort), another denominational official, from Boston (for wider perspective), and the chaplain at the University of Vermont (who wore a beard, as did the protagonist, and might be considered a spokesman for church youth). This panel appeared after the people had reassembled, and helped to define the issues. Discussion was lively. When the day was over, I felt that the program had gone well.

Starting in August, I'll be involved in film use on a still larger scale. I will then be the nonprint specialist for a private preparatory school in Pennsylvania. I will be responsible for encouraging sensible and stimulating film use. Therefore, I am particularly interested in building up a file of materials to recommend to teachers and students. I especially need film study materials which encourage what David Sohn in *Film: The Creative Eye* calls the three Cs: *Creativity—Communication—Change.*

> Upon those who step into the same
> rivers, different and ever different
> waters flow down.—*Heraclitus*

I am aware of three major influences in film use during the past ten years: Religious beginnings for film guide publishers; Revolutionary trends in education; and Rise of the effective short film.

Three major needs, identified by G. Howard Poteet in *The Compleat Guide to Film Study,* remain to be met in the years ahead: Definition of "film use"; Development of a new breed of film teachers; and Discovery of more useful materials.

First, the three Rs.

Religious Beginnings for Film Guide Publishers

Sheed and Ward, Herder and Herder, Paulist Press, and Pflaum were, ten years ago, conservative Roman Catholic publishers, with a list limited to pietistical and catechetical materials. Then: Sheed and Ward discovered Fischer; Herder and Herder discovered Wigal; Paulist Press discovered Heyer and Meyer; Pflaum discovered Schrank, Sohn, Kuhns, Amelio, Brown, Linton, Valdes, Crow, Goldman, Burnett, et al.

New publications appeared, intended to assist teachers of religion in parochial schools. These film books were a natural extension of a long-standing Roman Catholic emphasis on visual effects (as in the Mass, which was to be seen rather than heard). Protestants are traditionally more concerned with what can be heard (the music of Bach, the proclamation of the Word via preaching). Ecumenism was welcomed as (in effect) the reuniting of the delights of both eye and ear. Up until very recently, however, film publications and groups were often Roman Catholic. Example: The National Center for Film Study is a division of the Catholic Adult Education Center, the educational affiliate of the National Catholic Office for Motion Pictures. Example: John Culkin, now Director of the

Center for Understanding Media, used to be Father John Culkin, S.J. (i.e., Jesuit), of Fordham's National Film Study Project. More examples: Dalglish's *Media for Christian Formation* (soon abbreviated to *Media One,* then joined by *Media Two,* and now *Media Three*), McCaffrey's *Films for Religious Education* and *A Guide to Short Films for Religious Education* II, Cushing's *101 Films for Character Growth,* and Kuhn's *Themes: Short Films for Discussion* developed out of a desire to serve the Roman Catholic Church. Cox's *Audio Visual Resource Guide* (NCCC) was the only corresponding Protestant work.

It appears that the teachers of religion in parochial schools who were the intended audience of these church-related publications did not appreciate the value of these guides. A more general audience did, and the emphasis shifted to less religion, more films. Overtly religious film books are still being published, of course, but their market is ever more limited. Kahle and Lee's *Popcorn and Parable,* G. W. Jones's *Sunday Night at the Movies,* and Konzelman's *Marquee Ministry* are not likely to have much effect. The people who might have appreciated these books ten years ago are now reading Sarris and Schrank, and loving it.

Revolutionary Trends in Education

As Schrank says in *Media in Value Education,* a revolution is unquestionably under way. Witness such books as *Schools without Failure, The Underachieving School,* and *Teaching as a Subversive Activity.* The old style of education put the emphasis on *teaching* (or "teaching *to*"). The new style stresses *learning* (as in "learning *with*"), and *unlearning* (of such misconceptions as "I'm not important," "My feelings are not to be trusted," "Adults know best," and "I must become what adults want me to become"). There's a perception, now, of a new style of student, too. Frederick Goldman and Linda R. Burnett, in *Need Johnny Read?,* say: "One fact that is difficult for many adults to comprehend is that the youth of the world today have a much clearer understanding of local, national, and international affairs. This is not because they are more intelligent, but because they have been raised in an age of instant communications and instant news. The realities of politics, big business, and oppression are now seen and heard at an early age by anyone who has access to a television set or a transistor radio. To understand youth, one must try to communicate with them."

Given these new conditions, George B. Leonard, in *Education and Ecstasy,* recommends seven goals for schools of the future:

1. To learn the commonly agreed upon skills and knowledge of the culture and to learn it joyfully and to learn that it is all tentative
2. To learn how to bring creative change on all that is currently agreed upon
3. To learn delight rather than aggression, cooperation instead of competition, sharing instead of acquisition, and uniqueness instead of conformity
4. To learn heightened awareness and control of emotions, sense, and bodily states, and thereby empathy for others
5. To learn how to enter and enjoy varying states of consciousness
6. To learn to explore and enjoy the infinite possibilities in relations between people
7. To learn how to learn.

The relatedness of this coming revolution with films is sketched often by Schrank. In *Media in Value Education,* he gives us some of his "reflections on a murdered medium": "(Film) was given the back-breaking burden of overcoming all that was wrong with traditional education. Film was viewed as the long-sought 'answer' to student boredom. . . . Film carried this gargantuan burden for a time, but then teachers found that students began reacting to films as they had earlier to books. . . . Ultimately film died because teachers mishandled it and did not believe the warning words of film critic Pauline Kael, 'If you think movies can't be killed, you underestimate the power of education.' " Certainly not all teachers should be encouraged to use film, revolution or not!

Rise of the Effective Short Film

Less really *is* more! In *Need Johnny Read?*, Goldman and Burnett give their reasons for recommending exclusive use of short films: they introduce students gradually to film techniques and aesthetics; they do not require the untangling of a plot; they tend to be faster paced; they provide a wide range of form, freshness, and experimentation; they allow points to be stressed through repetition; they are cheaper to rent than features; and they can be shown and discussed without diminution of effect within the limits of a 45-minute class period. The short films being discussed are not didactic exercises such as the Yale Chronicles of America Photoplays. They are the "probes," aids to discovery, even works of art, which have appeared in quantity during the last decade. Sohn's *Film: The Creative Eye* lists some which have been especially effective.

Now, the three remaining necessities.

Definition of "Film Use"

In *The Compleat Guide to Film Study,* one finds this statement: "Clearly and concisely, we need to say what we aim for when we teach under the general banner of film study. Why are we doing it? With whom are we doing it? What is it exactly that we *are* doing?" Do we want to use film to support traditional academic pursuits (e.g., teaching composition), or do we hope to see greater visual literacy? Is the objective to clarify personal values, or to investigate the properties of the medium? Ralph Amelio in *Film in the Classroom* lists seven nonexclusive approaches that may be taken:

1. Comparative (comparing film with literature, for example)
2. Thematic (analyzing content)
3. Aesthetic (developing standards for evaluation)
4. Creative (making a film)
5. Psychological (measuring effect of film upon viewers)
6. Stylistic (recognizing elements of directors' and actors' style)
7. Historical (tracing development of film)

Other books examined later in this paper approach this problem differently and offer other good first answers.

Development of a New Breed of Film Teachers

The effective use of film is an acquired skill, yet both pre-service and in-service training are weak. According to Poteet, "It seems a vicious circle—lack of leadership fosters lack of leadership." The training of a new breed of film librarians is also, at present, discouraging. Paul Spehr in his article "Feature Films in Your Library" (*WLB,* April 1970) says "At the present time, film training and library science are separate disciplines, frequently unavailable at the same school. Only students with individual initiative can obtain training in both fields and almost no effort is made to relate the two. Furthermore, should the library science student prepare himself for work with films, there is little or no possibility that there are jobs waiting for him." GSLS (Graduate School of Library Service at Rutgers University) seems to be an exception in this area.

Discovery of More Useful Materials

Even the greatest film teacher must have proper materials. Most *films* are hard to get. Many *projectors* are hard to use. Adequate *projection facilities* are hard to find. *Supporting literature* is increasing rapidly, but as Poteet warns, actual needs must be discovered soon: "Some basic guidelines for the development of educational materials to support film education need to be written. Perhaps such guidelines would indicate a need for more writing on film criticism, or film history or aesthetics, or on practical film education matters. It seems unwise to leave all this to the chance production of the book publishers." (Chance is far less important than the law of supply and demand.)

I have attempted to analyze and describe more than three dozen examples of film study guides and related books. My comments are primarily *notes to myself*—reminders of the strengths and possible uses of certain books, some of which I have examined with great pleasure.

A brief comparison of study guides to individual films follows.

Study Guides to Individual Films

The Best and the Brightest

My recommendations to the beginning film teacher are, first, read Richard A. Lacey's *Seeing with Feeling,* then *Need Johnny Read?* by Frederick Goldman and Linda R. Burnett, then two by Jeffrey Schrank: *Teaching Human Beings* and *Media in Value Education.* These are the favored four.

1. Seeing with Feeling: Film in the Classroom by Richard A. Lacey (part of the Controversies in Education Series, from the University of Massachusetts School of Education). Simple premise: "To sensitize students to the medium of film and to make them more open to one another, we must discuss how and what each other sees" (p. 25). Offers a dozen devices, and fifteen guidelines: (1) make no assumptions; (2) content is style; (3) ask and offer feelings; (4) examine feelings surrounding whatever interests students at the moment; (5) use the "here and now wheel" (student writes feelings that he has NOW on each spoke of the wheel); (6) treat feelings as content; (7) try "before and after" exercises; (8) experiment with value clarification exercises; (9) ask for feedback; (10) compare and contrast films; (11) Concentrate on specific elements in a film; (12) stop film, freeze a frame; (13) experiment with sound; (14) use more than one screen; (15) try the "fishbowl" technique: two groups, one of which observes the other, as was the case when the Mahwah students visited GSLS for Citizen Kane Day. Teacher is perceived as enabler, not moderator. Need for a support group is explored. Objectives for film use are stated in behavioral terms. Stimulating examples: e.g., compare *Corral, Cattle Ranch, Dream of the Wild Horses*, and *Tamer of Wild Horses*. Good bibliography, addresses for distributors. A fine first guide to "What to do when the lights go on."

2. Need Johnny Read? Practical Methods to Enrich Humanities Courses Using Films and Film Study by Frederick Goldman and Linda R. Burnett. Demonstration that Lacey is right: movies generally enter schools on the coattails of other, established subjects. Claims that Johnny need not read. Reading is contrary to the realities of Johnny's life and interests. Efforts to make him read are not likely to succeed. However, Johnny needs to read to get through this book. It's mostly print. Not a "how-to-do-it" book, but a sound explanation of why films and television are the most influential media. Most readers will find it very convincing.

3. Teaching Human Beings: 101 Subversive Activities for the Classroom by Jeffrey Schrank. More than a study guide, *THB* offers ingenious suggestions for what to do until the educational revolution comes. Multimedia approach. Exercises are given. Books recommended. Films described include *The Searching Eye, The Big Shave, Bread, Leaf, Dream of the Wild Horses, Sky, Necrology*, in the section on Sense Education. Other sections deal with Hidden Assumptions (*The Invention of the Adolescent, The Things I Cannot Change, Why Man Creates*), Violence and the Violated (*Titticut Follies, High School, Night and Fog, The Selling of the Pentagon*), Chemicals and the Body (*A Walk in the Park*, possibly "the only really useful film in the whole area of drug education"; an interesting comment in light of the urging now of a moratorium on all drug education), Learning about Death (*The Day Grandpa Died, The Day Manolete Was Killed, The Red Kite, An Occurrence at Owl Creek Bridge*), and Subversive Activities (*Up Against the Wall Miss America, Radcliffe Blues*, and *Portrait of a Girl*). Fifteen simulation games are listed in an appendix. This book's effect is to make this reader want to meet Schrank and talk with him. He must be engaging, if not engrossing.

4. Media in Value Education: A Critical Guide by Jeffrey Schrank. Originally for teachers of religion, but useful by any teacher looking for stimulating ideas and encouragement. Seventy-five short films are reviewed. Discussion guide given for each. Section on music is now dated (refers to the Beatles, Ed Ames's *Who Will Answer, The Wozard of Iz*). Full of perceptive comments, such as this: "Some years back there was great interest in audio-visual aids in teaching. Many films, tapes, and filmstrips were produced. . . . But in the early stages of growth, many films, tapes, and filmstrips were produced that lacked sound artistic merit as well as a wise application of educational psychology. They were fine for developing the skills of the people who made them, but the products left students 'turned off.' Most importantly, these audio-visual aids failed to utilize the potential of their own media. Today audio-visual is 'out' and media is 'in.' Audio-visual has become something oe a 'dirty word' connoting boring visual lectures. . . . One has to sort through much of the debris of the a-v revolution to find the most worthwhile examples of the new direction in today's mass media." p. 19)

Once Is Not Enough

The first four books provide the rationale for film study, and some suggestion of its potential. The next six give practical directions, even step-by-step instructions, without insulting the intelligence of the reader.

5. Screen Experience: An Approach to Film, ed. by Sharon Feyen and Donald Wigal. Feyen, a journalism teacher, wrote one chapter and collaborated on a second. Wigal, Pflaum's editor, wrote two chapters, the discussion starters, expanded the film notes, and compiled the bibliography. It might be more his book than hers. Highly recommended for teachers. Six main parts:

Part I: An Introduction to Film

Part II: Putting It Down on Film (adaptation of novels and plays)

Part III: Forms of Film (Western, Comedy, Documentary . . .)

Part IV: The Art of Film (directing and editing)

Part V: Film Programming (very useful suggestions for a film series, etc.)

Part VI: Practical Information, including a classic description of film grammar and properties: (1) Montage; (2) Camera angle; (3) Camera position; (4) Camera movement; (5) Color; (6) Sound—natural, music; (7) Film devices—fade, dissolve, superimposition, etc.; (8) Categories—Documentary, Adaptation from stage or TV, Adaptation from novel, Animation, Social or moral or symbolic commentary, Pure film, e.g., *Clay*; (9) Cinéma vérité; (10) Introceptive camera—"The use of the camera to reveal psychological states," as in *Billy Budd*; (11) Character development; (12) Transitional phases; (13) Visual symbols; (14) Lighting; (15) Photographic images and composition; (16) Highly visual subjects, e.g., *Lawrence of Arabia.*

Appendix I is an annotated film list, running 68 pages. This is perhaps the most useful part of the book, although some will question the rave given *Oklahoma*!

6. Films Deliver: Teaching Creatively with Film, ed. by Anthony Schillaci and John M. Culkin. Discusses what films can do for teachers and students; how it's being done today, etc. Appendixes are most significant: Filmography of 16mm Features, Filmography of Short Films, Sample Guides. Big-time contributors: Putsch, Sohn, Maynard, Kuhns, and Powell, as well as the editors. Goes into details (virtues of xenon projection bulbs) and trends. A good second choice if the Feyen and Wigal is not available.

7. Film: The Creative Eye by David A. Sohn. Fifteen Pyramid films are used to awaken the wonder and creativity of anyone who picks up this beautiful book.

Sohn shows that the "study of processes in our environment is much more important than the accumulation of facts." He also provides insights into the creative process via interviews with Saul Bass, Charles Braverman, Ken Rudolph, David Adams, et al. The films are *The Searching Eye, Why Man Creates, Leaf, Dunes, Waters of Yosemite, Autumn: Frost Country, Art, American Time Capsule, World of '68, Home of the Brave, Deep Blue World, Moods of Surfing, Sky Capers, Catch the Joy, Ski the Outer Limits, Turned On, Full Fathom Five*. Possible activities are suggested after each film is discussed. Related quotes are tossed in. Could be used effectively as a text. As exciting as the Pyramid catalog.

8. Discovery in Film by Robert Heyer and Anthony Meyer. A beautifully put together discussion of 78 short films—how to use them, where to get them inexpensively. Six sections: (1) Communication—forms personal identity (*That's Me*), creates community (*The Detached Americans*), of nature's beauty (*Sky, Leaf*), rejected (*The Critic*); (2) Freedom—struggle for (*The Hand*), from death (*The Bespoke Overcoat*), from want (*Hunger in America*), etc.; (3) Love—sex and/or love (*Phoebe*), for self (*Time Piece*), etc.; (4) Peace; (5) Happiness; (6) The Underground. Plus two appendixes, outline of film course. For each of the 78 films, four perspectives are given: comment or critique, discussion questions, resource material, data. Intended for use in discussion situations in secondary schools. Students could handle it.

9. The Celluloid Curriculum: How to Use Movies in the Classroom by Richard A. Maynard. A handbook on how to use film effectively, based on actual courses. Sensitive to students' interests as well as teachers' needs. Three parts:

Part I. Film as an Independent Part of the Curriculum (sample units on Power and Revolution, Black America, Crime and Punishment, Sex Education, Responsibility, Ethics, Alcohol, Drugs, Mental Illness, Retardation, Sexual Deviation, Old Age, Poverty, Movies and Literature)

Part II. Film as an Object of Study (sample units on the Western, Cinematic Views of War, Myths about Tropical Africa Created by the Movies, The Black Man in the Movies, Movies and History, America the Violent)

Part III. A Practical Guide to Teaching with Films (stress on planning, finding funds, choosing equipment, booking films, etc.)

Provides a 32-page filmography. Most films are feature length. Annotations are often personal: "I guess by now it must seem that satire is the only kind of comedy I like." Includes *Joe, Midnight Cowboy*, and other films which are not likely to be rented for school use for a while. Excellent bibliography.

10. A Bookless Curriculum by Roland G. Brown. The 46 lesson outlines (covering 72 pp.) are the most important part of this slim volume intended for use by teachers. Very personal: "How I taught reluctant readers in Folsom, Pa." Spares no details. More pretentious and contrived than *Discovery in Film*. Themes covered fit Brown's objectives: Uniqueness of Individuals, Humor, Justice, Moral Choices, Animation, Propaganda, Legends, etc. Brown will probably give people ideas.

All Creatures Great and Small

While most of the recent film books are directed to teachers, two would make delightful students' texts.

11. The Media Works by Joan Valdes and Jeanne Crow. Traces the development and effect of nonprint media, with vivid graphics, clever text, brilliant design. Invites dipping-in anywhere. Four sections: (1) The Workings (radio formats, a trip behind the scenes, making it pay, etc.); (2) The Mass Message (Best sellers, Heroes: Do They Tell Us What We Want to Be?, etc.); (3) The Personal Message (alternative media, songs, still photography, etc.). Common directions: Dig (do research), React (suggestions given to appropriate reactions), Create (e.g., sketch a storyboard for the filming of a nursery rhyme), Do (similar to Create), and even Read. Paperback cover would be a problem, but otherwise, everything about this book is right. Obviously, Valdes and Crow listened to Schrank.

12. Exploring the Film by William Kuhns and Robert Stanley. Textbook, more directed to concerns of film courses than *The Media Works*. Fifteen chapters: Why Study Movies?, What's in a Movie?, Film History, How a Film is Made, Visual Language, Language of Motion, Sound, Characters, Drama, Fiction Films, Documentaries, Say It with Film, Film Criticism, TV, To Make a Film. It's all there. Probably my first choice.

13. Teaching Program: Exploring the Film by William Kuhns and Robert Stanley (a teacher's guide). Everything one could hope to have: goals and theory, commentary on the text (*Exploring the Film*), sources for suggested films, etc. Not for lazy teachers, but for eager ones.

Semi-Tough

Some books are aimed at skilled film teachers who are well past the beginning stage and concerned with understanding various philosophies and approaches to film study. Other material, while less intellectual, also represents a next step in film teaching. Five examples follow.

14. Perspectives on the Study of Film, ed. by John Stuart Katz (Boston: Little, Brown, 1971, 340 pp.). Includes articles by Balazs, Carpenter, McLuhan, Huxley, Kauffmann, Sarris, Schillaci, Sontag, and others. Uneven. Heavy going in places, brilliant elsewhere. Divided into four sections: Film Study and Education, The Film as Art and Humanities, The Film as Communications, Environment and Politics, and Curriculum Design and Evaluation in Film Study. Some perspectives are philosophical; e.g., "Film becomes the primary environment in which the hunger to know through experience is satisfied" (Schillaci, p. 218).

15. The School and the Art of Motion Pictures (rev. ed.) by David Mallery. "A discussion of practices and possibilities with an annotated list of films of special interest to schools. . . ." Not difficult, but not a book an individual teacher is likely to read often. Chiefly treats feature films.

16. The Compleat Guide to Film Study, ed. by G. Howard Poteet. A semi-stuffy introduction to "the ecology of film." Reviews rationale, history, language, literature, composition, how to introduce film into a high school curriculum. Filmography of films about movies and movie-making strangely omits *Basic Film Terms*. Not my favorite, but still a bargain at $4.75.

17. Film in the Classroom: Why Use It, How to Use It by Ralph J. Amelio. A middle-of-the-road manual. "Doubtlessly the most complete and up-to-date resource aid the newly appointed film teacher could hope to enlist," says the publisher's prospectus. Actually, it's a detailed report of the Willowbrook Cinema Study Project in Villa Park, Illinois, *not* a good book to hand a beginner. The section on rationale is very weak. Methods used are fairly exhaustive. Ten units of the film program are described in detail. For example, "The Adolescent: Through a Lens Starkly" took four to five weeks, covered *No Reason to Stay, The Summer We Moved to Elm Street, The 400 Blows, Phoebe, On the Waterfront* (How many "newly appointed film teachers" could do justice to *On the Waterfront*?). *The Sound of Trumpets, Summerhill, The Game,* and *King and Country* were added later. No explanation given as to why some obvious films (e.g., *The Invention of the Adolescent*) were not included. We do know how each film was used. I bought this book primarily because of its excellent, annotated, 18-page bibliography.

18. Movies with a Purpose: A Teacher's Guide to Planning and Producing Super-8 Movies for Classroom Use (Eastman Kodak Co.). An excellent introduction to making single-concept films. Planning emphasized. Behavioral objectives recommended. "Try defining your objectives in a single sentence that begins, 'After seeing the film, I want the student to . . .'." Variety stressed. "Don't just set your camera down in a fixed position and shoot." Casual style, but packed with information. Only weakness: unimaginative use of visuals; almost all pictures are one column wide. An essential reference for creative teachers.

Fourteen That Haven't Made the Best Seller List

Their appeal appears limited. Arrangement is alphabetical, by author.

19. Novels into Film: The Metamorphosis of Fiction into Cinema by George Bluestone. A classic study that concludes that film is a totally new medium, whatever the source of plots may be. Six examples of novels which are converted into new (film) entities: *The Informer, Wuthering Heights, Pride and Prejudice, The Grapes of Wrath, The Ox-Bow Incident, Madame Bovary.*

20. Our Modern Art: The Movies by Ernest Callenbach. A course outline (the Western, Animation, Syntax, Montage, Neorealism, Silent Comedy, etc.) still valid, after 18 years.

21. The War/Peace Film Guide by Lucy Dougall (Berkeley: World without War Council, 1970). Peace—Shalom. In no way is this guide dated by the ending of the Vietnam war. Four sections: (1) Short Films (the human cost of war, roots of war, nonviolence, conscientious objection and the draft, the effects of nuclear war, etc.); (2) Feature Films; (3) Program Development Guide; and (4) Planning Aids and Sources. Wise choices, valid suggestions, valuable list of sources for study guides. Good brief unbiased annotations (50 words or so each). Can be used in many different situations.

22. The Environment Film Review: A Critical Guide to Ecology Films (New York: Environment Information Center, 1972). This well-indexed annual guide, while not as exhaustive as claimed, is the best in the field by far. Reviews films in twenty categories plus "general." (*1985, America the Beautiful, Pollution in Perspective: Our Air and Water*, three films I wouldn't care to use, are rated "G" by *The EFR*.) In spite of its title, this is not a "critical" work. Does not "recommend or not recommend" specific films. The $20 for one year is a bit much to pay for another list of bland descriptions. Nevertheless, a place to begin.

23. The Screen Arts: A Guide to Film and Television Appreciation by Edward Fischer. Good suggestions for forming a film study group, better suggestions for developing discussion questions. Overall, too basic, and too dated to be of more than marginal value.

24. Film in Higher Education and Research: Proceedings of a Conference held at the College of Advanced Technology, Birmingham (England) **in September, 1964**, ed. by Peter D. Groves. Treats the role of film within a university, problems of distribution and use, instructional films, film as a research tool (i.e., high speed and time-lapse photography), and film production. Limited to Britain. Not essential.

25. Film Teaching: Studies in the Teaching of Film within Formal Education by Stuart Hall, et al. Four courses described in detail. Areas involved: liberal arts, teacher training, adult education, "university extramural courses" (outreach?). Dry and drab. Of little help for secondary schools.

26. Using Films: A Handbook for the Program Planner, ed. by James L. Limbacher. Short articles including a shallow and pointless 2½ page essay on "The School Film Program and Its Resources." Very irritating to anyone who knows anything at all about film use. Does suggest possible term paper topics: these essays need to be redone. Condescending, disappointing, and over-priced.

27. Practical Guide to Classroom Media by Dolores and David Linton. How to sell and finance a media program, which media to use; no background necessary. Hard to read (tightly bound, lines crowded together, sans serif type), few illustrations, not a very visual book. Still, contains some good advice. Gives addresses for free information. Explains the significance of current film enthusiasm with greater clarity than some more scholarly works. Worth getting.

28. The Filmviewer's Handbook by Emile G. McAnany and Robert Williams. History of film, vocabulary of film techniques, importance of a film society, survey of film societies, filmographies for 29 directors, extended bibliography. The most interesting chapter offers a sample film series: *High Noon, La Strada, On the Waterfront, Ikuru, The Set-Up, The Diary of a Country Priest* (all ca. 1949–1954). Background, suggestions for presentation, plot summaries are given for each film. No index. Out of print.

29. Films for Young Adults: A Selected List (New York Library Assn. Childrens' and Young Adult Services Section, 1966). Emphasis is on public library program. Offers criteria for selection from 1946, simple instructions, no appreciation of revolution in media and YA's taste, but strong 150-word annotations for older films (*Boundary Lines*, 1948, for example), and some films that aren't so old for which annotations are hard to find (such as *Guiseppina*, 1961). Suggestions offered for use and for related films and books. A supplementary film list, done intelligently.

30. Teaching about the Film by J. M. L. Peters. Attempts to sketch the content of film education and practical possibilities for film-teaching. Alas, since 1961 there have been many changes in the perceptiveness of youth, the needs and skills of the educators, the availability of short films and the standards used for critical evaluation. This volume makes these changes very apparent. Well meant, and good for its time, but now passé.

31. The Motion Picture and the Teaching of English by Marion C. Sheridan, et al. Introduces symbolism, point of view, sound use, etc. Basic materials, but not much related to the teaching of English. Does offer detailed analyses of *Citizen Kane* and *The Grapes of Wrath*, a brilliant appendix, "Film as Sharpener of Perception," and comments by Leonard Bernstein on his music for *On the Waterfront*. Fairly tedious, overall; now superseded.

32. Film Study in Higher Education by David C. Stewart. A report of a conference held at Dartmouth. Literate descriptions of film courses, plus noteworthy speech by Pauline Kael. Her speech alone is strong enough to carry the book. Her comment, "If you think movies can't be killed, you underestimate the power of education" (p.137), is widely used. There's much good sense here. Valid for high schools, too.

Five for Church Persons

33. Landing Rightside Up in TV and Film: An Unusual Experience in Screen Media Readiness for Teachers, Churchmen, and Youth-Serving Agencies by G. William Jones. Supposedly a programmed text, "arranged so that you can select only what is relevant to your special interest." Nonsense. An unfocused, uninformed irritant, with crude cartoons by Charles Cox.

34. Sunday Night at the Movies by G. William Jones. It's hard to believe that the author of this intelligently done introduction is also responsible for entry 33, above. Excellent film lists, "widely used in selecting films for youth groups, prisons and the armed forces" (according to Abingdon).

35. Popcorn and Parable: A New Look at the Movies by Roger Kahle and Robert E. A. Lee. An easy reader for returned missionaries and other church persons who have come home from an extended stay abroad, out of contact with modern media. Covers: How to Have a Film Festival, What Films Communicate, How to Use Reviews, etc. Elementary, but good of its kind.

36. Marquee Ministry: The Movie Theater as Church and Community Forum by Robert G. Konzelman. Pastors who want to transform local theaters into community forums may find this book helpful. For most of us, it's 15 years too late.

37. Environmental Man by William Kuhns (Harper & Row, 1969). An analysis of interactions between human beings and various environments, including films, and how these interactions may lead to new insights into Scripture and theology. Kuhns's film work is superior to his work in theology. Still, this is the most creative book in this set of five.

Hour of Gold, Hour of Lead

It may depend upon the study guide that is used!

A. Films in Depth Series, published by Pflaum, is among the best. Booklets (20–28 pp.) cost 50¢ each. A slipcased set of twelve with an "overview" is $6.95. Titles included:

> *An Occurrence at Owl Creek Bridge* (a study of visual language)
> *No Reason to Stay* (impact of film on education)
> *Overture* and *Overture/Nyitany* (music and film)
> *The Language of Faces* (documentary)
> *Orange and Blue* (editing)
> *Toys* (social comment via films)
> *Time Piece* (symbolism)
> *Night and Fog* (how film manipulates time)
> *Sunday Lark* (comedy)
> *Flavio* (use of still photos)
> *The Little Island* (animation)
> *A Stain on His Conscience* (film criticism).

Pflaum has a chart (see Table A) that shows how each film can be used in film courses. These attractive, inexpensive guides would not intimidate a student. Certain ones, such as *An Occurrence at Owl Creek Bridge* (*OOCB*, hereafter), contain material students should have (in this case, Ambrose Bierce's story, upon which the film was based). These 12 films would be ideal for a topical–technical film course.

B. Themes: Short Films for Discussion by William Kuhns. *Themes* includes (1) rationale for film use, (2) thematic and curriculum indices, (3) addresses of major film distributors, and (4) approximate rental charges. *Themes* is a continuing service; supplements are added about once a year, and notice is sent to each purchaser when a new supplement is ready. Treatment is usually superficial. For example, Kuhns's review of *OOCB* begins: "A Confederate soldier—perhaps a deserter—is about to be hanged." Those of us who have seen the film believe that Peyton Farquhar is a civilian. Bierce is sure of it. Suggestions are given for using each film, but there is little out of the ordinary. Discussion questions are ponderous. "What is the theme of *OOCB*?" However, the looseleaf pages can be given to students who need some priming. The form of the book appears to be its chief virtue.

Table A

	Human Dignity	Culture	Symbolism	Propaganda	Documentary	Editing	Art	Filmmaking	Social Studies	Communi-cations	English	Music	Photog-raphy
An Occurrence At Owl Creek Bridge	●		●			●	●				●		
No Reason to Stay	●	●		●	●	●		●	●				
Overture—Overture Nyitany						●		●	●			●	
The Language of Faces			●	●	●	●		●	●				
Orange and Blue			●	●			●	●					
Toys		●			●		●	●	●	●			
Time Piece	●	●	●				●	●	●				
Night and Fog	●			●	●	●		●					
Sunday Lark	●	●	●						●		●		
Flavio	●			●	●	●		●					●
The Little Island			●	●			●	●			●		
A Stain on His Conscience	●	●	●				●	●					

C. St. Clement's Film Association (423 W. 46 St., New York, N.Y. 10036) publishes some excellent study guides and commentaries, along with a monthly newsletter. For example, *Tora! Tora! Tora!* is seen as the basis for a high school unit on U.S.–Japanese relationships, U.S. foreign policy, Why Pearl Harbor?, propaganda, etc. These matters are treated with care, although briefly, in an attractive 9-page guide. Another example: discussion guide for *Billy Budd* is half as long and takes a totally different approach. Emphasis is on particular characters: Billy, Claggart and Vere, and on the difference between Law and Justice. The Association is worth joining.

D. National Center for Film Study (1307 S. Wabash Ave., Chicago, Ill. 60605) produces study guides as supplements to the *Catholic Film Newsletter*. These guides are among the few that list complete cast and credits. Questions aren't as provocative as those of Summers, but are superior to Kuhns's. For example, "In one of the statements of an interview, Pasolini said that he used 'the equivalent of what novelists call *indirect free speech*: it consists of putting oneself into someone's place and seeing the world with this person's eyes, and at the same time still being oneself.' What does he mean by 'indirect free speech'? Does this help to explain how an atheist can make a religious film?" Production matters and film techniques are also included.

E. Teaching Film Custodians (AV Center, Indiana Univ., Bloomington 47401) should be known in every school. This nonprofit organization provides pedantic guides (for teachers) on films that would otherwise go neglected or underused.

F. Foundation for Change (1619 Broadway, New York, N.Y. 10019) produces free material on certain social issues. It publishes film guides for films it deems guilty of racism, and uses these films as a spring-board to another analysis of racism in our society. For example, FFC's guide to *Tom Sawyer* includes role reversal exercises, historical survey of attitudes toward Indians, suggestions for an open-ended debate, etc. Technically, the guides are well done. They are not concerned with film as film, but with injustice, racism, and related issues.

G. The American Film Institute (JFK Center for the Performing Arts, Washington, D.C. 20566) has some carefully prepared "resources and questions towards a study of" certain feature films (*Ballad of a Soldier, Twelve Angry Men, Loneliness of the Long Distance Runner*, for example). Typically, each includes (1) credits, rental source, information on director, etc., (2) synopsis, (3) a sampling of critical comments, (4) "probes"—quotes, snatches of dialogue, and (5) intelligent discussion questions. What every study guide should be!

H. Consultants in Screen Education (c/o Film and Art, 554 Lexington St., Waltham, Mass. 02154) has guides available for *Lonely Are the Brave, Citizen Kane, The Bridge at Toko-Ri, The Sound of Trumpets, A Hard Day's Night, The Hustler, Nobody Waved Goodbye*, and *Raisin in the Sun*. Each is 50¢ (for 8 pp. 8½ × 5½ in). Excellent brief coverage of director, technical aspects, story, and how to teach the film. Hard to go wrong with these.

I. Screen Studies, Inc. (25 Steadman St., Chelmsford, Mass. 01824) published *The Hero, A Film Study Unit* by David Babcock, in 1968. This includes guides for *Hud, Stalag 17, The Maltese Falcon, All the Way Home*, and *Seven Days in May*. Plot summary, statement of theme, discussion guides and suggested activities are provided for each film. Screen Studies, Inc. probably has published other guides, but their bibliographic control is poor. The only other reference I can find is to *Youth in Contemporary Society, A Film Study Unit*, by Herbert Ostrach.

J. Producers put out guides to their films. I can recommend six:
ACI Films, 35 W. 45 St., New York, N.Y. 10036
Churchill Films, 662 N. Robertson Blvd., Los Angeles, Calif. 90069
Dimension (distributed by Churchill)
Pyramid Films, Box 1048, Santa Monica, Calif. 90406 (the guide for *The Conference* was prepared by Jeffrey Schrank)
Wombat Productions, 77 Tarrytown Rd., White Plains, N.Y. 10607
U.S. agencies such as U.S. Dept. of Commerce

Certainly there are others, and even more certainly, this is an area in which one must exercise extreme caution.

Material available from book publishers is, on the whole, more considered and easier to find and keep track of than the flyers and pamphlets put out, often in a hurry, by film distributors, producers, or societies. However, items of the sort mentioned in this section, along with periodical articles and film notes, do fill a need and should not be slighted. In the final analysis, commercially produced study guides, from whatever source, are no more than secondary stimuli for the development of personal plans to fit a particular situation, here and now. No guide should be appropriated without some sort of modification. No guide removes the need for local creativity. All we can do in (the best) study guides is tell each other what we found working for us.

An Untold Story

An Occurrence at Owl Creek Bridge is treated in many film guides, including:

Lacey (entry 1) pp. 29–47, 53–54, 75

Schrank (entry 3) p. 140; (entry 4) p. 20

Feyen and Wigal (entry 5) pp. 26, 37, 105, 120, 152, 166, 167, 216

Schillaci and Culkin (entry 6) pp. 89–93, 145–146, 151–152, 296

Heyer and Meyer (entry 8) pp. 160–162, 216

Maynard (entry 9) p. 96

Brown (entry 10) pp. 28–29, p. 44

Kuhns and Stanley (entry 12) p. 52

Amelio (entry 17) pp. 27–28

Entry A and B

Thus a film can be the standard by which study guides are measured. Such a comparison was made, in an informal fashion. A detailed analysis, however, lies beyond the scope of this discussion.

APPENDIX 3
A Basic Bibliography
for Film Service
and Use

The primary purpose of this bibliography is to enlarge, extend, and/or explain those portions of the text in which the reader has further interest or need. All those titles mentioned in the text, together with certain other recommended basic volumes and references, are annotated. Entries have been selected by their pertinence to the topic of film service and use and their correspondence with concepts, ideas, and statements made in the text. Although they are a selected group, the books described should serve to answer the majority of questions that might arise in any institution offering film service.

American Film Directors. Stanley Hochman, comp. and ed. New York: Frederick Ungar, 1974. 590 pp.

A source book of film criticism for some 65 film directors. Citing articles, excerpts, comments, etc., from some 300 film critics, the book offers an impressive general summary of the work of each director. Contains filmographies and indexes.

American Library Association Rules for Filing Catalog Cards, 2nd ed. Pauline A. Seely, ed. Chicago: American Library Assn., 1968. 94 pp.

A basic reference for librarians that addresses itself to methods and procedures for the filing of catalog cards.

The American Movies Reference Book: The Sound Era. Paul Michael. Englewood Cliffs, N.J.: Prentice–Hall, 1969. 629 pp. illus.

A large valuable reference book which contains separate sections on history (1929–1967), players (600), films (1,000), directors (50), producers (50), and awards. Profusely illustrated, the book deals with American sound films only.

Application and Operation of Audiovisual Equipment in Education. Fred J. Pula. New York: John Wiley, 1968. 360 pp. illus.

A discussion of the role of audiovisual technology in education is followed by explanations of the operation of projectors and other machines.

The Art of Make-up for Stage and Screen. Cecil Holland. Hollywood, Calif.: Cinematex, 1972. 102 pp. illus.

Lon Chaney provided the introduction to this volume.

The Art of the Film, rev. 2nd ed. Ernest Lindgren. New York: Collier, 1970 340 pp. illus.

An exploration of the art of the cinema which details the mechanics and techniques of editing, sound, image, and other film aesthetics. The contributions to film art by various directors are noted and some attention is given to film criticism.

The Audio-Visual Equipment Directory. National Audio-Visual Assn. Fairfax, Va.: National Audio-Visual Assn., 1954– . illus.

A growing annual which lists over 2,000 AV equipment items from almost 600 manufacturers in its twentieth edition (1974–1975). The machines are described by words, measurements, and pictures, but are *not* evaluated. Much information on related topics is offered in this essential reference book.

Audio-Visual Resource Guide, 9th ed. Nick Abrams, ed. New York: Friendship Press, 1972. 476 pp.

This volume includes evaluations of all types of nonprint media but the emphasis is on films. The reviews are lengthy, informative and most useful. Usually three sections are given—a synopsis, an evaluation, and some suggested uses. Although the material is prepared for use in religious education, the content is transferrable to all other areas which use films.

Audiovisual Equipment Self-Instruction Manual, 2nd ed. Stanton C. Oates. Dubuque, Iowa: Wm. C. Brown Co., 1971. 226 pp. illus.

Offers directions and advice on the operation of audiovisual machines.

Audiovisual Machines. Raymond L. Davidson. Scranton, Pa.: International Text Book Co., 1969. 266 pp. illus.

Deals with the operation of audiovisual equipment.

Audiovisual Market Place: A Multimedia Guide. J. A. Neal, ed. New York: Bowker, 1969–.

A guide to media producers, distributors, film festivals, equipment manufacturers, services, organizations, conventions, reference sources, and review media. Revised and updated annually.

AV Instruction: Technology, Media and Methods, 4th ed. James Brown, Richard Lewis, and Frederick Harcleroad. New York: McGraw–Hill, 1973. 624 pp. illus.

One of the basic texts in the education technology field, it is crammed with essential information about nonprint materials and their use in education.

AV Instructional Technology Manual for Independent Study, 4th ed. James Brown and Richard B. Lewis. New York: McGraw–Hill, 1973. 192 pp. illus.
Offers directions and advice on the operation of audiovisual machines.

(Filmguide to) The Battle of Algiers. Joan Mellen. Bloomington, Ind.: Indiana University Press, 1973. 82 pp.
One of the "Filmguide" series which offers a detailed analysis of the film along with information on the creative personnel involved in its making. There are suggestions for viewing and further study, as well as a bibliography.

Bibliography of Film Librarianship. Sam Kula. London: The Library Assn., 1967. 68 pp.
An annotated bibliography that deals with all aspects of film librarianship— training, administration, services, cooperatives, archives, cataloging, etc.

(Focus on) The Birth of a Nation. Fred Silva, ed. Englewood Cliffs, N.J.: Prentice–Hall, 1971. 184 pp. illus.
One of the "Focus on" series which offers reviews, essays, commentaries, etc., about the controversial film. A plot outline along with cast and credits is included along with an appreciation of director D.W. Griffith.

(Focus on) Blow-Up. Roy Huss, ed. Englewood Cliffs, N.J.: Prentice–Hall, 1971. 171 pp. illus.
One of the "Focus on" series which offers essays, reviews, criticism, etc., of the film along with a synopsis and cast credits. Contains the short story upon which the film was based.

(Focus on) Bonnie and Clyde. John Cawelti, ed. Englewood Cliffs, N.J.: Prentice–Hall, 1972. 176 pp. illus.
A "Focus on" book that offers reviews, essays, etc., on this controversial film. The plot is outlined and a script excerpt is included.

A Bookless Curriculum. Roland G. Brown. Dayton, Ohio: Pflaum, 1972. 136 pp.
Outlines a suggested high school course for nonreaders in which film and television are used instead of books.

The British Film Catalogue 1895–1970. Dennis Gifford. New York: McGraw–Hill, 1973. 967 pp.
This compilation lists over 14,000 films produced in England during the period from 1895 to 1970. The arrangement is chronological and by film title; cast and other credits are noted along with other information such as awards, censor's certificate, story source, etc.

Catalog of Shorts, Selected Features and Serial Films for Film Study. New York: Contemporary Films, 1973. 384 pp. illus.
Contemporary Films is associated with McGraw–Hill and both publish separate film catalogs. The more interesting total collection of films is found in this Contemporary catalog although many of the same films are listed in both. At-

tractive visuals taken from the films give added information about the content, style, etc. The annotations are descriptive rather than evaluative and they vary in length and quality. Occasionally there are critical quotes or a notation of the prizes won by the film. Technical data and credits are given in most cases.

The Celluloid Curriculum. Richard A. Maynard, New York: Hayden, 1971. 276 pp. illus.

An argument for the use of feature and short films in high school and college. Films are related to topics or areas of the English and social studies curriculum.

Church and Cinema: A Way of Viewing Film. James M. Wall. Grand Rapids, Mich.: Eerdmans Publishing, 1971. 135 pp.

Suggestions addressed to religious educators on ways of viewing film. Rather than church against film, the author advocates church with film.

The Cinema as Art. Ralph Stephenson and J. R. Debrix. Baltimore, Md.: Penguin Books, 1965. 268 pp. illus.

The language of film is discussed in depth and detail in this volume. The authors examine the manner in which a director uses the many cinema techniques to isolate what is significant in a particular situation. Much attention is given to the aesthetics of space, time, and sound.

Cinema Booklist. George P. Rehrauer. Metuchen, N.J.: Scarecrow Press, 1972. 473 pp.

An annotated evaluative bibliography of over 1,600 film books taken mostly from the period 1940 to 1970. Film scripts are given individual attention as are film periodicals. Indexed by subject and author.

Cinema Booklist—Supplement One. George P. Rehrauer. Metuchen, N.J.: Scarecrow Press, 1974. 405 pp.

Supplement One continues the work of the original with an additional group of over 900 titles taken mostly from the 1971–1973 period. Cumulative indexes are provided and special attention is paid to film scripts and souvenir books. An index to interviews of over 400 filmmakers is included.

Cinema Eye, Cinema Ear: Some Key Film-Makers of the Sixties. John Russell Taylor. New York: Hill & Wang, 1964. 294 pp.

Analyses of the work of six contemporary directors—Antonioni, Bergman, Bresson, Buñuel, Fellini, and Hitchcock.

(Focus on) Citizen Kane. Ronald Gottesman, ed. Englewood Cliffs, N.J.: Prentice-Hall, 1971. 178 pp. illus.

This "Focus on" book offers a wide sampling of opinion on the classic film with interviews, articles, commentaries, etc., about *Citizen Kane* and its director, Orson Welles. A detailed outline of the film plot and a script excerpt are also provided.

Classics of the Foreign Film: A Pictorial History. Parker Tyler. New York: Citadel, 1962. 253 pp. illus.

With text and more than 400 photographs, this book reviews 75 famous foreign films made between 1919 and 1961.

Classics of the Silent Screen: A Pictorial Treasury. Joe Franklin. New York: Citadel, 1959. 255 pp. illus.

Fifty well-known silent films (1903-1931) are recalled in text and photographs in the first section of this volume. The second part offers picture-text biographies of 75 silent screen personalities.

The College Film Library Collection. Emily Jones, ed. 2 vols. Williamsport, Pa.: Bro-Dart, 1971. 154 pp.

The first volume offers hundreds of EFLA type reviews of 16mm short films arranged by curriculum area or topic. Both a description and evaluation of the film are given. Lists of outstanding feature films and distributors are included along with a subject index. The second volume contains similar information on 8mm films and filmstrips.

A Companion to the Movies: From 1903 to the Present Day. Roy Pickard. New York: Hippocrene Books, 1974. 287 pp. illus.

A reference book that treats more than 1,000 films in some detail. Placed in a genre arrangement—westerns, musicals, comedies, etc.—each group is followed by a collection of mini-biographies of personalities who were identified with that particular genre. Appendixes for cameramen, famous film scores, original scripts, and Academy Awards are added. A name index helps to overcome the subjectivity of certain placements.

The Compleat Guide to Film Study. G. Howard Poteet, ed. Urbana, Ill.: The National Council of Teachers of English, 1972. 242 pp.

The use of film in the various curriculum areas is the theme of this anthology. Different approaches are offered with a filmography, bibliography, and an index.

The Complete Encyclopedia of Popular Music and Jazz 1900-1950. Roger D. Kinkle. 4 vols. New Rochelle, N.Y.: Arlington House, 1974.

A four-volume set covering the period 1900-1950, this reference work on popular music and jazz has much information on films of that period. Volume 1 is a chronological review on a yearly basis of shows, songs, musical films, casts, composers, etc. Volumes 2 and 3 contain biographies of those personalities associated with popular music and jazz in some capacity—performer, composer, arranger, band leader, etc. Four major indexes make up the final volume—song titles, personalities, movie musicals, and Broadway musicals.

Cooperative Film Services in Public Libraries. Patricia Blair Cory and Violet F. Myer. Chicago: American Library Assn., 1956. 127 pp.

A survey of film service as it existed in public libraries in the post-World War II period.

Creative Use of Films in Education. Duane Beeler and Frank McCallister. Chicago, Ill.: Roosevelt University, Labor Education Division, 1968. 86 pp. illus.

A Case Study of an Adult Educational Program for Union Leaders is the subtitle of this useful volume. The text considers training films, documentaries, and

feature films; the philosophy of using film is offered along with suggestions, recommendations, and some sample methodologies.

The Critical Index. John C. Gerlach and Lana Gerlach. New York: Teachers
College Press, 1973. 726 pp.

This bibliography of film articles covers the period from 1946 to 1973 and surveys some 22 periodicals. Generated by a computer, the material in the first portion is arranged under film titles and the names of film personalities, and in the
final section under film topics.

Designing for Visual Aids. Andrew Wright. New York: Van Nostrand Rein-
hold, 1970. 96 pp. illus.

A most useful volume for those who wish to design their own visual aids. Principles, concepts, examples, and advice are offered.

Dialogue with the World: A Modern Approach to the Humanities. Rev.
G. William Jones, ed. Wilmette, Ill.: Films, Inc., 1969. 206 pp. illus.

Individual study guides to 100 feature films are included in this most useful
volume. Although the film selection is limited to those distributed by Films, Inc.,
the classic films represented here are numerous. Offers credits, cast, a photo,
questions, plot outline, etc., on each film.

Directory of Film Libraries in North America. Joan E. Clark, ed. New
York: Film Library Information Council, 1971. 87 pp.

A listing of over 1,800 film libraries.

**A Directory of 16mm Film Collections in Colleges and Universities in
the United States.** Allan Mirwis. Bloomington, Ind.: Indiana University,
1972. 74 pp.

A listing of the colleges and universities located in the United States which
maintain film collections. The data is arranged by states, and those institutions
which rent to out-of-state users are noted.

Discovery in Film. Robert Heyer and Anthony Meyer. New York: Association
Press, 1969. 220 pp. illus.

This fine volume deals with the use of short films in discussion situations with
teenagers and adults. Films are divided into five categories, and comment, outline, questions, etc., are given for each film. Illustrations are impressive and several appendixes are included. *Discovery in Film, Book Two* (1973) continues
the work of the original volume.

Educational Film Guide, 11th ed. Frederic A. Krahn, ed. New York: H. W.
Wilson, 1953. 1,037 pp.

Begun in 1936, this was an early attempt to organize 11,000 educational films.
Supplements for 1954–1958 and 1959–1962 were issued after which publication
of the guide ceased.

Educational Films: Writing, Directing, and Producing for Classroom, Television, and Industry. Lewis Herman. New York: Crown, 1966. 338 pp.

The subtitle accurately describes the concern of this volume. Written with clarity and conciseness, the book offers both information and instruction.

Educational Media Index. The Educational Media Council, comp. 14 vols. New York: McGraw–Hill, 1964.

A misguided project consisting of 14 volumes which attempted to cover the entire field of nonprint materials. Its faults exceeded its virtues and it was discontinued after one edition.

Educational Media Organizations Directory. DCM Associates. New York: EFLA, 1974. 88 pp.

Describes 35 organizations by (1) personnel, (2) activities and/or services and/or periodicals, (3) permanent committees and/or task forces, (4) aims and/ or purposes and/or objectives, (5) membership and/or requirements.

Educational Media Yearbook. James W. Brown, ed. New York: Bowker, 1973– .

This annual publication contains a collection of articles on media and fine sections on organizations, foundations, federal granting agencies, and multimedia resources.

Educational Motion Pictures and Libraries. Gerald D. McDonald. Chicago: American Library Assn., 1942. 184 pp.

A pioneer survey and review of film service in libraries during the forties.

Educator's Guide to Free Films. Mary F. Horkheimer and John W. Diffor, comps. Randolph, Wis.: Educators Progress Service, 1940– .

A listing of more than 5,000 free films, this volume is revised and updated annually. The 36th edition is scheduled for 1976.

8mm Film Directory. Grace Ann Kone, comp. and ed. New York: Educational Film Library Assn., 1969. 532 pp.

Covers the 8mm film field (loops, reels, cartridges, silent, sound, regular-8, Super-8) with attention given to films in all these formats. The films are annotated, but not evaluated.

8mm Film for Adult Audiences. Geoffrey Bell. New York: (UNESCO) Unipub., 1968. 40 pp.

A report dealing with the use of 8mm film in training and in adult education. International in its coverage, the book examines the potential of 8mm film as a significant medium of instruction.

Elements of Film, 2nd ed. Lee R. Bobker. New York: Harcourt Brace Jovanovich, 1974. 267 pp. illus.

A discussion of the technical and aesthetic elements of the film medium. Attention is given to the roles of the director and the actor in the creative process. The work of some contemporary directors is discussed and a final section explores the function of film criticism.

Exploring the Film. William Kuhns and Robert Stanley. Dayton, Ohio: Pflaum, 1968. 190 pp. illus.

An excellent popular textbook on film study that has a clear, entertaining text and many attractive illustrations. Its appeal is to an audience that ranges from young adolescents to adults.

Faces, Forms, Films: The Artistry of Lon Chaney. Robert G. Anderson. New York: Barnes, 1971. 240 pp. illus.

After the short biography of Lon Chaney which opens this volume, much descriptive text and illustration is devoted to an analysis of his artistry—the makeup and character of his famous screen creations.

Feature Films on 8mm and 16mm. James L. Limbacher. New York: Bowker, 1974. 400 pp.

The fourth edition of this directory lists more than 15,000 feature films, giving the usual data about each—time, color, director, year, etc. Of major importance here is the rental-distributor information which, though incomplete, is a starting point. An index of directors with their films is included in this latest edition.

Film and Education: A Symposium on the Role of Film in the Field of Education. Godfrey Elliott, ed. New York: Philosophical Library, 1948. 597 pp.

An early anthology which deals with the nature and use of the educational film in the United States. Administrative problems and practices are discussed and some attention is given to educational film use in other countries.

Film and Television in Education for Teaching: A Report of a Joint Working Party of the Association of Teachers in Colleges and Departments of Education and the British Film Institute. London: British Film Institute, Undated. 66 pp.

An exploration of ways and means of introducing the study of film and television into teacher training courses and institutions. Film as a main course of study, a general course, and a curriculum course are some of the possibilities presented.

(Focus on) Film and Theatre. James Hurt, ed. Englewood Cliffs, N.J.: Prentice–Hall, 1974. 188 pp. illus.

A fine anthology which divides its articles into a historical survey and a collection of statements from artists who have worked in both media.

Film Cataloguing Rules. Film Production Librarians Group, Cataloguing Committee. London: Assn. of Special Libraries and Information Bureau, 1963. 71 pp. illus.

Another example of cataloging rules, this time from a London group specializing in film library activities. Contains examples, definitions, abbreviations, etc.

Film Evaluation Guide. New York: Educational Film Library Assn., 1965, 1968, 1972.

There are three volumes thus far in this series of evaluations of short films. The first book covers the period 1946–1964, while the first supplement handles 1965–1967 and the second covers 1967–1971. Each listing contains subject area, running time, release date, distributor, age level, synopsis, possible audiences, cost, technical rating, critical comment, and a final overall rating.

Evaluations tend to be somewhat "kind" and it must be noted that only a selected rather small percentage of all short films is reviewed. The three volumes cover about 7,000 films which is only a fraction of 24 years of short film production. Nevertheless, it is a quality reference and an essential for anyone who deals with short films constantly.

Film Evaluation—Why and How. Susan C. Zeitlan, ed. New York: Educational Film Library Assn., 1963. 32 pp.

A report on the EFLA Workshop held January 24–25, 1963 in Chicago, Illinois. The purpose of the workshop was a concentrated study of the film evaluation process.

The Film Experience—Elements of Motion Picture Art. Roy Huss and Norman Silverstein. New York: Dell, 1968. 172 pp. illus.

This volume offers well-written and illustrated descriptions of the principles and techniques of filmmaking. Continuity, visual and structural rhythm, imagery, tone, point of view, and theme are some of the major topics considered.

Film Form and **The Film Sense.** Sergei Eisenstein. New York: World Publishing Co., 1957 (1949, 1942). 272 pp., 296 pp. illus.

A double volume containing the most famous statements on the aesthetics of film. The reading is often difficult, but always rewarding.

The Film Idea. Stanley J. Solomon. New York: Harcourt Brace Jovanovich, 1972. 403 pp. illus.

The nature of the narrative film is explored in this recent book on the aesthetics of the film medium. Its development is traced from Edwin S. Porter to Ingmar Bergman, and some theories about film aesthetics are offered.

The Film in Education. Andrew Buchanan. London: Phoenix House, 1951. 256 pp. illus.

Deals with the history and development of the educational film in England.

Film in Higher Education and Research. Peter D. Groves, ed. New York: Pergamon Press, 1966. 332 pp. illus.

A report of a conference held in England in 1964 which considered the use of film in colleges and universities.

Film in the Classroom: Why Use It, How to Use It. Ralph J. Amelio. Dayton, Ohio: Pflaum, 1971. 208 pp. illus.

An explanation of an experimental film course designed for high school students. Units of study, organization, operation, and evaluation are considered.

The Film Index: Film as Art. Harold Leonard, ed. New York: Arno, 1966, (1941). 723 pp. illus.

A massive bibliography of film literature that covers the first 40 years of film history. More than 8,500 entries are well indexed.

Film Library Techniques: Principles of Administration. Helen P. Harrison. New York: Hastings House, 1973. 277 pp. illus.

This book concentrates on the administration of film libraries of all types—newsfilm, business, research, etc. Problems such as staffing, layout, planning, and economics are discussed, and attention is given to matters of cataloging, selection, handling, preservation, and copyright.

Film Makers on Film Making. Harry M. Geduld, ed. Bloomington, Ind.: Indiana University Press, 1967. 302 pp.

An anthology of excerpts written by 30 famous directors on the art and craft of filmmaking.

Film Music: From Violins to Video. James L. Limbacher. Metuchen, N.J.: Scarecrow, 1974. 835 pp.

A collection of articles, lists, and indexes all dealing with film music. Motion pictures with original scores are noted as are the composers and recordings made of these film scores.

Film News Omnibus. Rohama Lee, ed. vol. 1. New York: Film News, 1973. 270 pp. illus.

A collection of reviews of features and short films taken from past issues of *Film News* as far back as 1955.

Film Preservation: A Report of the Preservation Committee of the International Federation of Film Archives. Herbert Volkmann. London: The British Film Institute, 1965. 60 pp. illus.

Translated from the German language, this report considers film properties, magnetic tapes, storage problems, storage conditions, buildings, procedures, and film restoration. Qualifications for personnel concerned with film preservation are suggested, and a bibliography is included.

The Film Programmer's Guide to 16mm Rentals. Albany, Calif.: Reel Research, 1973. 164 pp.

This guide to film rentals lists 8,000 film titles—features, short films, and documentaries—along with selected information about each. For many films several distributors are noted.

Film Review Index See **International Index to Multi-Media Information**

The Film Sense See **Film Form** and **The Film Sense.**

Film Sneaks Annual. James L. Limbacher, ed. Ann Arbor, Mich.: Pierian Press, 1972. 121 pp.

This guide to 4,500 short films cumulates the ratings given in the previous seven years by evaluators from 40 major libraries in the United States. A typical entry indicates the title, distributor, and the number of evaluators who rated the films from excellent to poor. For some films, as few as two or three evaluations are noted, while for others the number approaches 20. (Short sections of *Film Sneaks* appear occasionally in *Film Library Quarterly*.)

Film—Space, Time, Light and Sound. Lincoln F. Johnson. New York: Holt, Rinehart & Winston, 1974. 340 pp. illus.

Not only does this volume deal with the aesthetics mentioned in its title, but it considers much more. Illustrations, a filmography, a bibliography, a glossary, an index, and notes support discussions on continuity, tense, structure, genre, filmmakers, and other film aesthetics.

Film Study—A Resource Guide. Frank Manchel. Cranbury, N.J.: Fairleigh Dickinson University Press, 1973. 422 pp.

A comprehensive bibliography and filmography arranged by chapters or topics pertinent to film study. Contains many helpful appendixes and indexes.

Film Study in Higher Education. David C. Stewart, ed. Washington, D.C.: American Council on Education, 1966. 174 pp. illus.

This anthology discusses the study of film as a contemporary art in institutions of higher education. Divergent plans and opinions are offered and the many appendixes are most useful. The book also has implication for the secondary school.

Film Teaching. Stuart Hall, Roy Knight, Albert Hunt, and Alan Lovell. Edited by Paddy Whannel and Peter Harcourt. London: British Film Institute, 1968. 107 pp. illus.

A description of film courses given in England in four areas of education—liberal studies, teacher training, adult education, and university extramural courses.

Film Technique and Film Acting, rev. and enlarged ed. V. I. Pudovkin. London: Vision, 1958. 388 pp. illus.

Two very famous statements on cinema theory and practice written by the famous Russian director who often played roles in his own films and those of others.

Film: The Creative Eye. David A. Sohn. Dayton, Ohio: Pflaum, 1970. 176 pp. illus.

A detailed discussion of seventeen short films to be used in a program for developing sensory awareness and increasing the perception of our environment.

Film Theory and Criticism. Gerald Mast and Marshall Cohen, eds. New York: Oxford University Press, 1974. 639 pp. illus.

A good collection of 54 articles dealing with film theory and criticism. Author representation is impressive and the book provides a solid introduction to film aesthetics.

Film Utilization Catalog. New York: Learning Corporation of America, 1973. 88 pp. illus.

A free catalog which offers study guides to 30 short films distributed by the publisher. Other short films are discussed.

Film World—A Guide to Cinema. Ivor Montagu. Baltimore, Md.: Penguin Books, 1964. 327 pp. illus.

In this volume, the nature of film is explored from four viewpoints—as a science, as art, as a commodity, and as a vehicle. Film history, film as compared to other arts, aesthetics, and the effect of business and finance on the development of the film medium are considered.

The Filmgoer's Companion, 4th ed. Leslie Halliwell. New York: Hill and Wang, 1974. 873 pp. illus.

Accurate information is offered on film personalities, topics, titles, etc., in this basic film reference which is revised and enlarged at irregular intervals. This latest edition offers over 10,000 entries and almost 500 illustrations.

Films by and/or about Women 1972. Berkeley, Calif.: Women's History Research Center, 1972. 72 pp.

A directory of films, filmmakers, and distributors that is concerned with films by or about women. Films are fully annotated under various categories—marriage, career, child care, etc.—and there is a section devoted to female filmmakers.

Films Deliver. Anthony Schillaci and John M. Culkin, eds. New York: Citation Press, 1970. 348 pp. illus.

An anthology of articles designed to encourage and improve film study and use in secondary schools. Filmographies, bibliographies, lists, etc., all contribute to the book's value.

Films for Children: A Selected List, 3rd ed. New York Library Assn. (Children's and Young Adult Services Section). New York: New York Library Assn., 1972. 32 pp.

A filmography of short films suggested for three possible audiences: four to eight years (P), nine to eleven years (I), and twelve to fourteen years (U).

Films for Libraries. American Library Assn. (Audio-Visual Committee). Chicago: American Library Assn., 1962. 81 pp.

An annotated filmography of short films recommended for public library use with children. In addition to the description and evaluation, technical and distributor information is given.

Films for Religious Education. Patrick J. McCaffrey. Notre Dame, Ind.: Fides Publishing, 1967. 106 pp. illus.

A collection of study guides for 72 short films designed for use in religious education. The approach is general and the material is well suited to use in any situation. *See also* the second volume, *A Guide to Short Films for Religious Education II.*

Films for Young Adults, rev. ed. New York Library Assn. New York: Educational Film Library Assn., 1970. 54 pp.

An annotated filmography of short films recommended for public library use with young adults. In addition to the description and evaluation, technical and distributor information is given.

Films in Children's Programs. Wisconsin Library Assn. (Film Committee of the Children's and Young People's Services Section). Madison, Wis.: Wisconsin Library Assn., 1972. 39 pp.
A filmography of 100 recommended films for children in grades three to six.

Films in Depth. Paul A. Schreivogel. 12 booklets. Dayton, Ohio: Pflaum, 1969–1970.
A boxed collection of 12 booklets, each of which is a detailed study guide to a classic short film. One additional booklet provides an introduction and an overview. (Booklets are also available individually from the publisher.)

Films Incorporated—1972–1973. Wilmette, Ill.: Films, Inc., 1972. 192 pp. illus.
In addition to publishing some fine supplemental catalogs at irregular intervals, Films, Inc. issues a yearly catalog which is also quite good. Emphasizing the feature films that the company distributes, the book offers information, visuals, data, and acceptable annotations.

Films Kids Like. Susan Rice, ed. Chicago: American Library Assn., 1973. 128 pp. illus.
An annotated filmography of 229 short films recommended for children from ages three to twelve years.

The Films of Alfred Hitchcock. George Perry. New York: Dutton/Vista, 1965. 160 pp. illus.
An attractive book in which the films and career of Alfred Hitchcock (up to 1964) are reviewed with text and illustrations.

Films—Too Good for Words. Salvatore J. Parlato, Jr. New York: Bowker, 1973. 192 pp.
A directory to nearly 1,000 nonnarrated films which offers description, but no evaluation. Several indexes are included to aid the user.

The Filmviewer's Handbook. Emile McAnany and Robert Williams. Paramus, N.J.: Paulist Press, 1965. 208 pp.
A collection of short chapters on various aspects of film study and use in schools, libraries, churches, etc. Film history, film language, film societies, film series, directors, and other related topics are considered.

The First Whole Library Catalog. The Films, Inc. staff. Wilmette, Ill.: Films, Inc., 1973. 96 pp. illus.
An unusual film catalog that offers information, advice, and suggestions on all aspects of film use and service. It is the first major company catalog to offer numerous feature films for lease.

(Filmguide to) The General. E. Rubinstein. Bloomington, Ind.: Indiana University Press, 1973. 96 pp. illus.
This title in the "Filmguide" series considers both *The General* and its director/star, Buster Keaton. Detailed analyses of the film and Keaton's comedy techniques are offered along with biographical data.

(Filmguide to) The Grapes of Wrath. Warren French. Bloomington, Ind.: Indiana University Press, 1973. 96 pp. illus.

A "Filmguide" title, this book painstakingly compares the film and the novel. In addition, much material about director John Ford is included along with an impressive annotated bibliography.

The Great Movies. William Bayer. New York: Grosset and Dunlap, 1973. 252 pp. illus.

Sixty selected films are divided into 12 genre categories and discussed in detail in this volume. A collection of fine visuals supports the interesting text.

Grierson on Documentary, rev. ed. Forsyth Hardy, ed. Los Angeles: University of California Press, 1966. 411 pp. illus.

A collection of essays which consider the philosophies and social attitudes of the documentary filmmaker. The background of the documentary movement, its founding in Britain, and its development in Canada are disucssed. This is an essential volume written by "the father of the documentary film" and offering the best information and thought on this film form.

A Guide to Short Films for Religious Education II. Patrick J. McCaffrey. Notre Dame, Ind.: Fides Publishing, 1968. 108 pp. illus.

A collection of study guides for 50 short films designed for use in religious education. The approach is general and the material is well suited for use in any situation. *See also* the first volume, *Films for Religious Education.*

Guidelines for Audiovisual Materials and Services for Public Libraries. Public Library Assn. Chicago: American Library Assn., 1970. 33 pp.

Discusses personnel, services, space, equipment, material storage, etc., for public libraries serving a population of 150,000 or more.

Guides to Newer Educational Media. Margaret F. Rufsvold and Carolyn Guss. Chicago: American Library Assn., 1973. 126 pp. illus.

A collection of catalogs, lists, bibliographies, services, periodicals, etc., which offer information on nonprint media. Films are treated extensively in many of the entries.

A Half Century of American Film. Wilmette, Ill.: Films, Inc., n.d. 160 pp. illus.

In this catalog, 500 feature films are grouped into five decades ending with the sixties. Cast, production personnel, technical data, a synopsis, and critical excerpts are given for each film. Illustrations are murky, but the informational text is excellent.

A Handbook of Canadian Film. Eleanor Beattie. Toronto: Peter Martin Associates, Ltd. 1973. 280 pp. illus.

A kind of dictionary that tries to bring together all kinds of information about film and filmmaking in Canada. Its 27 chapters consider such topics as film societies, film study, free films, children's films, festivals, archives, film catalogues, periodicals, professional associations, etc.

(Filmguide to) Henry V. Harry M. Geduld, ed. Bloomington, Ind.: Indiana University Press, 1973. 82 pp. illus.

This book in the "Filmguide" series provides information and detailed analysis of *Henry V.* An outline of the film, cast, credits, and a filmography for director/star Laurence Olivier are included.

A History of Instructional Technology. Paul Saettler. New York: McGraw–Hill, 1968. 399 pp. illus.

Includes a detailed explanation of instructional technology along with theoretical and methodological foundations and an account of historical development. Latter sections are devoted to instructional media research.

Hitchcock. François Truffaut. New York: Simon & Schuster, 1967. 256 pp. illus.

The extended interview of Alfred Hitchcock by French film director François Truffaut from which the reader learns much about both men.

How to Organize and Run a Film Society. Janet Weiner. New York: Collier, 1973. 210 pp. illus.

Contains good chapters on organization of a society, selection of films, publicity, and programming. Other sections are either redundant or unnecessary.

Ideas on Film. Cecile Starr, ed. New York: Funk and Wagnalls, 1951. 251 pp.

An early anthology on film use that has some material which is still pertinent. Much of the data and information and the film review section are of historical interest at this time.

Index to Instructional Media Catalogs. Olga S. Weber, ed. New York: Bowker, 1974. 272 pp.

Some 30,000 items from 630 publishers or producers are identified in this reference volume. Film catalogs appear throughout the many categories and headings. A subject index classifies instructional materials by media, grade level, and methodology and identifies their producers and publishers. A product and services index alphabetically lists over 100 types of equipment and services with the names of the companies providing each. A directory of represented companies is also included.

Index to 16mm Educational Films, 4th ed. The National Information Center for Educational Media (NICEM). 2 vols. Los Angeles, Calif.: NICEM, University of Southern California, 1973.

The fourth edition of this work describes 70,000 short films, giving all the usual data—running time, release date, distributor, etc. The annotations are taken mostly from producer catalogs and it must be stressed that *no* evaluation of the film is made. All types of short films are covered, but the listing is still a selective one.

It is not unusual to search for a film here and not find it. The index is generated via a computer which can only retrieve those titles placed within it. It is, nevertheless, a good information source for the short film.

The Influence of the Cinema on Children and Adolescents. Department of Mass Communications. New York: UNESCO, 1961. 106 pp.

An international bibliography that considers such topics as attitudes, analysis of content, influence, after-effect, and educational effect.

The Information Film. Gloria Waldron. New York: Columbia University Press, 1949. 281 pp.

A study made in the late forties which surveyed the use of film in some 60 public libraries, this volume was one of the "Public Library Inquiry Reports." The purpose of the reports was to examine the basic issues and problems facing the public library at that time.

Instructional Film Research 1918–1950 (Rapid Mass Learning). Charles Hoban and Edward Van Ormer. New York: Arno Press, 1970 (1950).

A reprint of the summary and evaluation of three decades of research on instructional film. Done originally at Pennsylvania State University and sponsored by the Army and the Navy.

The International Encyclopedia of Film. Roger Manvell and Lewis Jacobs. New York: Crown, 1972. 574 pp. illus.

An essential basic reference book with 1,280 entries treating film terminology, individual biographies, and national cinemas. A chronological outline of film history, a lengthy bibliography, and several indexes complete the book. It is profusely illustrated with both black-and-white and color photographs.

International Index to Film Periodicals 1972. Karen Jones, ed. New York: Bowker, 1973. 344 pp.

Some 7,000 entries which appeared in some 60 film periodicals during 1972 are indexed in this book. Entries are annotated and classified under 11 major headings. *International Index to Film Periodicals 1973* continues the work of the original volume and was edited by Michael Moulds.

International Index to Multi-Media Information. Wesley A. Doak, ed. Pasadena, Calif.: Audio-Visual Associates, 1965– .

This annual index, which prior to 1973 was the *Film Review Index*, is published in quarterly cumulative installments. The fourth issue is the compilation for the complete year. More than 60 publications are indexed, and in addition to films, a range of nonbook media such as slides, transparencies, filmstrips, games, and kits is considered.

Media are first arranged alphabetically by title, a second listing is by subject, and a final section gives distributor information. In the case of films, information is given about the format (16mm, 8mm, feature, videotape, etc.), the type of review entry (review, annotation, or mention), and the reviewing publication (volume, issue, date, page, reviewer's name, and a very short excerpt), but there is no indication of any rating or evaluation by the reviewers. (A compilation for 1970–1972 is available directly from R. R. Bowker Company.)

International Motion Picture Almanac. Charles S. Aaronson, ed. New
York: Quigley Publication Co., 1928–
An essential reference book published yearly which contains thousands of
short biographies, feature film lists, award and poll winners, data on distributor,
exhibition, and production, etc. The 46th edition is scheduled for 1975.

Landing Rightside-Up in TV and Film. G. William Jones. Nashville,
Tenn.: Abingdon Press, 1973. 128 pp. illus.
A programmed approach along with some cartoon illustrations is used in this
discussion of the problems of communicating with young people via film and television.

Leading Film Discussions, 3rd ed. Madeline S. Friedlander. New York: The
League of Women Voters of the City of New York, 1972. 42 pp.
Deals with selecting, securing, and using films in effective programs. How to
discuss films and how to train leaders are among other topics considered.

Library of Congress Catalog: Motion Pictures and Filmstrips. Washington, D.C.: Library of Congress, 1953–
Published quarterly with annual and quinquennial cumulations, these volumes list Library of Congress catalog cards issued for all educational and instructional films released in the United States and Canada. The volumes offer information, but no evaluation. Published cumulation volumes include: Volume 24
(1948–1952); Volume 28 (1953–1957); Volumes 53 and 54 (1958–1962); and
Volumes 71 and 72 (1963–1967). For other volumes published by the federal
government, see *Motion Pictures.*

The Liveliest Art: A Panoramic History of the Movies. Arthur Knight.
New York: Macmillan, 1957. 352 pp. illus.
This general film history takes the reader only up to the mid-fifties. Its style
and comprehensiveness have made it one of the most popular film books ever
written.

A Manual for Evaluators of Films and Filmstrips. Mary L. Allison, Emily
S. Jones and Edward T. Schofield. Paris: UNESCO, 1956. 23 pp.
An early guide to film evaluation prepared under EFLA's auspices and pub-
lished by UNESCO.

Manual on Film Evaluation. Emily S. Jones. New York: Educational Film
Library Assn., 1974. 32 pp.
Advice and direction on the evaluation of films.

**Marquee Ministry: The Movie Theater as Church and Community Fo-
rum.** Robert G. Konzelman. New York: Harper & Row, 1972. 128 pp. illus.
An argument for using commercial films in religious teaching and for cooperating with local theater owners in using their buildings for this purpose.

Mass Communication: A Sociological Perspective. Charles R. Wright.
New York: Random House, 1959. 124 pp.
A basic book which explains a complex subject in a clear provocative text. Discusses the functions of mass communication, the mass audience, etc.

Media for Christian Formation. William A. Dalglish, ed. Dayton, Ohio:
Pflaum, 1969. 393 pp. illus.
Hundreds of reviews of nonprint media appear in this resource book designed
for use in religious education. The evaluations of the films have pertinence for
professionals in all fields.

Media in Value Education: A Critical Guide. Jeffrey Schrank. Chicago:
Argus Communications, 1970. 168 pp.
The use of nonprint media in education is the theme of this volume in which
many short films are described and recommended.

Media Two for Christian Formation. William A. Dalglish, ed. Dayton,
Ohio: Pflaum, 1971. 502 pp. illus.
A volume which supplements and complements the original *Media for Christian Formation*, this book contains over 400 reviews of nonprint media. The film
reviews are most impressive and have pertinence for professionals in all fields.

The Media Works. Joan Valdes and Jeanne Crow. Dayton, Ohio: Pflaum,
1973. 282 pp. illus.
Mass media such as films, television, newspapers, radio, magazines, etc., are
examined in this volume and many suggestions are offered for their inclusion in
the curriculum of the secondary school.

Mediaware—Selection, Operation and Maintenance. Raymond Wyman.
Dubuque, Iowa: Wm. C. Brown Co., 1969. 188 pp. illus.
Information and suggestions are offered on the selection, operation, and main-
tenance of audiovisual machinery.

The Motion Picture and the Teaching of English. Marion C. Sheridan,
Harold H. Owen, Jr., Ken Macrorie, and Fred Marcus. New York: Apple-
ton–Century–Crofts, 1965. 168 pp.
An early attempt to encourage the use of film in English courses in secondary
schools. Although the authors were well-intentioned, the volume reveals an
overly cautious approach and contains many factual errors.

**Motion Picture Directors: A Bibliography of Magazine and Periodical
Articles, 1900–1972.** Mel Schuster. Metuchen, N.J.: Scarecrow Press, 1973.
418 pp. illus.
An essential bibliography which lists articles about film directors appearing in
some 340 periodicals from 1900 to 1972. The material is arranged for user convenience and the volume will save any film researcher many hours of searching.

**Motion Picture Performers —A Bibliography of Magazine and Period-
ical Articles, 1900–1969.** Mel Schuster. Metuchen, N.J.: Scarecrow Press,
1971. 702 pp.

An essential bibliography which lists articles about film performers contained in some 300 periodicals which appeared between 1900 and 1969. Performers are listed alphabetically with the articles arranged chronologically beneath each name by year.

Motion Pictures 1894-1912. Howard Lamarr Walls. Washington, D.C.: Government Printing Office, 1953. 92 pp.
———**1912-1939.** 1951. 1256 pp.
———**1940-1949.** 1953. 599 pp.
———**1950-1959.** 1960. 494 pp.
———**1960-1969.** 1971. 744 pp.

These volumes are based on the applications submitted to the Copyright Office. The data and the format in which they are presented vary from volume to volume, but the books are invaluable in locating information that is not available elsewhere. (For other volumes published by the federal government, see *Library of Congress Catalog: Motion Pictures and Filmstrips.*)

Movies and Morals. Anthony Schillaci. Notre Dame, Ind.: Fides, 1970. 181 pp.

An argument for the knowledgeable use of films which offers suggestions on workshops, film series, etc.

Movies for Kids. Edith Zornow and Ruth M. Goldstein. New York: Avon, 1973. 224 pp. illus.

An annotated filmography of 125 feature films and 75 short films recommended for children ages nine to thirteen.

Movies on TV, 6th ed. Steven H. Scheuer, ed. New York: Bantam Books, 1971. 408 pp.

Over 8,000 feature films which are available for showing on television are described in this volume which is updated at frequent intervals. A short synopsis, rating, a few cast names, year of release, etc., are given for each.

Movies with a Purpose. Kodak editors. Rochester, N.Y.: Eastman Kodak, 1972. 28 pp. illus.

A guide to planning and producing Super-8mm movies for classroom use.

The Moving Image. Robert Gessner. New York: Dutton, 1968. 444 pp. illus.

An attempt to explain and improve cinematic literacy, this volume emphasizes the film script as the key element in any film. Excerpts from many film scripts are included and the supporting appendixes are most helpful.

A Multi-Media Approach to Children's Literature. Ellin Greene and Madalynne Schoenfeld. Chicago: American Library Assn., 1972. 262 pp.

A selective list of films, filmstrips, and recordings based on children's books. Some 175 films are listed for the total of 425 books considered.

Multi-Media Reviews Index. Ann Arbor, Mich.: Pierian Press, 1970–

This annual index to reviews of nonprint media includes film, along with records, tapes, games, etc. Several hundred periodicals are indexed and the entry information offers some evaluation data in the form of a plus (+), minus (–), or asterisk (*) symbol placed before each review citation.

The index is a particularly essential reference source for any institution which uses film. A typical film entry gives the title, producer, year of release, gauge, running time, sound or silent, color or black and white, and a detailed listing of reviews, e.g., + Film News, V.30, N.4, Sept. '73, p. 20.

In addition to the annual volume, the index is available in quarterly cumulations, and abbreviated sections of the index appear each month in *Audiovisual Instruction*, the journal of the Association for Educational Communications and Technology (AECT), 1201 16 St., N.W., Washington, D.C. 20036. Annual volumes available at this writing are: Volume 1 (1970) 10,000 reviews from 70 journals; Volume 2 (1971) 20,000 reviews from 120 journals; Volume 3 (1972) 30,000 reviews from 214 journals; Cumulative Subject Indexes (1970–1972); and Volume 4 (1973) 40,000 reviews from 300 journals.

Museum Media. Paul Wasserman and Esther Herman, eds. Detroit: Gale Research, 1974. 455 pp.

A directory and index of publications and audiovisuals available from United States and Canadian museums. Films are included along with filmstrips, slides, reproductions, etc. A subject index, a geographic index, and a title-keyword index are provided.

Need Johnny Read? Frederick Goldman and Linda R. Burnett. Dayton, Ohio: Pflaum, 1971. 238 pp. illus.

This book challenges the dominance of print materials in the educational systems of America and suggests courses, methods, and activities which support visual literacy.

The New Film Index. Richard Dwyer McCann and Edward S. Perry, New York: E. P. Dutton, 1975. 522 pp.

This bibliography dealing solely with magazine articles in English from 1930 to 1970 is a most valuable reference. It does, however, differ considerably from its namesake, *The Film Index*.

A New Pictorial History of the Talkies. Daniel Blum and John Kobal. New York: G. P. Putnam's, 1973. 392 pp. illus.

The history of talking pictures (mostly American) is presented in this classic volume which consists of thousands of photographs and some brief connecting narrative.

The New York Times Directory of the Film. Arno/Random House, 1971 1,243 pp. illus.

A huge essential reference volume derived from the six-volume edition of the *New York Times Reviews*. Contains not only 500 reviews of important films from 1913 to 1960, but an index of film personalities and their work, a list of awards, and 2,000 small photographs.

The New York Times Guide to Movies on TV. Howard Thompson, ed. Chicago: Quadrangle, 1970. 225 pp. illus.

About 2,000 illustrated reviews of feature films which are available for showing on television. The period covered is 1950–1968 and each review is descriptive and critical. The majority of these films are also available for 16mm rental.

Non Book Materials: The Organization of Integrated Collections. Jean Riddle Weihs, Shirley Lewis, and Janet MacDonald. Ottawa: Canadian Library Assn., 1973. 107 pp.

Rules and suggestions for cataloging nonprint materials. The book is a result of the cooperative efforts of several concerned professional organizations.

Non-Theatrical Film Distributors: Sales–Service–Policies. Carol A. Emmens, comp. New York: EFLA, 1974. 66 pp.

Describes 137 selected film distributors as to type of films, sales-preview policy, and replacement-discount policy.

Novels into Film. George Bluestone. Berkeley, Calif.: University of California Press, 1961. 237 pp.

A classic volume about the translation of novels into motion pictures. Using six titles, the author makes detailed analyses of the two forms and finds they are autonomous.

(From Fiction to Film) An Occurrence at Owl Creek Bridge. Gerald R. Barrett, Thomas L. Erskine. Encino, Calif.: Dickenson Publishing, 1973. 216 pp. illus.

A study of the translation of Ambrose Bierce's short story into film terms. The short story and the scripts of the two short films it inspired are presented along with critical reviews of each.

101 Films for Character Growth. Jane Cushing. Notre Dame, Ind.: Fides, 1969. 110 pp.

A collection of more than 100 study guides for short films which can be used profitably in many situations and settings.

Operating Audiovisual Equipment, 2nd ed. Sidney Eboch and George W. Cochern. San Francisco: Chandler Publishing Co., 1968. 75 pp. illus.

The operation, care, and maintenance of audiovisual machines is discussed in this volume.

Our Modern Art: The Movies. Ernest Callenbach. Chicago, Ill.: Center for the Study of Liberal Education for Adults, 1955. 116 pp.

The use of films in adult education is the concern of this volume. Programs using feature films are emphasized but there are some examples dealing with the use of short films.

Our Movie-Made Children. Henry James Forman. New York: Macmillan, 1933. 288 pp.

A popularized summary of the 12 independent research investigations that were sponsored by the Payne Fund. From 1929 to 1933 studies were made concerning motion pictures and their effect on children and youth. Topics included morality, getting ideas, content, attendance, emotional response, social attitudes, character development, sleep, conduct, delinquency, and crime.

(Filmguide to) La Passion de Jeanne d'Arc. David Bordwell. Bloomington, Ind.: Indiana University Press, 1973. 83 pp. illus.
Another "Filmguide" title, this book describes and analyzes the famous silent film. In addition, much attention is given to director Carl Dreyer and his film-making techniques.

Performing Arts—Books in Print. Ralph Newman Schoolcraft. New York: Drama Book Specialists, 1973. 761 pp.
An updating of *Theatre Books in Print*, this bibliography has a large section on motion picture books. An author index and a title index facilitate its use.

A Pictorial History of the Silent Screen. Daniel Blum. New York: Putnam, 1972 (1953). 334 pp. illus.
This classic volume consists of thousands of photographs arranged in a yearly chronology which covers the first three decades of film history. The emphasis is on American films and the narrative is brief and unobtrusive.

Popcorn and Parable. Roger Kahle and Robert E. A. Lee. Minneapolis: Augsburg, 1971. 128 pp. illus.
This volume urges the consideration of modern feature films as aids in the teaching and discussion of religious truths. Comments are offered on censorship, sex, violence, fads, exploitation, etc.

Practical Guide to Classroom Media. Dolores and David Linton. Dayton, Ohio: Pflaum, 1971. 118 pp. illus.
Encouragement for the use of nonprint materials in classroom teaching is offered in this book. The chapter which deals with film covers many pertinent topics—choosing a projector, film language, criticism, student filmmaking, etc.

Projectionist's Manual (Nav. Pers. 91983-A). Washington, D.C.: Government Printing Office, 1964. 96 pp. illus.
A guide to the operation of audiovisual machines written for naval personnel. The diagrams are most effective and the material is clear and concise.

(Filmguide to) Psycho. James Naremore. Bloomington, Ind.: Indiana University Press, 1973. 96 pp.
A book in the "Filmguide" series, this volume contains credits, a plot outline, a section on Hitchcock, a long analysis of the film and a final summary critique.

Public Library Subject Headings for 16mm Motion Pictures, rev. ed. The Audiovisual Chapter of the California Library Assn. Sacramento, Calif.: CLA, 1974. 49 pp.
A subject heading list developed specifically for films. Useful in preparing printed film catalogs and in the cataloging process.

(Focus on) Rashomon. Donald Ritchie, ed. Englewood Cliffs, N.J.: Prentice-Hall, 1972. 185 pp. illus.

A title in the "Focus on" series, this book contains reviews, essays, interviews, and comments pertinent to *Rashomon.* A filmography for director Akira Kurosawa is included.

Rediscovering the American Cinema. James Leahy and William Routt, eds. Wilmette, Ill.: Films, Inc., 1970. 112 pp. illus.

This catalog uses a film study textbook approach dividing films into categories such as aesthetics, auteur, personality, and genre. Bibliographies accompany many of the subdivisions and the annotations are intelligent, informative, and rewarding. A short supplement is also available.

The Resource Guide—For Adult Religious Education. Mary Reed Newland. Kansas City, Mo.: National Catholic Reporter Publishing Co., 1974. 196 pp.

A guide to multimedia resources suitable for use with adult audiences. Considers films along with books, filmstrips, TV programs, etc. Materials are placed in a category arrangement, e.g., war, poverty, ecology, racism. The volume is somewhat limited by its lack of a title index.

Retrospective Index to Film Periodicals 1930–1971. Linda Batty. New York: Bowker, 1975. 950 pp.

Announced as an index, covering the period 1930 to 1971, to articles and reviews in over 20 English-language film periodicals. Arranged by title, the entries are also indexed by author and subject.

(From Fiction to Film) The Rocking Horse Winner. Gerald R. Barrett and Thomas L. Erskine. Encino, Calif.: Dickenson, 1974. 238 pp. illus.

A "From Fiction to Film" title, this volume offers the D. H. Lawrence short story and the script of the feature film based upon it. Critical reviews of both the story and the film are also included.

Rules for Use in the Cataloguing Department of the National Film Archive, 5th rev. ed. London: The British Film Institute, 1960. 46 pp. illus.

Another example of cataloging rules, this book describes procedures used at the National Film Archive. Attention is given to all aspects and there are samples and indexes to complement the text.

(Filmguide to) The Rules of the Game. Gerald Mast. Bloomington, Ind.: Indiana University Press, 1973. 85 pp.

A title in the "Filmguide" series, this volume contains a detailed analysis of the film along with other pertinent information. A filmography for director Jean Renoir is included.

Scholastic's Literature of the Screen. Richard A. Maynard, ed. New York: Scholastic Book Services, 1974. illus.

The initial production of this series consists of five volumes. Each of the first four, *Identity, Power, Men and Women,* and *Values in Conflict,* contains three feature film scripts. Suggestions and advice on using the individual scripts with a showing of the film are offered in the final volume along with distributor information and a short bibliography.

The School and the Art of Motion Pictures, rev. ed. David Mallery. Boston: National Assn. of Independent Schools, 1966. 147 pp.

The major portion of this volume is devoted to describing specific feature films which are recommended for use in classroom teaching. Supporting sections help to make it a good general reference book.

The Screen Arts. Edward Fischer. New York: Sheed and Ward, 1960. 184 pp.

A guide to film and television appreciation with the emphasis on film topics such as film grammar, the director, the screen writer, the actor, standards of quality, etc.

Screen Experience: An Approach to Film. Sharon Feyen and Donald Wigal, eds. Dayton, Ohio: Pflaum, 1969. 273 pp. illus.

A most valuable book on film and its use. After offering some background chapters on film history, genres, adaptations, etc., attention is given to selection, evaluation, and programming. A fine annotated filmography concludes the book.

The Second Whole Library Catalog. The Films, Inc. staff. Wilmette, Ill.: Films, Inc., 1974. 144 pp. illus.

An enlargement of the initial volume, this catalog retains the same imaginative format, but offers a new list of suggested films along with additional information on many other film topics.

Seeing with Feeling: Film in the Classroom. Richard A. Lacey. Philadelphia: Saunders, 1971. 118 pp. illus.

How to use film effectively in a classroom situation is the theme of this book. The suggestions along with the resource appendixes provided are most valuable.

(Focus on) The Seventh Seal. Birgitta Steene, ed. Englewood Cliffs, N.J.: Prentice–Hall, 1972. 182 pp. illus.

A title in the "Focus on" series, this volume contains reviews, essays, and commentaries on *The Seventh Seal.* There are interviews and a filmography for director Ingmar Bergman, and *Wood Painting,* the original play which inspired the film, is reprinted.

(Focus on) Shoot the Piano Player. Leo Braudy, ed. Englewood Cliffs, N.J.: Prentice–Hall, 1972. 182 pp. illus.

A title in the "Focus on" series, this volume contains five reviews and thirteen essays and commentaries on *Shoot the Piano Player.* Final sections offer a plot outline, a script excerpt, and other pertinent materials for studying the film.

The Short Film: An Evaluative Selection of 500 Films. George Rehrauer. New York: Macmillan Information, 1975. 199 pp. illus.

A detailed filmography of 500 top-rated short films from all subject areas covering the period from the 1930s to the present day. Films were chosen on the basis of recommendations found in 36 books dealing specifically with the short film. Contains full film descriptions along with a bibliography, a subject index, and a distributor list.

(From Fiction to Film) Silent Snow, Secret Snow. Gerald R. Barrett and Thomas L. Erskine. Encino, Calif.: Dickenson, 1972. 193 pp. illus.

A title in the "From Fiction to Film" series, this book contains the original short story by Conrad Aiken and the script of the short film directed by Gene Kearney. Critical reviews of the film and the story are included.

16mm Collection of International Cinema 1974-75. The staff of Macmillian Audio Brandon Films. Mount Vernon, N.Y.: Macmillian Audio Brandon, 1973. 630 pp. illus.

This beautiful volume resembles a Sears-Roebuck catalog and is packed with all kinds of film information. As the title indicates, it is international in scope and deals with feature films and short films in both the sound and silent formats. Visuals are plentiful and this book will satisfy many questions that cannot be answered elsewhere. It is more rewarding than many of the trade film books put out by commercial publishers.

Sixty Years of 16mm Film 1923-1983: A Symposium. Evanston, Ill.: Film Council of America, 1954. 220 pp.

An attempt to survey the field of the 16mm film in 1954. The Film Council of America sponsored this volume and it contains articles on film use by labor, churches, colleges, museums, schools, etc.

Standards for Cataloging Non-Print Materials, rev. ed. Assn. for Educational Communications and Technology. Washington, D.C. : National Education Assn., 1971. 56 pp.

A range of instructional media is considered in these guidelines for cataloging.

Standards for School Media Programs. American Assn. of School Librarians–ALA. Ed. by Department of Audiovisual Instruction–NEA. Chicago: American Library Assn., 1969. 80 pp.

The standards were created by DAVI and AASL as a guide for library programs in elementary and secondary schools. They are pertinent for the creation of new media centers or the conversion of existing print libraries into media centers.

The State of the Art of Instructional Films. Charles F. Hoban. Stanford, Calif.: ERIC, Stanford University, 1971. 34 pp.

A report which notes developments and advancements in the making, acceptance, and use of short educational films. Theoretical developments and research implications are also treated.

Sunday Night at the Movies. G. William Jones. Richmond, Va.: Knox Press, 1967. 126 pp.

A book that argues for a sensible informed approach to the screen arts by church audiences. Film aesthetics, discussion techniques, film selection, and other related topics are treated.

A Survey of British Research in Audio-Visual Aids, 1945–1971. Helen Coppen. London: National Committee for Audio-Visual Aids in Education, Educational Foundation for Visual Aids, 1972. 271 pp.

A section of this survey is devoted to film. Each entry consists of a purpose, a procedure, and a conclusion. A supplement covering the 1972–1973 period is also available.

Teaching about the Film. J. M. Peters. New York: Columbia University Press, 1961. 120 pp. illus.

A guide to developing film study courses, this book considers first the content of such courses and then the appropriate methodologies. A valuable book for anyone concerned with film study or use.

Teaching Human Beings. Jeffrey Schrank. Boston: Beacon Press, 1972. 192 pp.

Many short films are evaluated in this volume which is divided into topical sections with certain nonprint media recommended for each topic.

Teaching Program: Exploring the Film. William Kuhns and Robert Stanley. Dayton, Ohio: Pflaum, 1968. 94 pp.

A resource book that offers many suggestions, this volume was designed for teachers who use *Exploring the Film* as a text. It is, however, a valuable aid to anyone dealing with film.

Themes: Short Films for Discussion. William Kuhns. 3 vols. Dayton, Ohio: Pflaum, 1968.

A collection of study guides to short films published in a loose-leaf format. The original group (82 films) was enlarged by two supplements (30 films and 22 films). A synopsis is given for each film followed by some discussion questions. *Themes Two* (1974) continues the work of the original by offering 100 more short films, but in a somewhat different format. The author has dropped the "possible use" and "suggested questions" sections and offers only a narrative review-outline of each film. Instead of loose-leaf pages, the collection now comes in a bound paperback book.

Theories of Film. Andrew Tudor. New York: Viking Press, 1973. 168 pp. illus.

An exploration of the wide field of film theory. Not only are the major statements of Eisenstein, Grierson, Bazin, Kracauer, Arnheim, and others presented, but attention is given to genre theory and auteur theory. Conclusions and implications are offered.

Theory of Film—The Redemption of Physical Reality. Siegfried Kracauer. New York: Oxford University Press, 1965 (1960). 364 pp. illus.

This significant book on film aesthetics puts forth an important theory of film which uses still photography as a base and develops the major characteristics, areas, and elements of the film medium in considerable depth.

(Judith Crist's) TV Guide to the Movies. Judith Crist. New York: Popular
Library, 1974. 415 pp.

Although the annotations are clear, witty, and perceptive, the coverage by
critic Crist is limited to about 1,500 entries. Selection is often questionable, but
she includes some films made for television not easily found elsewhere.

TV Movies. Leonard Maltin, ed. New York: Signet, 1974. 669 pp.

Some 10,000 feature films are described in this volume designed for television
viewers. Since nearly all of the films are available for rental, lease, or purchase,
the book offers valuable information to the user of film. This second edition contains over 300 made-for-television films and about 2,000 new feature film titles
which did not appear in the earlier volume.

(Filmguide to) 2001: A Space Odyssey. Carolyn Geduld. Bloomington, Ind.:
Indiana University Press, 1973. 96 pp. illus.

A title in the "Filmguide" series, this volume contains much background material about the film and its director, Stanley Kubrick. A lengthy analysis is offered and other critical reaction is noted.

Understanding Media: The Extensions of Man. Marshall McLuhan. New
York: McGraw–Hill, 1964. 365 pp.

McLuhan's provocative book which likens media to extensions of man. His
theories about hot and cool media, the global village, and the medium as the message are offered.

U. S. Government Films. The National Audiovisual Center. Washington,
D.C.: General Services Administration, 1969. 165 pp. (Supplements issued on
an irregular basis.)

A catalog of films and filmstrips for sale by the National Audiovisual Center.
Films are arranged under subject headings, but a consolidated list is given at the
end of the book. Prices for these films are much lower than equivalent commercial films since the government has amortized much of the production cost.

U.S. Government Films for Public Educational Use (Circular No. 742).
Seerley Reid and Eloyse Grubbs. Washington, D.C.: Government Printing
Office, 1968. 532 pp.

A basic book on government films in which 6,000 films and filmstrips are annotated giving the agency source, a summary, technical data, and loan-rental-
purchase information. Films are not evaluated.

Using Films: A Handbook for the Program Planner. James Limbacher,
ed. New York: Educational Film Library Assn., 1967. 130 pp.

An anthology about using films which covers some basic concepts in an elementary and unsophisticated manner.

Who Was Who on Screen. Evelyn Mack Truitt. New York: Bowker, 1974.
384 pp.

This unique, detailed necrology covers the period from 1920 to 1971 and considers over 6,000 film performers. Personal data are included with a chronologically arranged filmography.

Women in Focus. Jeanne Betancourt. Dayton, Ohio: Pflaum, 1974. 186 pp. illus.

A reference book that deals with films which present real women rather than stereotypes. Film annotations are lengthy, but complete, and are supplemented by an index of filmmakers. A theme index, some programming suggestions, a bibliography, and a distributor list complete the book.

World Encyclopedia of the Film. Tim Cawkwell and John M. Smith, eds. New York: World, 1972. 444 pp. illus.

A fine reference book that consists of two main parts, a biographical section with 2,000 entries and a listing of about 20,000 films with basic cast and credits data provided for each. The book covers up to 1971 and is international in scope.

Young Cinema: 21 Years of the Children's Film Foundation. London: Children's Film Foundation, Ld., 1972. 20 pp. illus.

This is the most recent volume to deal with the work of the Children's Film Foundation, a nonprofit, sponsored organization that is the major producer of children's films in the western world. Other volumes on the same topic include *Saturday Morning Cinema* (1969) and *Children's Film Foundation: Catalogue and Index of Films* (1972).

APPENDIX 4
Selected
Film Periodicals

Any listing of periodicals must be selected and suspect. Announcements of new magazines arrive with as much frequency as sad notices of the demise of others. Changes take place in the frequency of publication, and formats are always being redesigned. Any inquiries about the following periodicals should be directed to the address noted.

Action (6/yr)
7950 Sunset Blvd.
Hollywood, Calif. 90046

Adult Jewish Education (irreg)
218 E. 70 St.
New York, N.Y. 10021

Advertising and Sales Promotion
(12/yr)
740 Rush St.
Chicago, Ill. 60611

After Dark (12/yr)
10 Columbus Circle
New York, N.Y. 10019

The American Biology Teacher
(9/yr)
National Assn. of Biology Teachers
1420 N St., N.W.
Washington, D.C. 20005

American Cinematographer
(12/yr)
American Soc. of Cinematographers
1782 N. Orange
Hollywood, Calif. 90028

American Journal of Nursing
(12/yr)
10 Columbus Circle
New York, N.Y. 10019

American School and University
(12/yr)
134 N. 13 St.
Philadelphia, Pa. 19107

Argosy (12/yr)
205 E. 42 St.
New York, N.Y. 10017

Athletic Journal (10/yr)
1719 Howard St.
Evanston, Ill. 60202

Audio-Visual Communications
(12/yr)
750 Third Ave.
New York, N.Y. 10016

Audiovisual Instruction (10/yr)
1201 16th St., N.W.
Washington, D.C. 20036

Booklist (23/yr)
American Library Assn.
50 E. Huron St.
Chicago, Ill. 60611

Boxoffice (52/yr)
Associated Publications, Inc.
825 Van Brunt Rd.
Kansas City, Mo. 62124

Business Screen (6/yr)
757 Third Ave.
New York, N.Y. 10017

Canyon Cinemanews (12/yr)
Box 637
Sausalito, Calif. 94956

Catholic Educator (12/yr)
53 Park Place
New York, N.Y. 10007

Catholic Film Newsletter (26/yr)
405 Lexington Ave.
New York, N.Y. 10017

Christian Century (52/yr)
407 S. Dearborn St.
Chicago, Ill. 60605

Cinéaste (4/yr)
244 W. 27 St.
New York, N.Y. 10001

Cinéfantastique (4/yr)
7470 Diversey
Elmwood Park, Ill. 60635

Cinema (3/yr)
9667 Wilshire Blvd.
Beverly Hills, Calif. 90212

Cinema Canada (6/yr)
Canadian Society of Cinematographers
2533 Gerrard St., E.
Scarborough, Ont., Can.

Cinema Journal (2/yr)
Radio–TV–Film Div.
University of Maryland
College Park, Md. 20742

Classic Film Collector (4/yr)
734 Philadelphia St.
Indiana, Pa. 15701

Clearing House (10/yr)
Fairleigh Dickinson University
Teaneck, N.J. 07666

Coast FM and Fine Arts (12/yr)
291 S. La Cienega Blvd.
Beverly Hills, Calif. 90211

Commonweal (26/yr)
Commonweal Publishing Co.
232 Madison Ave.
New York, N.Y. 10016

Community Mental Health Jour-
nal (4/yr)
2852 Broadway
New York, N.Y. 10025

Consumer Reports (12/yr)
Consumers Union of U.S., Inc.
Box 1000
Mount Vernon, N.Y. 10050

Consumers' Research (12/yr)
Consumer's Research, Inc.
Washington, N.J. 07882

Continental Film Review (12/yr)
Eurap Publishing Co., Ltd.
385 High Rd., Woodgreen
London N22, Eng.

Cosmopolitan (12/yr)
Hearst Corp.
224 W. 57 St.
New York, N.Y. 10019

Count Dracula Society Quarterly (4/yr)
22 Canterbury St.
East Hartford, Conn. 06118

CTVD: Cinema-TV-Digest (4/yr)
Hampton Books
Hampton Bays, N.Y. 11946

Cue (52/yr)
20 W. 43 St.
New York, N.Y. 10036

Cultural Information Service (12/yr)
2900 Queen Lane
Philadelphia, Pa 19129

Daily Variety (5/wk)
154 W. 46 St.
New York, N.Y. 10036

Ebony (12/yr)
1820 S. Michigan Ave.
Chicago, Ill. 60616

Educate (12/yr)
33 W. 60 St.
New York, N.Y. 10023

Educational Screen and AV Guide (12/yr)
434 S. Wabash Ave.
Chicago, Ill. 60605

Elementary English (8/yr)
1111 Kenyon Rd.
Urbana, Ill. 61801

Encounter (12/yr)
British Publications, Inc.
11–03 46 Ave.
Long Island City, N.Y. 11101

English Journal (9/yr)
1111 Kenyon Rd.
Urbana, Ill. 61801

Esquire (12/yr)
Esquire, Inc.
488 Madison Ave.
New York, N.Y. 10022

Evergreen Review (12/yr)
80 University Place
New York, N.Y. 10003

The Exploiter (52/yr)
2715 N. Pulaski Rd.
Chicago, Ill. 60639

Family Circle (12/yr)
488 Madison Ave.
New York, N.Y. 10022

Film (4/yr)
British Federation of Film Societies
81 Dean St.
London, W1, Eng.

Film and Television Daily (5/wk)
(formerly *Film Daily*)
1600 Broadway
New York, N.Y. 10019

Film Comment (4/yr)
100 Walnut Place
Brookline, Mass. 02146

Film Critic (4/yr)
(formerly *Film Society Review*)
American Federation of Film Societies
333 Ave. of the Americas
New York, New York 10014

Film Culture (4/yr)
GPO Box 1499
New York, N.Y. 10001

Filmfacts (24/yr)
Box 213, Village Sta.
New York, N.Y. 10014

Film Fan Monthly (12/yr)
77 Grayson Place
Teaneck, N.J. 07666

Film Heritage (4/yr)
Box 652
University of Dayton
Dayton, Ohio 45409

Film Information (12/yr)
Broadcasting and Film Commission
Box 500, Manhattanville Sta.
New York, N.Y. 10027

The Film Journal (4/yr)
121 Varick St.
New York, N.Y. 10013

Film Library Quarterly (4/yr)
Box 348, Radio City Sta.
New York, N.Y. 10019

Filmmakers Newsletter (11/yr)
41 Union Sq. W.
New York, N.Y. 10003

Film News (6/yr)
250 W. 57 St.
New York, N.Y. 10019

Filmograph (4/yr)
7926 Ashboro Dr.
Alexandria, Va. 22309

Film Quarterly (4/yr)
2223 Fulton St.
University of California Press
Berkeley, Calif. 94720

Films and Filming (12/yr)
Hanson Books
Artillery Mansions
75 Victoria St.
London, SW1, Eng.

Films in Review (9/yr)
National Board of Review of Motion
   Pictures, Inc.
210 E. 68 St.
New York, N.Y. 10021

Film Society Bulletin (9/yr)
333 Ave. of the Americas
New York, N.Y. 10011

Focus (4/yr)
5811 S. Ellis Ave.
Chicago, Ill. 60637

Focus on Film (5/yr)
Tantivity Press
108 New Bond St.
London W1, Eng.

Glamour (12/yr)
420 Lexington Ave.
New York, N.Y. 10017

Good Housekeeping (12/yr)
Box 517
New York, N.Y. 10019

Grade Teacher (9/yr)
22 W. Putnam Ave.
Greenwich, Conn. 06830

**Greater Amusements and Inter-
national Projectionist** (12/yr)
Gallo Publishing Corp.
1600 Broadway, 514-D
New York, N.Y. 10019

Harper's Bazaar (12/yr)
Box 552
New York, N.Y. 10019

Harper's Magazine (12/yr)
381 W. Center St.
Marion, Ohio 43302

Holiday (6/yr)
1100 Waterway Blvd.
Indianapolis, Ind. 46202

Hollywood Reporter (5/wk)
6715 Sunset Blvd.
Hollywood, Calif. 90028

Humanist (6/yr)
4244 Ridge Lea Rd.
Amherst, N.Y. 14226

Illinois Education (4/yr)
100 E. Edwards St.
Springfield, Ill. 62704

Independent Film Journal (26/yr)
1251 Ave. of the Americas
New York, N.Y. 10020

Industrial Photography (12/yr)
750 Third Ave.
New York, N.Y. 10017

Ingenue (12/yr)
Dell Publishing Co.
750 Third Ave.
New York, N.Y. 10017

Instructor (10/yr)
7 Bank St.
Dansville, N.Y. 14437

International Journal of Religious Education (12/yr)
475 Riverside Dr.
New York, N.Y. 10027

Inter/View (12/yr)
33 Union Sq. W.
New York, N.Y. 10003

Journal of the American Medical Association (52/yr)
535 N. Dearborn St.
Chicago, Ill. 60610

Journal of Geography (9/yr)
111 W. Washington St.
Chicago, Ill. 60602

Journal of Reading (8/yr)
6 Tyre Ave.
Newark, Del. 19711

The Journal of the Popular Film (4/yr)
University Hall, Rm. 101
Bowling Green State University
Bowling Green, Ohio 43403

Journal of the University Film Association (4/yr)
156 W. 19 Ave.
Columbus, Ohio 43210

Junior Scholastic (30/yr)
Scholastic Magazines
902 Sylvan Ave.
Englewood Cliffs, N.J. 07632

K–Eight (10/yr)
134 N. 13 St.
Philadelphia, Pa. 19107

Ladies' Home Journal (12/yr)
Box 1695
Des Moines, Iowa 50306

Liberty (4/yr)
635 Madison Ave.
New York, N.Y. 10022

Maclean's Magazine (12/yr)
Maclean–Hunter, Ltd.
481 University Ave.
Toronto, Ont. M5W 1A7, Can.

Mademoiselle (12/yr)
Box 5204
Boulder, Colo. 80302

Man, Society, Technology (8/yr)
Industrial Arts Assn.
1201 16 St., N.W.
Washington, D.C. 20036

Mass Media Ministries Newsletter (26/yr)
2116 N. Charles St.
Baltimore, Md. 21218

Media and Methods (9/yr)
134 N. 13 St.
Philadelphia, Pa. 19107

Media Mix Newsletter (8/yr)
221 W. Madison
Chicago, Ill. 60611

Medical and Biological Engineering (6/yr)
44–01 21 St.
Long Island City, N.Y. 11101

Mental Hygiene (4/yr)
10 Columbus Circle
New York, N.Y. 10019

Mise en Scène (irreg.)
4080 Crawford Hall
Case Western Reserve University
Cleveland, Ohio 44106

Modern Screen (12/yr)
750 Third Ave.
New York, N.Y. 10017

Monthly Film Bulletin (12/yr)
British Film Institute
81 Dean St.
London W1, Eng.

Motion Picture Daily (104/yr)
Quigley Publishing Co., Inc.
1270 Ave. of the Americas
New York, N.Y. 10020

Motion Picture Herald (13/yr)
Quigley Publishing Co., Inc.
1270 Ave. of the Americas
New York, N.Y. 10020

Motion Picture Magazine (12/yr)
205 E. 42 St.
New York, N.Y. 10017

Movie (4/yr)
188 High St.
Nutley, N.J. 07110

Movieland and TV Times (12/yr)
21 W. 26 St.
New York, N.Y. 10010

Movie Life (12/yr)
295 Madison Ave.
New York, N.Y. 10017

Movie Mirror (12/yr)
315 Park Ave. S.
New York, N.Y. 10010

Movies International (4/yr)
Press Arts, Inc.
7805 Deering Ave.
Canoga Park, Calif. 91304

Movie Stars (12/yr)
295 Madison Ave.
New York, N.Y. 10017

Ms. (12/yr)
Majority Enterprises, Inc.
370 Lexington Ave.
New York, N.Y. 10017

Nation (52/yr)
Nation Associates, Inc.
333 Ave. of the Americas
New York, N.Y. 10014

National Observer (52/yr)
200 Burnett Rd.
Chicopee, Mass. 01021

National Review (26/yr)
150 E. 35 St.
New York, N.Y. 10016

Nation's Schools (12/yr)
230 W. Monroe St.
Chicago, Ill. 60606

New Leader (26/yr)
212 Fifth Ave.
New York, N.Y. 10010

New Republic (52/yr)
381 W. Center St.
Marion, Ohio 43302

Newsweek (52/yr)
Newsweek Bldg.
Livingston, N.J. 07039

New Times (24/yr)
One Park Ave.
New York, N.Y. 10016

New York (52/yr)
New York Magazine Co.
207 E. 32 St.
New York, N.Y. 10016

New Yorker (52/yr)
25 W. 43 St.
New York, N.Y. 10036

Nursing Outlook (12/yr)
10 Columbus Circle
New York, N.Y. 10019

Oui (12/yr)
919 N. Michigan Ave.
Chicago, Ill. 60611

**Parents' Magazine and Better
Family Living** (12/yr)
52 Vanderbilt Ave.
New York, N.Y. 10017

The Pedagogic Reporter (4/yr)
101 Fifth Ave.
New York, N.Y. 10003

Penthouse (12/yr)
909 Third Ave.
New York, N.Y. 10022

Photo Methods for Industry
(12/yr)
33 W. 60 St.
New York, N.Y. 10023

Photon (6/yr)
801 Ave. C
Brooklyn, N.Y. 11218

Photoplay (12/yr)
205 E. 42 St.
New York, N.Y. 10017

Photo Screen (12/yr)
315 Park Ave. S.
New York, N.Y. 10010

Playboy (12/yr)
919 N. Michigan Ave.
Chicago, Ill. 60611

Playgirl (12/yr)
1801 Century Park E.
Suite 2300
Century City
Los Angeles, Calif. 90067

Preview (4/yr)
Indiana University AV Center
Bloomington, Ind. 47401

Previews (9/yr)
1180 Ave. of the Americas
New York, N.Y. 10036

PTA Magazine (10/yr)
National Congress of Parents and
Teachers

700 N. Rush St.
Chicago, Ill. 60611

Ramparts (12/yr)
2054 University Ave.
Berkeley, Calif. 94704

Rap (12/yr)
Box 667
Dayton, Ohio

Redbook (12/yr)
230 Park Ave.
New York, N.Y. 10017

Rolling Stone (26/yr)
625 Third Ave.
San Francisco, Calif. 94107

Saturday Review (26/yr)
488 Madison Ave.
New York, N.Y. 10022

Scholastic Teacher (9/yr)
Scholastic Magazines, Inc.
50 W. 44 St.
New York, N.Y. 10036

School Management (12/yr)
22 W. Putnam Ave.
Greenwich, Conn. 06830

**School Musician Director and
Teacher** (9/yr)
4 E. Clinton St.
Joliet, Ill. 60431

School Product News (12/yr)
614 Superior Ave. W.
Cleveland, Ohio 44113

School Progress (12/yr)
481 University Ave.
Toronto, Ont., Can.

Science Activities (10/yr)
8150 N. Central Park Ave.
Skokie, Ill. 60076

Science and Children (8/yr)
National Science Teachers Assn.
1201 16th St., N.W.
Washington, D.C. 20036

Science News (52/yr)
Science Service, Inc.
231 W. Center St.
Marion, Ohio 43302

The Science Teacher (10/yr)
1201 16th St., N.W.
Washington, D.C. 20036

Screen (4/yr)
Society for Education in Film and
   Television
81 Dean St.
London W1V 6AA, Eng.

Screen Actor (4/yr)
7750 Sunset Blvd.
Los Angeles, Calif. 90048

Screen Facts (6/yr)
Box 154
Kew Gardens, N.Y. 11415

See (5/yr)
38 W. Fifth St.
Dayton, Ohio 45402

Senior Scholastic (30/yr)
902 Sylvan Ave.
Englewood Cliffs, N.J. 07632

Seventeen (12/yr)
Triangle Communications, Inc.
Radnor, Pa. 19088

Show Business (52/yr)
136 W. 44 St.
New York, N.Y. 10036

Sight and Sound (4/yr)
Eastern News Distributors
155 W. 15 St.
New York, N.Y. 10011

Sightlines (5/yr)
17 W. 60 St.
New York, N.Y. 10023

SMPTE Journal (12/yr)
Society of Motion Picture and Television Engineers
862 Scarsdale Ave.
Scarsdale, N.Y. 10583

Social Education (8/yr)
1201 16th St., N.W.
Washington, D.C. 20036

Soviet Film (12/yr)
V/O Sovexportfilm, 14
Kalashny Pereulok
Moscow K-9, USSR

Spectrum (6/yr)
475 Riverside Dr.
New York, N.Y. 10027

The Speech Teacher (4/yr)
Speech Assn. of America
Statler Hilton Hotel
New York, N.Y. 10001

Take One (6/yr)
Box 1778, Sta. B
Montreal 110, Can.

Teen Magazine (12/yr)
8490 Sunset Blvd.
Los Angeles, Calif. 90069

Time (52/yr)
541 N. Fairbanks Court
Chicago, Ill. 60611

Today's Catholic Teacher (8/yr)
38 W. Fifth St.
Dayton, Ohio 45402

Today's Filmmaker (4/yr)
250 Fulton Ave.
Hempstead, N.Y. 11550

Training in Business and Industry
   (12/yr)
One Park Ave.
New York, N.Y. 10016

True (12/yr)
Fawcett Publications, Inc.
Fawcett Bldg.
Greenwich, Conn. 06830

TV and Movie Screen (12/yr)
315 Park Ave. S.
New York, N.Y. 10010

Variety (52/yr)
154 W. 46 St.
New York, N.Y. 10036

Views and Reviews (4/yr)
633 W. Wisconsin Ave.
Milwaukee, Wis. 53203

Village Voice (52/yr)
80 University Place
New York, N.Y. 10003

Vocational Guidance Quarterly (4/yr)
1607 New Hampshire Ave., N.W.
Washington, D.C. 20009

Vogue (12/yr)
Conde Nast Publications, Inc.
Box 5201
Boulder, Colo. 80302

Women and Film (3/yr)
2802 Arizona Ave.
Santa Monica, Calif. 90404

Your Church (6/yr)
Box 397
Valley Forge, Pa. 19481

APPENDIX 5
Selected
Film Associations
and Organizations

There are hundreds of national organizations that are concerned either totally or in part with film. They range from professional societies to information rating services. Some are directly concerned with filmmaking, others with film use, and still others with film evaluation. Below is a selected listing of some organizations whose rationale for being depends to a large extent on films. Groups such as the Association for Educational Communication and Technology (AECT) are not named since film represents only one facet of their numerous interests.

For more detailed information on organizations dealing with film, it is suggested that the reader consult Encyclopedia of Associations, *edited by Margaret Fisk, Detroit: Gale Research Co., 1972 or* Audiovisual Market Place, *edited by J. A. Neal, N.Y.: Bowker, 1974.*

Academy of Motion Picture Arts and Sciences, 9038 Melrose Ave., Los Angeles, Calif. 90069
Major aim is to improve film quality—annual awards, promotion of theatrical features, shorts, etc. Library includes screenplays, clippings, other original materials for research.

American Federation of Film Societies, 333 Ave. of the Americas, New York, N.Y. 10014.
Information clearinghouse for film societies, e.g., film availability, costs, study guides, etc. Publishes *Film Critic* (formerly *Film Society Review*).

American Film Institute (AFI), John F. Kennedy Center for the Performing Arts, Washington, D.C. 20566
Dedicated to establishing and advancing film as an art form. Restores films, locates lost films, sponsors programs, encourages new filmmakers. Active in publishing books, periodicals, and newsletter. Becoming the major repository for American films.

American Science Film Association, 7720 Wisconsin Ave., Bethesda, Md. 20014

Devoted to film as a research tool, as a communication of research findings, and as an aid to science education and to helping audiences understand and appreciate science. Publishes a newsletter.

American Society of Cinematographers, 1782 N. Orange, Hollywood, Calif. 90028

Professionals concerned with cinematography. Publications include manuals and a monthly periodical, *American Cinematographer.*

British Film Institute (BFI), 81 Dean St., London W1, Eng.

The British institution which serves as a model for other nations to emulate. Source of film information, circulates films for educational use. Publishes books, pamphlets, etc., and the film periodical *Sight and Sound.*

British Universities Film Council (BUFC), Royalty House, 72 Dean St., London IV, Eng.

Dedicated to exploration and encouragement of film use in higher education. Evaluates films, gathers information for publications, clearinghouse for research on film use.

Canadian Science Film Association, c/o Canadian Educational Media Council, 252 Bloor St., W. Toronto, Ont. M5S IV5, Can.

Concerned with the science film in all its forms—educational, recreational, documentary, etc. Promotes use of science films, supplies information, publishes bulletin, encourages research.

Center for Understanding Media (CUM), 75 Horatio St., New York, N.Y. 10014

Dedicated to media and education, performs research, designs experimental programs, publishes findings, provides information.

Center for Visual Literacy, c/o College of Education, Taylor Hall, University of Rochester, Rochester, N.Y. 14627

Concerns itself with information, research projects, and activities relating to visual literacy.

Conference on Visual Literacy, c/o Samuel B. Ross, Green Chimneys School, Brewster, N.Y. 10509

Research and dissemination of information about visual literacy.

Consortium of University Film Centers (CUFC), c/o Visual Aids Service, University of Illinois, 1325 S. Oak St., Champaign, Ill. 61820

Concerned with film centers of all kinds, their problems, programs, information exchange, research, standards, etc.

Council on International Nontheatrical Events (CINE), 1201 16th St., N.W., Washington, D.C. 20036

Selects short films for participation in foreign film festivals. Continual screening and evaluation of short films with awards given each year.

Dance Films Association, 250 W. 57 St., New York, N.Y. 10019
Dedicated to preservation of dance via media. Produces and rents dance films, sponsors dance film festivals.

Educational Film Library Association (EFLA), 17 W. 60 St., New York, N.Y. 10023
The parent film organization which serves as a clearinghouse for information about short films. Evaluates films, sponsors American Film Festival each year, offers EFLA services through film evaluation cards, publishes information in books, pamphlets and a periodical, *Sightlines.*

Encyclopedia Cinematographica, c/o Audio-Visual Services, Pennsylvania State University, University Park, Pa. 16802
Rents science films which show phenomena that could not be observed otherwise. Part of an international association with film libraries throughout the world.

Farm Film Foundation, 1425 H St., N.W., Washington, D.C. 20005
Goal is to interpret rural America to audiences through films. Produces and sponsors films many of which are available without charge.

Film Library Information Council (FLIC), Box 348, Radio City Sta., New York, N.Y. 10019
Dedicated to improving film service in public libraries. Sponsors programs, workshops, etc; publishes periodical, *Film Library Quarterly,* and other informational materials.

International Federation of Film Archives, 74 Galerie Ravenstein, 1000 Brussels, Belgium
Encourages establishment of film archives in all countries and cooperation between them. Indexes 61 film periodicals (published by R.R. Bowker) and issues manuals on film preservation, establishing archives, and film cataloging.

Mass Media Ministries, 2116 N. Charles St., Baltimore, Md. 21218
Deals with films that can be used in religious education. Rents films and offers an information service.

Motion Picture Association of America (MPA), 522 Fifth Ave., New York, N.Y. 10036
Link between film industry and public, responsible for rating of films and other public relations efforts.

Museum of Modern Art Film Library (MOMA), 11 W. 53 St., New York, N.Y. 10019
Film archive dates back to the 30s. Rents some films, sponsors special showings in museum, and publishes books, film notes, and guides. Has large collection of stills, periodicals, books on films.

National Audiovisual Center c/o National Archives and Record Service (NARS), General Services Administration, Pennsylvania Ave. & Eighth St., N.W., Washington, D.C. 20408

Aims for best possible use of federally funded films. Sells films, publishes catalogs, provides information on government films.

National Board of Review of Motion Pictures, Inc., 210 E. 68 St., New York, N.Y. 10021
Organized in 1909, its aim is to develop discrimination in viewing films. Publishes periodical, *Films in Review.* Gives yearly awards to outstanding feature films.

National Catholic Office for Motion Pictures, 405 Lexington Ave., Suite 4200, New York, N.Y. 10017
A previewing organization which evaluates films for Catholic audiences and others. Publishes *Catholic Film Newsletter.*

National Center for Film Study, 1307 S. Wabash Ave., Chicago, Ill. 60605
Encourages the establishment and improvement of film studies in schools and colleges. Publishes information on trends, films, etc.

National Council of Churches, Broadcasting and Film Commission, 475 Riverside Dr., New York, N.Y. 10027
Concerns itself with the use of media in religious education. Publications include *The Audio-Visual Resource Guide* now in its ninth edition. Film evaluators are from all religious denominations.

National Film Board of Canada (NFBC), 1251 Ave. of the Americas, New York, N.Y. 10020
Parent of Canadian Studios that make many short films. Goal is to produce films that interpret Canada to audiences. Films do that and much, much more.

The New York State Council on the Arts, 250 W. 57 St., New York, N.Y., 10019
Assists institutions involved with film study by commissioning study guides for films.

Psychological Cinema Register (PCR), c/o Audiovisual Services, Pennsylvania State University, University Park, Pa. 16802
Collects films on behavorial sciences pertinent to college research and study. Rents and sells certain films.

St. Clement's Film Association, 423 W. 46 St., New York, N.Y. 10036
Aims to assist members in obtaining, using, and appreciating films. Publishes study guides and other materials.

Scottish Film Council, 16-17 Woodside Terrace, Charing Cross, Glasgow G3 7XN, Scot.
Aim is to improve Scottish education via media. Maintains a large film library, publishes film bulletins, sponsors workshops, conferences, courses, etc.

Society for Cinema Studies, Radio–TV–Film Div., University of Maryland, College Park, Md. 20742
Dedicated to film history, scholarship, criticism, etc. Publishes periodical, *Cinema Journal,* and other film materials.

Society of Motion Picture and Television Engineers (SMPTE), 862
Scarsdale Ave., Scarsdale, N.Y. 10583
Association of technical professionals which publishes books and other materials about the mechanics of filmmaking and showing.

Teaching Film Custodians (TFC), AV Center, Indiana University, Bloomington, Ind. 47401
With cooperation of film producers, makes short excerpts from feature films available. Also publishes study guides and other materials.

University Film Association (UFA), Department of Communication Arts,
University of Windsor, Windsor, Ont. 9NB 3P4, Can.
Concerned with film for instruction and communication. Publishes material, encourages film production, and is most concerned with film study in schools and colleges.

APPENDIX 6
Selected
Film Distributors

This list of film distributors is a selected one, but an attempt has been made to include those which the author feels are the major ones. In periods of economic uncertainty, the tenure of some film distribution companies becomes short-lived and dissolutions, mergers, and name changes may occur. Should any discrepancy arise pertaining to a distributor name or address, the reader is directed to an annual reference volume such as Audiovisual Market Place *(Bowker) for information on recent changes.*

The difference between a producer and a distributor should be noted. A producer is engaged in the business of creating films, while a distributor's major interest is renting, loaning, selling, or leasing them. Some producers prefer to act as their own distributor.

As indicated in the text, distributors are a primary source of catalogs which offer much information on all types of films. A single request will usually place the writer on the mailing list.

ABC Media Concepts
1001 N. Poinsetta Pl.
Hollywood, Calif. 90046

ABC Merchandising
1330 Ave. of the Americas
New York, N.Y. 10019

ACI Films
35 W. 45 St.
New York, N.Y. 10036

Arizona State University
Central Arizona Film Coop.
Matthews Hall
Tempe, Ariz. 85281

Association–Sterling
866 Third Ave.
New York, N.Y. 10022

Audio Film Center
34 MacQuesten Pkwy. S.
Mount Vernon, N.Y. 10550

Baylis Glascock Films
1901 Ave. of the Stars
Los Angeles, Calif. 90067

Benchmark Films
145 Scarborough Rd.
Briarcliff Manor, N.Y. 10510

BFA Educational Media
2211 Michigan Ave.
Santa Monica, Calif. 90404

Blackhawk Films
1235 W. Fifth St.
Davenport, Iowa 52808

Boston University
Krasker Memorial Film Library
765 Commonwealth
Boston, Mass. 02215

Stephen Bosustow Productions
1649 11th St.
Santa Monica, Calif. 90404

Brigham Young University
Film Marketing Dept. of Motion Picture Production
Provo, Utah 84601

Cambridge Film Corp.
Box 126
Cambridge, Mass. 02139

Canyon Cinema Filmmakers' Cooperative
Industrial Center Bldg.
Sausalito, Calif. 94965

Carousel Films
1501 Broadway
New York, N.Y. 10036

Center Cinema Cooperative
540 N. Lakeside Dr.
Chicago, Ill. 60611

Center for Mass Communication
of Columbia University Press
562 W. 113 St.
New York, N.Y. 10025

Churchill Films
662 N. Robertson Blvd.
Los Angeles, Calif. 90069

Columbia Cinematique
711 Fifth Ave.
New York, N.Y. 10022

Connecticut Films
6 Cobble Hill Rd.
Westport, Conn. 06880

Contemporary Films/McGraw-Hill
1221 Ave. of the Americas
New York, N.Y. 10020

Continental 16
241 E. 34 St.
New York, N.Y. 10036

Coronet Films
65 E. South Water St.
Chicago, Ill. 60601

Creative Film Society
7237 Canby Ave.
Reseda, Calif. 19335

Dartmouth College Films
Office of Instructional Services
Fairbanks Hall
Hanover, N.H. 03755

Louis de Rochemont Associates
1600 Broadway
New York, N.Y. 10019

Walt Disney Productions
500 S. Buena Vista Ave.
Burbank, Calif. 91503

Doubleday Multimedia
1371 Reynolds Ave.
Santa Ana, Calif. 92705

Eastern New Mexico University
Film Library
Portales, N. Mex. 88130

Embassy Pictures
1301 Ave. of the Americas
New York, N.Y. 10019

Encyclopedia Britannica Educational Corp.
425 N. Michigan Ave.
Chicago, Ill. 60611

Family Theater
7201 Sunset Blvd.
Hollywood, Calif. 90029

Film Images
17 W. 60 St.
New York, N.Y. 10023

Filmmakers' Cooperative
175 Lexington Ave.
New York, N.Y. 10016

Films, Inc.
1144 Wilmette Ave.
Wilmette, Ill. 60091

Fishtail Sky Productions
331 Laurel Ave.
San Anselmo, Calif. 94960

Florida State University
Audiovisual Center
Tallahassee, Fla. 32306

Franciscan Communication Center
1229 S. Santee St.
Los Angeles, Calif. 90015

Grailville
Loveland, Ohio 45140

Grove Press, Inc.
Film Division
53 E. 11 St.
New York, N.Y. 10003

Hartley Productions
Cat Rock Rd.
Cos Cob, Conn. 06807

Image Resources
267 W. 25 St.
New York, N.Y. 10001

Indiana State University
Audiovisual Center
Terre Haute, Ind. 47809

Indiana University
Audiovisual Center
Bloomington, Ind. 47401

Iowa State University
Media Resources Center
Ames, Iowa 50010

Institute of Communicative Arts
Emory University
Atlanta, Ga. 30333

Institutional Cinema Service, Inc.
29 E. Tenth St.
New York, N.Y. 10003

Interlude Films
524-C E. Glenoaks Blvd.
Glendale, Calif. 91207

International Film Bureau, Inc.
332 S. Michigan Ave.
Chicago, Ill. 60604

International Film Foundation
475 Fifth Ave.
New York, N.Y. 10017

I Q Films, Inc.
689 Fifth Ave.
New York, N.Y. 10022

Janus Films
745 Fifth Ave.
New York, N.Y. 10022

Kent State University
Audiovisual Service
Kent, Ohio 44242

Learning Corporation of America
711 Fifth Ave.
New York, N.Y. 10022

McGraw–Hill Films
1221 Ave. of the Americas
New York, N.Y. 10020

Macmillan Audio Brandon
Subs. of Macmillan, Inc.
34 MacQuesten Pkwy. S.
Mount Vernon, N.Y. 10550

Macmillan Films
34 MacQuesten Pky. S.
Mount Vernon, N.Y. 10550

Maryknoll Fathers
Maryknoll, N.Y. 10545

Mass Media Ministries
2116 N. Charles St.
Baltimore, Md. 21218

Michigan State University
Audiovisual Center
East Lansing, Mich. 48823

Modern Talking Picture Service
2323 New Hyde Park Rd.
New Hyde Park, N.Y. 11040

Museum of Modern Art
11 W. 53 St.
New York, N.Y. 10019

National Audiovisual Center
General Services Administration
Washington, D.C. 20409

National Council of Churches
475 Riverside Dr.
New York, N.Y. 10027

National Film Board of Canada
1251 Ave. of the Americas
New York, N.Y. 10020

NBC Educational Enterprises
30 Rockerfeller Plaza
New York, N.Y. 10020

New York University
Film Library
26 Washington Pl.
New York, N.Y. 10003

Northern Illinois University
Div. of Communication Services
Altgeld Hall, Rm. 114
Dekalb, Ill. 60115

Ohio State University
Film Library
156 W. 19 Ave.
Colombus, Ohio 43210

Oklahoma State University
Audiovisual Center
Stillwater, Okla. 74074

Pennsylvania State University
AV Aids Library
University Park, Pa. 16802

Perennial Education
1825 Willow Rd.
Northfield, Ill. 60093

Phoenix Films
470 Park Ave. S.
New York, N.Y. 10016

Purdue University
Audiovisual Center
Lafayette, Ind. 47907

Pyramid Films
Box 1048
Santa Monica, Calif. 90406

Radiant Films
220 W. 42 St.
New York, N.Y. 10036

Radim Films
17 W. 60 St.
New York, N.Y. 10023

Walter Reade 16
214 E. 34 St.
New York, N.Y. 10016

Rembrandt Film Library
267 W. 25 St.
New York, N.Y. 10001

ROA's Films
1696 N. Astor St.
Milwaukee, Wis. 53202

Serious Business Co.
1927 Marin Ave.
Berkeley, Calif. 94707

South Dakota State University
Audiovisual Center
Brookings, S.Dak. 57006

Southern Illinois University
Learning Resources Service
Carbondale, Ill. 62901

State University of New York, Buffalo
Instructional Communication Center
Media Library
22 Foster Annex
Buffalo, N.Y. 14214

Sterling Educational Films
241 E. 34 St.
New York, N.Y. 10016

Swank Motion Pictures
201 S. Jefferson Ave.
St. Louis, Mo. 63166

Syracuse University
Film Library
1455 E. Colvin St.
Syracuse, N.Y. 13210

Teaching Film Custodians
Audio Visual Center
Indiana University
Bloomington, Ind. 47401

Teleketics
St. Francis Productions
1229 S. Santee St.
Los Angeles, Calif. 90015

Texture Films
1600 Broadway
New York, N.Y. 10019

Time-Life Films
43 W. 16 St.
New York, N.Y. 10011

Twyman Films
Box 605
Dayton, Ohio 45401

United Artists 16
729 Seventh Ave.
New York, N.Y. 10019

United States Information Agency
1750 Pennsylvania Ave., N.W.
Washington, D.C. 20547

Universal Education and Visual Arts
Division of Universal City Studios, Inc.
100 Universal City Plaza
Universal City, Calif. 91608

Universal 16 United World Films
2001 S. Vermont Ave.
Los Angeles, Calif. 90001

University of Arizona
Bureau of Audiovisual Services
Tucson, Ariz. 85721

University of California
Extension Media Center
2223 Fulton St.
Berkeley, Calif. 94720

University of California Film Productions
University Extension
Berkeley, Calif. 94720

University of Colorado
Film Library
Stadium Bldg., Rm. 320
Boulder, Colo. 80302

University of Connecticut
Audiovisual Center
Storrs, Conn. 06268

University of Illinois
Visual Aids Service
1325 S. Oak St.
Champaign, Ill. 61820

University of Iowa
Audiovisual Center
Div. of Extension Services
Iowa City, Iowa 52240

University of Kansas
Audiovisual Center
6 Bailey Hall
Lawrence, Kans. 66044

University of Kentucky
Audiovisual Services
Porter Bldg.
Lexington, Ky. 40506

University of Maine
Audiovisual Center
Shibles Hall
Orono, Maine 04473

University of Michigan
AV Education Center
416 Fourth St.
Ann Arbor, Mich. 48103

University of Minnesota
Dept. of Audiovisual Extension
2037 University Ave., S.E.
Minneapolis, Minn. 55455

University of Mississippi
Educational Film Library
School of Education
University, Miss. 38677

University of Missouri
University Extension Div.
203 Whitten Hall
Columbia, Mo. 65201

University of Nebraska
Instructional Media Center
Nebraska Hall, 421
Lincoln, Nebr. 68508

University of New Hampshire
Dept. of Media Services
University Library
Durham, N.H. 03824

University of South Dakota
Film Library
Vermillion, S.Dak. 57069

University of South Florida
Films–Educational Resources
Tampa, Fla. 33620

University of Texas
Visual Instruction Bureau
Box Drawer W
University Sta.
Austin, Tex. 78712

University of Utah
Educational Media Center
Milton Bennion Hall, 207
Salt Lake City, Utah 84112

Warner Brothers/7 Arts
Film Exchange
165 W. 46 St.
New York, N.Y. 10017

Washington State University
Audiovisual Center
Pullman, Wash. 99163

Wayne State University
Audiovisual Center
5448 Cass Ave.
Detroit, Mich. 48208

Weston Woods Studios, Inc.
Weston Woods, Conn. 06880

Wholesome Film Center
20 Melrose St.
Boston, Mass. 02116

Clem Williams Films, Inc.
2240 Noblestown Rd.
Pittsburgh, Pa. 15205

Wisconsin State University
Film Rental Library
Audiovisual Center
La Crosse, Wis. 54601

David Wolper Productions
8720 Sunset Blvd.
Hollywood, Calif. 90069

Xerox Films
High Ridge Pk.
Stamford, Conn. 06904

Yeshiva University
Film Library
526 W. 187 St.
New York, N.Y. 10033

APPENDIX 7
Selected Film Equipment Manufacturers

The equipment manufacturers listed here are limited to those mentioned in this book. Catalogs of the products that they manufacture/sell are available on request. Many local distributors have franchises for the sale of audiovisual hardware in certain geographic territories. National distributors such as Bro-Dart handle the products of several equipment manufacturers. The reader is once more directed to The Audio-Visual Equipment Directory, published annually by the National Audio-Visual Association, for the latest data on audiovisual machines and equipment.

Allied Impex Corp.
168 Glen Cove Rd.
Carle Place, N.Y. 11514

A.V. Systems, Inc.
44 Railroad Ave.
Glen Head, N.Y. 11545

A.V.E. Corp.
250 W. 54 St.
New York, N.Y. 10019

Bell & Howell, Audio-Visual Products Division
7100 McCormick Rd.
Lincolnwood, Ill. 60645

Bell & Howell Canada, Ltd.
125 Norfinch Dr.
Downsview, Ont., Can.

Brewster Corp.
50 River St.
Old Saybrook, Conn. 06475

Brumberger Co.
1948 Troutman St.
Brooklyn, N.Y. 11237

Da–Lite Screen Co., Inc.
State Rd. 15 N.
Warsaw, Ind. 46580

A.B. Dick Co.
5700 W. Touhy Ave.
Chicago, Ill. 60648

Draper Shade and Screen Co.
Box 908
Spiceland, Ind. 47385

DuKane Corp.
2900 DuKane Dr.
St. Charles, Ill. 60174

Eastman Kodak Co.
343 State St.
Rochester, N.Y. 14650

R. Friedman Associates
28349 Chagrin Blvd.
Cleveland, Ohio 44122

GAF Corp.
140 W. 51 Street
New York, N.Y. 10020

Karl Heitz, Inc.
979 Third Ave.
New York, N.Y. 10022

Honeywell, Inc.
Photographic Products Div.
5501 S. Broadway
Littleton, Colo. 80120

Hudson Photographic Industries, Inc.
2 S. Buckhout St.
Irvington, N.Y. 10533

Information Handling Services
Box 1154
Englewood, Colo. 80110

International Audio Visual, Inc.
119 Blanchard St.
Seattle, Wash. 98121

Jayark Instruments Corp.
Subs. of Jayark Corp.
420 Madison Ave.
New York, N.Y. 10017

Kalart Victor Corp.
Box 112
Hultenius St.
Plainville, Conn. 06062

Keystone—Division of Berkey Photos, Inc.
Keystone Place
Paramus, N.J. 07652

Knox Manufacturing Co.
111 Spruce
Wood Dale, Ill. 60191

Charles Mayer Studios, Inc.
140 E. Market St.
Akron, Ohio 44308

Media Systems Corp.
250 W. Main St.
Moorestown, N.J. 08057

Minolta Corp.
200 Park Ave. S.
New York, N.Y. 10003

North American Philips Co.
100 E. 42 St.
New York, N.Y. 10017

Paillard Inc.–Bolex & Hasselblad
1900 Lower Rd.
Linden, N.J. 07036

Ponder & Best, Inc.
1630 Stewart
Santa Monica, Calif. 90404

Producers Service Corp.
1200 Grand Central Ave.
Glendale, Calif. 91201

Purpose Film Center
2625 Temple St.
Los Angeles, Calif. 90026

Radiant Manufacturing Co.
8220 N. Austin Ave.
Morton Grove, Ill. 60053

Retention Communication Systems
2 Pennsylvania Plaza
New York, N.Y. 10001

Riker Communications
142 Central Ave.
Clark, N.J. 07066

Singer Education Systems
3750 Monroe Ave.
Rochester, N.Y. 14603

Viewlex, Inc.
Broadway Ave.
Holbrook, N.Y. 11741

Wilcox–Lange, Inc.
3925 N. Pulaski Rd.
Chicago, Ill. 60641

GLOSSARY

The terms selected for this glossary are derived from the text and are presented here for clarification and convenience. An attempt was made to explain the terms with brevity, clarity, and simplicity. Detailed expositions were avoided as were complex technical statements. In order to follow this plan, some compromises were necessary. It is recognized that certain definitions may be deemed partial or vulnerable; what description, for instance, of documentary film will satisfy everyone? It is hoped, however, that the major elements presented in each explanation will be helpful.

Acetate   A slow-burning cellulose base used for motion picture films.

Action   The movement of people or objects in front of the camera lens.

Adaptation   The transformation of a play, poem, short story, or novel into cinematic language.

Angle   The position in space taken originally by the camera and ultimately by the viewer.

Animation   An illusion of motion accomplished usually by single frame shooting rather than by photographing continuously. Examples include a series of many drawings made to show all the minute movements in a single action; the manipulation of inanimate objects in hardly perceptible steps; drawing directly on film, etc.

Art film   A film whose style is consciously experimental or artistic. Known also as avant-garde, underground.

Aspect ratio   A comparison of the width of the film frame with its height.

Auteur   The author of a film; a filmmaker whose body of cinematic work is identifiable by common characteristics of technique or by his use of recurrent themes.

B&W   A black and white film; a film containing images made up of tones of gray as opposed to color.

Booking   Reserving a film for use on a specific date.

Boom shot   Shot made with a camera that is positioned on a moving cantilever beam or on a crane, so that it can travel through space in any direction.

Can   Circular container, often made of metal, in which a film reel is stored and transported.

Cartoon   A film made of animated drawings.

Cartridge   A container for film. Certain projector cartridges contain a continuous loop of film which moves in only a forward direction; other cartridges can be reversed or rewound.

Cassette   A miniaturized reel-to-reel system for tape, film, etc., enclosed in a sealed plastic container.

Cinéma vérité   A film style often characterized by use of a hand-held camera. Both natural language and actions are used rather than a prepared script and directions.

Circuit   A group of libraries or other institutions joined together for the purchase, exhibition, and distribution of mutually chosen films. The activities of a circuit are performed according to a planned schedule.

Commentary   Explanatory talk that accompanies a film (also called *narration*).

Commercial films   Films produced for showing in motion picture theaters that charge admission.

Compatibility   With reference to audiovisual materials, the ability of different systems or machines to decode the same type of software is meant. For example, 16mm sound projectors are compatible but 8mm sound cartridge projectors are not.

Compilation film   A complete film made from bits of other films, i.e., shots, scenes, and sequences.

Composition   The arrangement of the elements that are to be photographed.

Contrast   A comparison between the lightest and the darkest areas of a shot.

Cooperative   Two or more institutions joined together to provide a specific service at reasonable cost.

Credits   The names of those persons who have made important professional and creative contributions to a film; usually presented at the beginning or end of a film.

Cut   The immediate substitution of one shot for another.

Deep focus   The use of special lenses to provide a great depth of field in which the objects in the immediate foreground and the objects in the far background are seen as clear sharp images.

Definition   The clarity, sharpness, or distinctness of an image.

Dissolve   The fading of one shot as it is gradually replaced completely by a new shot; melting one shot into a following one.

Distributor A person or an organization that lends, rents, leases, and/or sells films.

Documentary film A film of fact or a film dealing with a topic of sociological significance which makes use of nonactors. It is made from real or reconstructed situations and events. The natural drama of the world is interpreted by a creative shaping of selected film footage.

Educational film An informative or factual film designed primarily for use in an educational context.

Emulsion A coating placed over the cellulose base of motion picture film. It is sensitive to light and is made from silver salts and gelatin.

Exhibition The act of showing films to an audience.

Experimental film A film which tries something new, unconventional, or different in technique, style, etc. This name is often used interchangeably with underground film and avant-garde film, although some differences exist.

Fade The slow disappearance of a shot into darkness or the gradual emergence of a shot from darkness into full definition.

Fast motion An exaggerated illusion of speeded-up motion obtained by operating the camera at a slow rate.

Feature film For the purposes of this volume, a film that uses 61 or more minutes in telling a narrative story. Other definitions based on time or footage are used.

Fiction film A film that tells a story. Made from a prepared script using professional actors and staged action, it is sometimes called a narrative film.

Film A thin flexible strip with perforations on one or both sides placed at regular intervals. The strip is made of a cellulose base which has been coated with a light-sensitive emulsion.

Film librarian A professional person who selects, acquires, catalogs, stores, and ultimately makes film available to patron-users.

Film library A collection of films built by a qualified professional to satisfy the specific needs of a defined audience; or a specific location in an institution where films are stored.

Film society A group of people organized for the purpose of seeing films of their choice.

Flashback A break in a chronological narrative by a visualized recollection of something in the past by a character in a film, or the repetition of earlier moments in the film used as a reminder to the viewer.

Focus Adjustment of a lens in order to produce a sharp clear image.

Frame The simplest unit of a motion picture film; the single still picture which is flashed for a fraction of a second on the screen. Each foot of 16mm film consists of 39 frames (or 39 still pictures) and, at a sound speed of 24 frames per second, 36 feet of film travel through the projector each minute.

Frame enlargement The photographic blow-up of individual frames taken directly from a print of a motion picture film. The use of frame enlargements as illustrations for film books has increased lately.

Freeze frame   Extended printing of a single frame at the end of a shot.

Gauge   The width of motion picture film stock expressed in millimeters. The commonest gauges are 35mm, 16mm, and 8mm.

Iconographic film   A film whose movement originated only within the camera. The subjects of the films are inanimate objects such as a drawing, painting, sculpture, or building.

Instructional film   A film designed to provide information, knowledge, or training in the acquisition of a skill.

Leader   Blank colored film attached to the beginning of a reel of motion picture film for protection and identification. The leader rather than the film itself is used for threading, and it is color-keyed to indicate the beginning of a reel and to show that the film has been rewound.

Magnetic sound track   The film's accompanying sound encoded on a ferromagnetic wire or strip embedded lengthwise along one edge of the film.

Montage   The assembling and editing of shots and sounds—a part of the filmmaker's creative activity; or a special effect achieved by using several different shots arranged to show a transition in time, place, experience, etc.

Negative   A reversal of the dark and light areas of a picture or a positive film.

Nontheatrical films   Films produced for showing in locations other than motion picture theaters.

One sheet   A poster made to advertise a film; a one sheet measures 27 by 41 inches, a three sheet measures 41 by 81 inches, a six sheet measures 81 by 81 inches.

Optical printer   A photographic device used to create dissolves, fades, superimpositions, and many other special effects.

Optical sound track   A thin band of contrasting lines and areas that are printed on one side of the motion picture film.

Packet   Six or more films placed together for use on a film circuit.

Pan shot   Shot taken when the camera is anchored or mounted on a base and then rotated in a horizontal plane.

Parallel editing   Two separate actions developed nearly simultaneously by showing fragments of each one alternately.

Persistence of vision   The retention of an image by the retina of the eye for a fraction of a second after the light stimulus has been removed.

Photostasis film   A short film or sequence made by the flashing of many different shots in very rapid succession.

Pool   A collection of films available from a permanent repository. Access to the collection is usually by membership fee rather than by individual film rental.

Positive print   Made from a negative, this film shows a true picture and is used for projection.

Print   A positive copy of a film made from the film's negative.

Producer   A person or an organization whose primary function is to underwrite the cost of making films.

Projection   A pictorial display or image made by throwing light rays on a reflecting surface.

Projector   Machine that produces an image on a screen, wall, or other reflecting surface.

Propaganda film   A film with a strong discernible opinion, usually designed to persuade or convince a viewer who is already sympathetic to that opinion.

Pure film   A film which does not undergo the developing process.

Raw stock   Light-sensitized film that has not yet been exposed in a camera.

Reel   A plastic or metal holder, consisting of a hub with two circular flanges, on which film is wound; the length of a film is sometimes approximated by the number of reels it requires.

Research film   A film made to facilitate the observation and interpretation of natural or scientific phenomena.

Rewind   The process of returning film back to the feed reel in order that it again be ready for projection.

Running time   The number of minutes needed to project a complete film at its intended speed.

Scene   Several shots arranged or ordered to create a unit in time.

Screen   A diffusive reflecting surface made of opaque white or silver material upon which an image may be projected with brilliance and clarity.

Sequence   The film equivalent of a chapter in a book, composed of several scenes combined to develop one incident, one experience, one subject, etc.

Shipping container   A square package or box in which film is shipped. It is often made of fiberboard, with metal corners and crossed webbing straps added for protection and safety.

Shooting a film   The use of a motion picture camera to photograph actions or objects. The expression was probably first used in connection with Marey's invention, the photographic gun, in 1882.

Short film   For the purposes of this volume, the short film is defined as a film with a running time of 60 minutes or less. Other definitions based on time or length are used.

Shot   A length of film exposed during one single running of the camera; of indeterminate length, it can last from a fraction of a second to several minutes.

Single frame photography   The exposure of a single frame of film at one time or running of the motion picture camera. This technique is used in animation.

Slow motion   The operation of a camera at a fast speed so that the resulting film action will appear slower than normal when projected.

Special effects   Unusual or "trick" photography that cannot be done via regular filming techniques. This type of photography employs devices such as optical printers, matte boxes, models, etc.

Speed-projection   The number of frames per second at which a film is projected. The most common projector speeds for 8mm film and 16mm film are 18 frames per second (silent speed) and 24 frames per second (sound speed); 36 feet of 16mm film pass through the projector in one minute at sound speed.

Splicer　A manual or automatic machine used to join pieces of motion picture film together.

Split screen　A special effect that enables more than one shot to be projected simultaneously.

Still　A specially posed or taken still photograph which is used to advertise a film. It is not the same as a frame enlargement.

Stop motion　Stopping the camera, rearranging some part of the scene, and then restarting the camera.

Superimposition　Two or more shots that share the screen simultaneously, in an overlay arrangement.

Take-up reel　The reel which receives and holds that portion of the film which has been projected.

Threading　The correct placement of film in the projector.

Tilt shot　A shot taken when the camera is anchored or mounted on a base and moves up or down in a vertical plane.

Tracking shot　A shot made by moving the camera toward, away from, or parallel with the subject. A wheeled vehicle or dolly is used to move the camera.

Trailer　A length of blank film, usually colored, placed at the end of a reel for protection or identification; or a short advertisement placed at the end of a film.

Wipe　The removal or wiping off of one shot by the use of traveling lines, patterns, or designs.

Zoom shot　A shot which contains a fast movement toward or away from a subject.

INDEX